The problem of literary value

Manchester University Press

MANCHESTER MEDIEVAL LITERATURE AND CULTURE

Series editors: Anke Bernau, David Matthews and James Paz

Series founded by: J. J. Anderson and Gail Ashton

Advisory board: Ruth Evans, Patricia C. Ingham, Andrew James Johnston, Chris Jones, Catherine Karkov, Nicola McDonald, Haruko Momma, Susan Phillips, Sarah Salih, Larry Scanlon, Stephanie Trigg and Matthew Vernon

Manchester Medieval Literature and Culture publishes monographs and essay collections comprising new research informed by current critical methodologies on the literary cultures of the global Middle Ages. We are interested in all periods, from the early Middle Ages through to the late, and we include postmedieval engagements with and representations of the medieval period (or 'medievalism'). 'Literature' is taken in a broad sense, to include the many different medieval genres: imaginative, historical, political, scientific and religious.

Titles available in the series

40. *Sleep and its spaces in Middle English literature: Emotions, ethics, dreams*   Megan G. Leitch

41. *Encountering* The Book of Margery Kempe   Laura Kalas and Laura Varnam (eds)

42. *The narrative grotesque in medieval Scottish poetry*   Caitlin Flynn

43. *Painful pleasures: Sadomasochism in medieval cultures*   Christopher Vaccaro (ed.)

44. *Medieval literary voices: Embodiment, materiality and performance*   Louise D'Arcens and Sif Ríkharðsdóttir (eds)

45. *Bestsellers and masterpieces: The changing medieval canon*   Heather Blurton and Dwight F. Reynolds (eds)

46. *Hybrid healing: Old English remedies and medical texts*   Lori Ann Garner

47. *The heat of* Beowulf   Daniel C. Remein

48. *Difficult pasts: Post-Reformation memory and the medieval romance*   Mimi Ensley

The problem of literary value

Robert J. Meyer-Lee

MANCHESTER UNIVERSITY PRESS

Copyright © Robert J. Meyer-Lee 2023

The right of Robert J. Meyer-Lee to be identified as the author of this work has been asserted in accordance with the Copyright, Designs and Patents Act 1988.

Published by Manchester University Press
Oxford Road, Manchester M13 9PL

www.manchesteruniversitypress.co.uk

British Library Cataloguing-in-Publication Data
A catalogue record for this book is available from the British Library

ISBN 978 1 5261 6794 1 hardback

First published 2023

The publisher has no responsibility for the persistence or accuracy of URLs for any external or third-party internet websites referred to in this book, and does not guarantee that any content on such websites is, or will remain, accurate or appropriate.

An electronic version is also available under a Creative Commons (CC BY-NC-ND) licence, which permits non-commercial use, distribution and reproduction provided the author(s) and Manchester University Press are fully cited and no modifications or adaptations are made. Details of the licence can be viewed at https://creativecommons.org/licenses/by-nc-nd/4.0/. This has been made possible thanks to TOME (Toward an Open Monograph Ecosystem) – a collaboration of the Association of American Universities, the Association of University Presses and the Association of Research Libraries – and the generous support of Agnes Scott College, Emory University and the Andrew W. Mellon Foundation. Learn more at the TOME website, available at: http://openmonographs.org/

Typeset by Newgen Publishing UK

For Elaine

Contents

Preamble: what this book is about	*page* viii
Acknowledgements	xi
List of abbreviations	xiii
Introduction: the problem of literary value	1
1 Literary value and the object of Chaucer studies	19
2 A preliminary theory of literary valuing	70
3 Loose binding and its affordances	99
4 Canonicity	135
5 Interpretation	189
Postscript: losing my religion	237
References	242
Index	260

Preamble: what this book is about

These preliminary remarks aim to calibrate potential readers' expectations about a book that possesses the broad title of *The problem of literary value* but nonetheless appears within Manchester University Press's Medieval Literature and Culture Series.

Most fundamentally, this book is about the challenges that literary value presents for the general field of literary studies, and hence I hope that, regardless of their areas of specialisation, readers concerned about these challenges will find the book's various considerations of this topic of interest. Yet, by far most of the specific examples of these challenges that the book examines involve the study of medieval literature and, most often and more narrowly, Chaucer studies. In the course of the book's consideration of the general problem of literary value, therefore, it also supplies an extended reflection on the state of Chaucer studies over the last several decades in respect to some of the issues, ideas and practices that have been prominent within the subfield.

Doubtlessly, my choice to so limit the scope of my examples attenuates in some regards the applicability of the book's most general arguments. But obviously I have proceeded on the assumption that more has been gained than lost. Chaucer studies, in particular, in several ways serves as a perspicacious synecdoche for the general field of literary studies in respect to the problem of literary value. Because Chaucer, on the one hand, has enjoyed long and enduring canonicity in Anglophone literary studies – figured from soon after his death up to the present as the genial progenitor of a patrilineal English literary history – and, on the other hand, possesses a somewhat marginal position in the field as a medieval author for whom there are historical and linguistic obstacles of access, the problem of literary value has been especially salient in Chaucer studies. Indeed, in recent years, within a changing landscape of Anglophone literary studies that for crucial reasons has sought to become more inclusive, the pressure on Chaucer's paradoxically marginal centrality has become intense. In some quarters, the combination of his standing as a fountainhead of a Eurocentric conception of literary value and the perception of his language and culture as forbiddingly alien to modernity has urgently brought to the fore the question of his value. Accordingly, in very practical ways, as in, say, revising the content of a university's English major curricula, that question has become, in miniature, the question of value for the field as a whole. While literary value is ultimately no more or no less of a problem for Chaucer studies than for literary studies generally, this corner of the field thus provides a ready vehicle for thinking through some of the problem's myriad complexities.

There are, moreover, more practical reasons for the book's restriction of the scope of its examples. This book attempts to treat in individual chapters topics – the critical edition, canonicity, interpretation – that are, obviously, massive in scope, that quickly ramify into all sorts of conceptual difficulties and that possess accordingly vast traditions of commentary. Even if I were able to master those traditions, any sustained engagement with them would quickly overwhelm the relatively modest aims of this book. The pragmatic approach that I describe in this book's introduction hence serves as a kind of throttle on the expansiveness of these topics, as this approach tries to stay close to concrete scholarly and pedagogical practices and does not attempt to account for the full conceptual landscapes in which these reside. This concreteness depends in part on specificity, which the repeated returns to Chaucer studies supply. Relatedly, the blinders imposed by the focus of the book's examples aim for a compensatory perceptual clarity by way of those examples' consistency. By usually limiting itself to a narrow slice of the literary studies pie (to use a different metaphor), the book may explore the intricacies of the problem of literary value as they emerge in diverse endeavours that nonetheless share the same object. In this way the book both keeps in check the generation of ramifications peculiar to different slices of that pie (say, those that would emerge from a consideration of editions of *Frankenstein*) and provides common points of reference across the endeavours that it considers.

Readers who have been convinced enough by these remarks to keep reading to this point may still be sceptical, however, about the book's decision to centre Chaucer. No matter how germane Chaucer is to the topic, in simply granting the place of honour to such a traditional object of literary value – at a moment in the history of Anglophone literary studies when the field has now for some time striven to unmask and overcome the regressive ideological dimensions of its investments in such objects – has not this book in effect already solved the problem that it sets out to explore, and in a way that ought rightly ensure its early obsolescence? In fact, the very terms of this question involve several of the dimensions of the problem of literary value that this book considers, and thus my best response to it is to encourage such sceptical readers to venture forth into its pages. For example, in Chapter 4, I suggest that the troubles of canonicity – which include, say, the inevitable traffic between literary and political value – have not been overcome through the retirement of traditional canonical texts and authors. Nonetheless, here at the outset, let me be clear that my choice to centre Chaucer is by no means intended as a defence of his continuing canonicity, but rather, as I have indicated, that choice has been prompted by the analytical utility of the currently vexed status of that canonicity. Whether the overall effect of the book tends towards an apologia for the study of Chaucer or actually further erodes that study's presumed value is a question that I ultimately will leave to my readers, although I offer a few brief reflections on the topic in the book's postscript.

Acknowledgements

Even more so than my other publications, this book was born out of many years of conversation, very frequently of the informal, spontaneous variety, with colleagues, mentors, students, friends and family. Any list of those to whom I owe thanks will thus necessarily be hopelessly incomplete, but of course what always follows that caveat in this context is just such a list. Mine includes Charlotte Artese, Sarah Buss, Ardis Butterfield, Chris Cannon, Seeta Chaganti, Ruth Evans, Matthew Giancarlo, James Goldstein, Frank Grady, Lee Kahan, Kathryn Kerby-Fulton, Ashby Kinch, David Matthews, Gabriel, Jackson and Lucas Meyer-Lee, Mark Miller, Cathy Sanok, Kyoko Takanashi, Peggy Thompson, Peter Travis and Claire Waters. To all the rest of you who have helped to make this book a reality, I am sorry that my memory fails me. And, obviously, none of those named deserves blame for any of the book's dubious opinions or faulty thinking.

Meredith Carroll of Manchester University Press has been a great pleasure to work with. I am thrilled to join the other authors in the Manchester Medieval Literature and Culture series, and I am grateful to the series editors and the exceptionally perceptive and helpful anonymous readers for supporting this somewhat odd bird of a book.

Initial work on the book was facilitated by financial support from Indiana University's New Frontiers in the Arts & Humanities Program. Its completion was made possible by a sabbatical granted by Agnes Scott College and the support of the college's Miriam Francis Smith Scholar fund.

An earlier version of Chapter 1 appeared as 'Manuscript Studies, Literary Value, and the Object of Chaucer Studies', *SAC*, 30 (2008), 1–37. © 2008 New Chaucer Society.

An earlier version of Chapter 2, as well as portions of the introduction and Chapter 3, appeared as 'Toward a Theory and Practice of Literary Valuing', *NLH*, 46:2 (2015), 335–55. © 2015 Johns Hopkins University Press.

Abbreviations

ChR	*The Chaucer Review*
JEGP	*Journal of English and Germanic Philology*
MLQ	*Modern Language Quarterly*
NLH	*New Literary History*
PMLA	*Publications of the Modern Language Association*
SAC	*Studies in the Age of Chaucer*

Introduction: the problem of literary value

Not so long ago – and to the surprised consternation of many outside the field of literary studies – literary value was a topic rarely broached in the most prestigious literary critical journals and, in many departments of literature, was a concern that stigmatised its holder as old-fashioned or naïve. In many if not all quarters today, however, this attitude itself now appears old-fashioned, as over the last couple of decades literary value has become the focus of considerable and increasing critical energy. This book contributes to this trend but not in one of the fashions that most other contributions typically assume. In particular, the book neither presents an argument for what specifically constitutes the most important or defining values of literature nor conversely provides a historical account of how certain values have come to be identified with literature. The book is neither a celebration of literary value nor a critique of its fabrication and ideological complicity. Instead, the book seeks to come to grips, pragmatically, with what it understands to be for the field of literary studies the inevitable and inevitably problematic concept of literary value and, more crucially, the practice of literary valuing. Towards this end, the book develops a preliminary theory of literary valuing and explores the nature and consequences of these problematic inevitabilities for three of the field's most basic aspects.

In these explorations, the principal intent is to be practical and diagnostic, to provide a better understanding of the problem of literary value as it affects our everyday activities of scholarship and teaching. My most basic hope is that these diagnoses may be of some use in my readers' unavoidable grappling with the problem of literary value. Because I do not believe that the problem is one that lends itself to a resolution – at least not to a generally applicable one – readers will not find in this book long, prescriptive exhortations. Instead, towards the end of most of the subsequent chapters I provide some suggestions for or examples of possible responses to the problem, ones that aim to harness that problem as a source of critical energy rather than allowing it to produce within our practices unhelpful, sometimes damaging incoherencies, of which we are in some cases only minimally aware. Most of these responses will be variations on the recommendation to incorporate reflexivity into one's scholarly and pedagogical praxis – a recommendation that is, obviously, scarcely novel. My hope is that the specificities of this recommendation's formulations in the terms of this book will make it more practicable than it often is, as I suspect that reflexivity has been much easier to espouse than actually to realise. Here and there in the book I go beyond such practical responses and offer suggestions for how the framework that I develop might help to address one or more of the many ills of the field of literary studies, the continuing existence of which plainly constitutes one of this book's principal prompts. I list of few these ills below; here perhaps they may be collectively signalled by the results of a survey conducted by the American Academy of Arts and Sciences that Judith Butler discusses in a recent *MLA Newsletter*. As Butler observes, while the results show encouragingly that '84% of Americans ... have a positive view of literature', they also attest, discouragingly, to the view of many 'that the teaching of literature at the college or university level is a "waste of time" or cost[s] too much'.[1] This discrepancy exemplifies the sort of incoherence, or gap, that has motivated this book.

While I will consider value in a number of ways in the pages that follow, by the phrase 'literary value' I mean, most often and most basically, the value of the literary as a category or, to adapt denotations from the *Oxford English Dictionary*, 'The relative worth, usefulness, or importance of [the category of the literary], the estimation in which [that category] is held according to its real or supposed desirability or utility'; 'the quality of [the category] considered in respect of its ability to serve a specified purpose or cause a particular effect'.[2] I take this as my basic topic rather than the category of the literary itself for reasons that will become evident by Chapter 2 but most simply because literary value is the more historically persistent troublemaker, despite the seeming logical priority of the adjective in its label. While the distinctive concept of and associated terminology for literary value appear to have been products of the rise of aesthetic discourse in the eighteenth century, 'the emergence of a named concept in historical time', as Maura Nolan reminds us, 'does not necessarily indicate a point of origin'.[3] And in this instance the historical record plainly shows that a concern with a phenomenon recognisable as literary value in the sense above goes back at least as far as Plato's negative judgement of it.

I suspect that what constitutes the nature of the category of the literary, either in the abstract or in respect to the practices of a specific place or time, will remain a thorny question, one that – however fruitful the many answers it has elicited have been – is likely permanently intractable. Yet this difficulty has never prevented considerations of its value, which have been both socially more pervasive and rhetorically more urgent in their articulations. In this respect, it is simply like any other value-laden category, which easily beckons judgement regardless of how much the judging individual understands the nature of the category. Indeed, in the history of literary theory it has been defences of literary value, triggered by attacks upon it (such as Sir Philip Sidney's response to Stephen Gosson), that have very often served as the impetus behind the most searching and innovative attempts to define the nature of the literary. This book takes as its informing rationale this continuous – if not of course unchanging – concern with the value of the literary, in whatever more-or-less culturally distinct form the latter category of writing has taken. It does not attempt to trace the waxing and waning of historically specific features of the discourse of literary value, such as those crucial ones that arose in concert with the discourse of economic value in the writings of, say, Adam Smith and Karl Marx, which have been treated extensively by others.[4] It also does not primarily consider literary value in the sense of the comparative merit of specific works, although it will explore, especially in Chapters 1 and 4, some of the practical and conceptual ramifications of the fact that that sense is a necessary corollary of the one above, and so the problem of literary value encompasses both.

This book's point of departure is the observation that literary value has been a problem, in the sense of a prominent and current area of investigation and debate, from no later than Plato's impugning of it. But just as importantly it recognises, as I have suggested, that literary value has been at various times, and is at present very much so, a problem in the more ordinary sense of a perplexity causing distress. The rather stark reemergence of this latter kind of problem over the last third of the twentieth century, indeed, has likely prompted the recent renewed attention given to the former kind. As we are all acutely aware, the field of literary studies, still in the process of setting its new bearings and centres of gravity following the late twentieth-century self-questioning of its basic aims and objects of study, finds itself confronting declining undergraduate majors, vanishing tenure-track lines, open hostility from the administrative and legislative bodies that control much of its funding, and so on.[5] In this dispiriting context, the value of literature as the field's legitimating principle no longer appears to possess an institutional and public relations efficacy as potent as it once held (witness the aforementioned survey results). Hence, confronting these practical problems, many literary scholars have not coincidentally returned with vigour to the more academic question of what the value of literature is, how it has historically evolved and how it has functioned within and without the field, in the past and present, and how it might so function in the future.

Most simplistically, some commentators have placed the blame for the practical problems on the field's putative abandonment of literary value — because of theory, historicism, cultural studies, politically activist approaches and whatever other bogeymen might be the culprits.[6] This book wholly rejects this view as a fruitlessly nostalgic one that misconceives as a fall from grace what was instead a pivotal and necessary, if turbulent, moment in which the field recognised and sought to ameliorate many of its conceptual and institutional blind spots. And I suspect, too, that the practical problems that the field faces ultimately have less to do with anything internal to the field itself as much as with the large-scale transformation of the scope and thus also the actual and perceived functions of the institutions of higher education that have, for well over a century, been the field's principal domicile.[7] The latter topic, however, is for a very different book from this one. Here I address not the reasons for the transformation of higher education, whatever they may be, but how in this context literary value operates and some of the implications of that operation.

In the remainder of this introduction, I locate in a little more detail the academic problem of literary value amid the anxieties rife within the field of literary studies. Looking back to work that emerged in response to this problem over the last few decades, I characterise two of the prominent and rather antithetical critical trends in this response (the ones already hinted at above). Against that backdrop I then provide a fuller explanation of the project of this book.

In the Anglo-American academy since about the mid-1990s, theoretical considerations of literary value have steadily become more common and are now perhaps more widespread than they ever have been, and in retrospect this reemergence should come as no surprise. As Gerald Graff and others have described, since the modern institutionalisation of literary studies in the nineteenth century the academy has never been entirely comfortable with value, which – as transmitted by canonical authors such as Chaucer and Shakespeare – at once both justified the study of literature (for various and competing humanistic and philological reasons) and threatened to exile it, by reducing it to a matter of taste rather than reason.[8] If value was therefore not very often directly theorised, it was scarcely ever questioned. New Criticism, more alert to the issue than its methodological predecessors, proved particularly adept at negotiating the dilemma of value, establishing a balancing act between judgement and interpretation, in which a reasoned determination of the principles of relative artistic unity at the same time implicitly determined relative literary merit.

This balancing act, of course, turned out to be rather fragile. The critiques of the literary canon that shook the academy in the 1970s (especially in the US) disclosed this harmony of interpretation and judgement to be propped up by a canon whose assumed value justified a practice of criticism that – aside from local areas of contestation, especially around the canonical margins – merely and predictably confirmed canonical value. Revealed to be conceptually aporetic, ideologically freighted (usually more-or-less covertly) and historically and culturally relative, literary value, unprecedentedly, appeared no longer able to function as a half-concealed underpinning of the discipline. David F. Bell, recalling this viewpoint in his contribution to *PMLA*'s 2002 series of essays on the question 'Why

Major in Literature – What Do We Tell Our Students', distils it to the query 'What group has the right to decide the value of a literary text? Is this decision not always an oppressive move to control what is permitted in discourse?' In response, the field's 'best solution' was, he notes, 'to forgo the question of value and to broaden the spectrum of the literary as much as possible'.[9] And to different degrees and in different ways, certain kinds of cultural studies, historicism and book history or manuscript studies (to name a few of the pertinent approaches) emerged as shrewd recalibrations of the field's object of study, ones for which value is (putatively) incidental rather than defining, or at most an object of sociohistorical inquiry. In short, the field recovered its rationale by pushing value aside.[10]

These shifts in the object of study became prevalent enough that they provoked an identity crisis for a field that still (at least in most institutional instances) featured the term *literature* in its denomination. As then *PMLA* editor Carlos J. Alonso remarked in respect to the aforementioned series on 'Why Major in Literature', '[T]here is no longer a consensus on the object of literary studies or on the justifications for pursuing this field as an intellectual project ... we are confronted with the weakness that arises from our dismantling of our own house.'[11] Alonso is recognising that by the mid-1990s, these shifts – coinciding with perceived declines in research funding, student enrolments and public prestige – seemed to many to have constituted a grave, ill-conceived error. Backward-looking apologists, such as Harold Bloom in *The Western Canon*, issued elegiac accounts of value that had wide dissemination, although little impact in the academy.[12] More accurate barometers of the field's tipping point were the anguished voices of critics such as George Levine, who by and large accepted the terms of the critique of the canon but nonetheless called for a restoration of the centrality of literature and its value in the discipline.

Levine's succinct and candid expression of these views in a 1993 *Profession* essay may stand for the sentiments of many others in the same period. The founding director of the Center for the Critical Analysis of Contemporary Culture at Rutgers, Levine first describes the field's shift in its object of study that the name of his own centre appears to consolidate:

> Nominally, we teach in English departments or literature departments. But many of the best-known in our field are professionally interested

in things that are only marginally related to English or literature ... in much of the best-known criticism in recent years, the first objective, however mediated by a study of texts, is social or political change; literature ... is often regarded as a kind of enemy of change and serves primarily to be demystified, denaturalized, and shown to be complicit with dominant ideologies whose traces it seeks invariably to efface.

Yet, however much he accepts the rationale for this shift and appreciates its energies, he goes on to characterise it as a dire threat, even if just for largely practical reasons:

> by carrying out these multiple and often conflicting activities under the protection of English departments, we have left the profession particularly vulnerable to popular chastising and threatening. Moreover, I believe that we need to consider some of these anomalies in the discipline now, in practical institutional terms. We must examine the value of the literary and the aesthetic ... if English, as a profession sustained by publicly and privately endowed institutions, is to survive.[13]

Levine's repeated references to the 'best-known' critics and criticism as evidence of the shift in the field's object, however, suggest that this shift was never as hegemonic as it may have felt from within the enclaves of Research I English departments. Out of the spotlight but nonetheless residing within very influential locales – such as in the headnotes in the *Norton Anthology of English Literature* – the field's traditional commitment to value persisted throughout the period, even if the canon itself underwent transformation, reconception and a degree of abandonment.[14] As Steven Connor perspicaciously remarked in 1992, 'value and evaluation have not so much been exiled as driven into the critical unconscious, where they continue to exercise force but without being available for analytic scrutiny'.[15] From this perspective, our current critical climate, with its variety of (to name just a few trends) new formalisms, new aestheticisms, ethical criticisms, reparative readings, and so on, represents the inevitable return of the repressed, either as laudable kind of disciplinary talking cure or as a regressive neurosis, depending on where one's critical sympathies lie.[16]

Yet there is more operative in this perhaps inevitable critical rebound than just field-internal psychodynamics. For, as most of us are painfully aware, the now decades-long external sources of Levine's anxiety have not abated but in fact have intensified. As Rita

8   *The problem of literary value*

Felski has queried, 'In such an austere and inauspicious climate, how do scholars of literature make a case for the value of what we do? How do we come up with rationales for reading and talking about books without reverting to the canon-worship of the past?'[17] And even if we were able to evade such questions issuing from outside the academy, they are increasingly omnipresent within, most mundanely, perhaps, from the demands of quantitative programme assessment to produce straightforward answers to such questions and to develop mechanisms for measuring their success. Obviously, this institutional imperative, as well as the external demands for justification, may be more easily met if the field actually were to conceive of its nominal object of study as valuable. Hence not coincidentally over the last couple of decades there has been an ever-increasing proliferation of publications that take up exactly the project that Levine and others called for.

Such publications range in scope and audience from the MLA 'Report to the Teagle Foundation on the Undergraduate Major in Language and Literature', to special issues of journals somehow devoted to the topic (both generally and for subfields, as in issues of, respectively, *MLQ* and *ChR*), to a flurry of monographs that similarly treat the topic both broadly (such as Gregory Jusdanis's *Fiction Agonistes*) and for specific subfields (such as Peggy Knapp's *Chaucerian Aesthetics*).[18] The bibliography, indeed, has grown to intimidating proportions in a relatively short time.[19] Hence, in lieu of a survey, I will let the Teagle Report speak for the group, since, given its practical, programmatic aims, it conveys the basic sentiment (if not of course the specific rationales) of this trend of publications in a particularly unguarded manner. '[W]ithout literature,' the report asserts, 'there is no in-depth understanding of narratives that lead to the discovery of other cultures in their specificities and diversity and to the understanding of other human beings in their similarities and differences.' Therefore, '[w]hile we advocate incorporating into the major the study of a variety of texts, we insist that the most beneficial among these are literary works, which offer their readers a rich and challenging – and therefore rewarding – object of study.' While the canon and its supposed universal values are nowhere to be found in the report, literature and its universal value (for example, its ability to provide an 'imaginative context through which readers gain insight into politics, history, society, emotion, and the interior life') have returned to centre stage.[20] A similarly motivated report from a group of Harvard humanities professors – including, from English, Homi Bhabha and James Simpson – more boldly recommends restoring a canon to the undergraduate curriculum, albeit one whose value is evident precisely in its ideological flexibility.[21]

These voices of advocacy, despite their current prominence and growing frequency, obviously do not constitute a consensus. As a casual glance at many publishers' 'new and forthcoming' lists makes evident, and as hallway conversations with one's colleagues may easily confirm, much scholarship and teaching continues to proceed within a cultural studies or historicist paradigm, in which literature serves as merely one form evidence among others.[22] Moreover, those who seek to revalorise literature must contend with the powerful critique of the discourse of literary value that emerged in the aftermath of the 1970s canon debates, and which possesses continuing influence and articulation. Like the voices of advocacy, these counter-voices recognise the centrality of literary value to the field and seek to account for it, but in contrast take a more neutral and sometimes even hostile approach. As exemplified by the seminal triumvirate of Terry Eagleton's *Literary Theory: An Introduction*, Stanley Fish's *Is There a Text in This Class* and Barbara Herrnstein Smith's *Contingencies of Value*, these studies – as different in their focuses, methods and conclusions as they are – share an emphasis on the constructedness, relativity and instrumentality of literary value.[23] According to Eagleton, for example, 'There is no such thing as a literary work or tradition valuable *in itself*, regardless of what anyone might have said or come to say about it. "Value" is a transitive term: it means whatever is valued by certain people in specific situations, according to particular criteria and in light of given purposes.' For Eagleton these 'given purposes', as embodied in 'value-judgements', are most fundamentally ideological: 'They refer in the end not simply to private taste, but to the assumptions by which certain social groups exercise and maintain power over others.'[24] Critiques such as this one may be more-or-less accepting of value as an ineradicable aspect of the field, but they seek to disclose its mystifying seductions, which typically occur in the form of universalising and essentialising claims.[25]

Subsequent critiques have put particular emphasis on the historical genesis and function of the discourse of literary value, being less concerned about its relativity than about the nature and implications of its specific determinations. In remarkably intricate detail, these critiques have traced the emergence of this discourse in specific historical circumstances in relation to other discourses, and they have followed the transmutations of this discourse and its functions through subsequent periods, up to the present. For example, one of the first of such critiques – Ian Hunter's Foucauldian study of the emergence of literary education – identifies the discourse of value as part of the moral disciplinary mechanisms of the state apparatus of public education.[26] Even more influentially, John Guillory, adapting the work of Pierre Bourdieu, traces the discourse of literary value from its precipitation from more general eighteenth-century accounts of value to its current, but waning, function as the underpinning of literary cultural capital.[27] (In general, Bourdieu's studies of the operation of cultural value in France – particularly *Distinction* and *The Field of Cultural Production* – have had tremendous impact on Anglo-American thinking on this topic and are often sourced for definitions of the meaning and function of literary value in a considerably less nuanced manner than in Guillory's adaptation.[28]) More recently, Mary Poovey has revisited the eighteenth-century emergence of a distinct discourse of literary value and its subsequent entanglements with the discourse of economic value, with consequences for both.[29] Interestingly, in the final sections of this study, addressing the implications of her findings for current practices of literary criticism, Poovey turns back to Hunter to develop a method of critical analysis, 'historical description', that does not depend on the category of literary value that she finds still haunts New Historicist readings, since only a method free of this category can delineate that category's historical operation. Wholly devoted to the topic of value, her study seeks to be, at least in respect to literature, value-neutral.

I will return to these two rather different approaches to literary value – simply put, advocacy and critique – in Chapter 2, where, as points of departure for my preliminary theory of literary valuing, I will give them better labels, scrutinise some of their implications and interdependencies and indicate some of what they leave out. At this point, I just suggest that while these two kinds of approaches by no means encompass all recent treatments of literary value, they do account for two of the most prominent and urgently pursued argumentative tendencies. And, while these tendencies are not incompatible (indeed, they not infrequently coexist within the same study), they are logically antithetical. Hence they tend to reproduce each other, with the conceptual lacunae of the one serving as the prompt for the other, resulting in a dialectical ping-pong match with no ready synthesis in sight. I do not mean this whimsical characterisation to be slighting; this dialectical ping-ponging has in fact generated a remarkable volume of important work. I merely mean to emphasise that this present study articulates and explores the implications of an approach to literary value that seeks to play neither side.

This book adopts a pragmatic approach to literary value, one that recognises the potential validity of the claims of both the affirmative and suspicious approaches but brackets those claims by focusing on the practical implications of our everyday activities as scholars and teachers of a thing that we continue to call literature. This book argues that regardless of how literary value is formulated in advocacies of its importance, interrogated in critiques of its function or history or simply obscured or pushed aside, as a category operating pragmatically it remains inextricably essential to the field of literary studies, simply because that category is an ineluctable participant in the apprehension of an object as literary. In this light, the problem of literary value becomes not much how to define it or to find a substitute for it, but rather, in the myriad activities that we pursue as literary scholars and teachers, how to reconcile its ineluctability with our understandable uncertainty regarding its precise nature and our wary cognisance of its complicities.

As I mentioned at the outset, however, in the chapters that follow I do not attempt to prescribe sure remedies for accomplishing this reconciliation. While the book does propose some possibilities in this regard, I devote most of its pages to the more basic work of accounting for some of the several dimensions in which the problem of literary value is felt. Specifically, the book offers, as an explanation of its view regarding the ineluctability of the category of literary value, a preliminary, pragmatic theory of literary valuing, and it explores the implications and ramifications of this ineluctability for three prominent aspects of the field of literary studies in the practical formations that they take at present and have taken in the recent past. These three aspects will serve as sites or case studies in which the sprawling complexities of the problem of literary value may be reconnoitred within a specific focus and in some depth.

Perhaps a bit counterintuitively, the first chapter does not supply the theory of literary valuing but instead the first case study: most basically, it considers literary value in relation to the edition of a literary work and specifically the Chaucer edition. The basis of this chapter is an article that I published in 2008. In reworking this material, I have sought to transform it from a reflection on the implications of what was then an ongoing critique of the Chaucer edition from the perspective of manuscript studies into a reflection on the implications of the brushing aside of that critique in the years that followed. It locates that critique at a moment in literary critical history when one set of still dominant trends (historicism in particular) was beginning to yield to others, most of which remain current today. The chapter thus looks backward and forward from 2008, showing how the problem of literary value has remained a problem throughout and arguing that the continued operation of the problem constituted one of the principal reasons why the critique of the edition never gained traction. This chapter has earned the opening slot not merely out of the convenience of its compositional chronology, therefore, but because of the way its exploration of the critique of the edition runs headlong into the problem of literary value, thereby providing an initial limning of the contours of that problem that the subsequent chapters will elaborate. In effect, it illustrates why the book's theory of literary valuing is needed. More so than the other chapters, this one spends most of its time within the confines of Chaucer studies, although its more general implications are, I believe, readily evident.

Chapters 2 and 3 develop the book's preliminary theory of literary valuing. Not aspiring towards the formulation of a full-blown theory, these chapters instead follow the prompts of Chapter 1 in order to identify a set of principles that they formalise in various ways, with the aim of thereby establishing a conceptual ground for this book's treatment of the problem of literary value. Chapter 2, to provide additional context and rationale for this preliminary theory, first revisits the literary value theoretical ping-pong match mentioned above. Staking out an alternative, it then presents a framework for understanding literary valuing. It argues, in a nutshell, that when pragmatically considered, literary value is the effect of an activity of mediation wholly coincident with its conception as a quality, an activity performed by actors within a network that shapes all individual instances, and an activity that is a social fact integral to the phenomenon of the literary and yet neither singular nor necessarily stable in character.

As the lexis of the preceding formulation signals, my preliminary theory of literary valuing relies upon some key concepts from Actor-Network Theory. Chapter 3 makes this and other theoretical debts more explicit in its effort to expand upon the preliminary theory in a few important ways. In particular, Chapter 3 considers the implications of a broadly characteristic (if not necessary) feature of the activity of literary valuing, which it names loose binding. To accomplish this, it first makes explicit its understanding of value as a general category, for which it draws from the work of Georg Simmel and later theorists of value in his vein, blending Simmel's ideas with those from Actor-Network Theory to present a fundamentally differential, dynamic account of value. Elucidating loose binding in those terms, the chapter then develops a pragmatic framework for understanding how different kinds of value mutually determine one another and, as an illustration of these several points, considers Giovanni Boccaccio's reflections on the value of poetry, as exemplified by Dante. The chapter closes with two sections that begin to answer the question of 'so what'. The first of these does this by way of clarifying the relation between the concept of loose binding and the hoary formalist one of defamiliarisation, while the second suggests that the axiological framework that I am proposing might serve as the 'big tent' that the field of literary studies no longer possesses.

While this book offers its preliminary theory of literary valuing for whatever utility it may possess on its own, the theory also informs the following two chapters. Chapter 4 tackles one of the most troubling aspects of the problem of literary value, its ideological complicity (as acutely evident in, e.g., colonialist, white supremacist and androcentric ideologies), considering this in respect to the idea and practice of canonicity. For this purpose it revisits the canon wars of the late twentieth century, but its main aim is to identify how, and then explore the implications of the fact that, the ineluctability of canonicity and simultaneously its inescapable complicity remain with us. Towards this end, it draws on the preceding chapters' preliminary theory of literary valuing to describe several concrete manifestations of how canonicity ineluctability emerges despite attempts to evade or to identify an alternative to it, and, conversely, of how canonicity's ideological complicity inevitably haunts explicit efforts to defend it as a principle. The chapter concludes by providing an example of how this dilemma, although not resolvable, might become generative rather than merely perplexing, and thereby constitute one of the field's distinctive disciplinary contributions.

The topic of the book's final chapter is interpretation, understood in its most general sense as the activity that we perform when ascribing any sort of meaning to a literary text. As in Chapter 4, to manage the (even more) sprawling nature of this topic, the chapter keeps its focus trained on specific manifestations of the problem of literary value, here in instances of interpretation or reflections on interpretation. It examines such instances from several decades ago up to the present, using them to elucidate a foundational problem of interpretation in the terms of Chapter 2 and 3's preliminary theory of literary valuing. In particular, it emphasises that one essential facet of the infamous hermeneutic circle is that value ascription inaugurates the activity of interpretation, is its outcome and pervades it at each step. The chapter then takes a close, sustained look at the efforts of one celebrated medievalist, Lee Patterson, to come to grips with this very problem in his efforts to establish a firm grounding for academic literary study, seeking to trace in Patterson's response the challenges and pitfalls that such efforts may entail. In its final section, the chapter considers a pair of recent medievalist interpretations that point toward a way of leveraging those challenges as a source of critical insight while keeping at bay entanglements in paradox.

In a brief postscript, I seek to take my own advice of pursuing a reflexive critical practice and lay my cards on the table, so to speak, in regard to literary value in general and Chaucer's value in particular.

Notes

1 Judith Butler, 'The Future of the Humanities Can Be Found in Its Public Forums', *MLA Newsletter*, 52:4 (2020), 2–3.
2 *OED value* n., 6.a and 6.c.
3 Maura Nolan, 'Making the Aesthetic Turn: Adorno, the Medieval, and the Future of the Past', *Journal of Medieval and Early Modern Studies*, 34:3 (2004), 549–75 (571).
4 E.g., John Guillory, *Cultural Capital: The Problem of Literary Canon Formation* (Chicago: University of Chicago Press, 1993); and Terry Eagleton, *The Ideology of the Aesthetic* (Malden: Blackwell, 1990).
5 James F. English, *The Global Future of English Studies* (New York: John Wiley, 2012), casts doubt on this ubiquitous narrative of crisis and decline when English Studies is considered in a global context. Yet the experiences that I list are widely enough attested, at least in North America, to suggest that even if the rhetoric of crisis may be overwrought, the field is going through a basic transformation in respect to the institutional and discursive contexts in which it has for many decades existed. Such basic transformations are, of course, typically experienced as crisis and decline by those with an investment in the status quo.
6 This view is particularly common in journalistic forums. See, e.g., Verlyn Klinkenborg, 'The Decline and Fall of the English Major', *New York Times* (23 June 2013), New York edition, p. SR10.
7 Consider, e.g., the massive expansion in North America of the number of individuals whom higher education serves, the consequent effect on employment qualifications and the consequent change in public perception of what a university degree accomplishes. English, *Global Future*, treats these and related phenomena under the heading 'massification', arguing that a vision of universal higher education realised at something akin to the level of R1 universities or elite liberal arts colleges was always a fantasy. For a well-known different diagnosis, see Bill Readings, *The University in Ruins* (Cambridge, MA: Harvard University Press, 1996).
8 Gerald Graff, *Professing Literature: An Institutional History* (Chicago: University of Chicago Press, 1987).
9 David F. Bell, 'A Moratorium on Suspicion?', *PMLA*, 117:3 (2002), 487–90 (488). Bell goes on to oppose this view.
10 For one of the book-length accounts of this disciplinary 'paradigm shift', see Antony Easthope, *Literary into Cultural Studies* (London: Routledge, 1991).

11 Carlos J. Alonso, 'Editor's Column: My Professional Advice (to Graduate Students)', *PMLA*, 117:3 (2002), 401–6 (401). Cf. the observation of James F. English, 'Literary Studies', in Tony Bennett and John Frow (eds), *The SAGE Handbook of Cultural Analysis* (London: SAGE, 2008), pp. 126–44, from a few years later that 'according to what has lately become a persistent and intensifying complaint, literary study has practically disappeared from many higher-educational institutions, and the true literary scholar is today a largely residual figure' (p. 126).

12 Harold Bloom, *The Western Canon: The Books and School of the Ages* (New York: Harcourt Brace, 1994).

13 George Levine, 'The Real Trouble', *Profession* (1993), 43–5 (43, 43–4). See also Levine's more extensive consideration of the issue around this same time in 'Introduction: Reclaiming the Aesthetic', in George Levine (ed.), *Aesthetics and Ideology* (New Brunswick: Rutgers University Press, 1994), pp. 1–28, some of the contributions to which collection perform the very demystification about which Levine is both understanding and anxious; and, more recently, see George Levine, 'Saving Disinterest: Aesthetics, Contingency, and Mixed Conditions', *NLH*, 32:4 (2001), 907–31. For another mid-nineties collection that as a whole voices similar ambivalence toward literary value, see James Soderholm (ed.), *Beauty and the Critic: Aesthetics in an Age of Cultural Studies* (Tuscaloosa: University of Alabama Press, 1997).

14 For one particularly lucid diagnosis of the sometimes hyperbolic perceptions of the demise of literary studies at the hands of cultural studies, see Rita Felski, 'The Role of Aesthetics in Cultural Studies', in Michael Bérubé (ed.), *The Aesthetics of Cultural Studies* (Malden: Blackwell, 2005), pp. 28–43.

15 Steven Connor, *Theory and Cultural Value* (Oxford: Blackwell, 1992), p. 14.

16 For one representative sampling of value-friendly literary critical approaches, see *PMLA*, 125:4 (2010), a special issue on 'Literary Criticism for the Twenty-First Century' guest edited by Jonathan Culler.

17 Rita Felski, *Uses of Literature* (Malden: Blackwell, 2008), p. 2.

18 MLA Teagle Foundation Working Group, 'Report to the Teagle Foundation on the Undergraduate Major in Language and Literature', *Profession* (2009), 285–312; *MLQ*, 72:3 (2011), a special issue on 'Literary Value'; *ChR*, 39:3 (2005), a special issue on 'Chaucer and Aesthetics'; Gregory Jusdanis, *Fiction Agonistes: In Defense of Literature* (Stanford: Stanford University Press, 2010); Peggy A. Knapp, *Chaucerian Aesthetics* (New York: Palgrave Macmillan,

2008). Also symptomatic in this regard is the fact that beginning in 2007 the MLA forum for The Teaching of Literature sponsored an annual session on the rather forum-existential topic of 'Why Teach Literature Anyway'. The series extended through 2020, although the 'Anyway' disappears from the title in 2012.
19 I cite additional studies of this sort in later chapters.
20 Teagle Working Group, 'Report', pp. 289, 289, 290. Cf. Jusdanis's neo-Horatian formula of literary value – 'to provide pleasure and a social purpose at the same time': 'On the one hand, we derive much enjoyment and excitement as we step into an illusory world. Yet from its fictional universe, we are also able to gaze back at the actual one, criticize it, see alternatives, or seek to transform it' (*Fiction Agonistes*, p. 3).
21 Harvard Humanities Working Group, 'The Teaching of the Arts and Humanities at Harvard College: Mapping the Future', https://scholar.harvard.edu/files/sdkelly/files/mapping_the_future_12_april_2013.pdf (2013; accessed 4 January 2020). For example, the report states, 'As the profiles of our disciplines shrink, we might also turn to those works that magnify the discipline, sometimes known as the canon ... A revisited canon could, however, be more flexibly sensitive to the conviction that works of enduring force and fame remain worth reading not least because great works of art never speak with unequivocal voice for one, closed position. That open-ended self-division is the very condition of their greatness' (p. 31).
22 Thus, to offer a single anecdote, when hearing about the topic of this book, my former colleague Jake Mattox – a scholar and teacher of nineteenth-century American Literature – quizzically rejoined, 'But aren't most English departments training people to challenge the whole question of value?'
23 Terry Eagleton, *Literary Theory: An Introduction* (Minneapolis: University of Minnesota Press, 1983); Stanley Fish, *Is There a Text in This Class?: The Authority of Interpretive Communities* (Cambridge, MA: Harvard University Press, 1980); Barbara Herrnstein Smith, *Contingencies of Value: Alternative Perspectives for Critical Theory* (Cambridge, MA: Harvard University Press, 1988).
24 Eagleton, *Literary Theory*, pp. 11, 16. Those who have followed Eagleton's career know that on this topic his views have continued to evolve. See, e.g., Terry Eagleton, *The Event of Literature* (New Haven: Yale University Press, 2012).
25 For a succinct history of the wider domain of axiological theory that traces the emergence of this anti-essentialist position, see John Fekete, 'Introductory Notes for a Postmodern Value Agenda', in John

Fekete (ed.), *Life after Postmodernism: Essays on Value and Culture* (New York: St. Martin's Press, 1987), pp. i–xix. Notably – and, in retrospect, presciently – as a whole the essays in this collection pivot between this anti-essentialism and something closer to advocacy.
26 Ian Hunter, *Culture and Government: The Emergence of Literary Education* (Basingstoke: Macmillan Press, 1988).
27 Guillory, *Cultural Capital*.
28 Pierre Bourdieu, *Distinction: A Social Critique of the Judgement of Taste*, trans. Richard Nice (Cambridge, MA: Harvard University Press, 1984); Bourdieu, *The Field of Cultural Production*, ed. Randal Johnson (New York: Columbia University Press, 1993).
29 Mary Poovey, *Genres of the Credit Economy: Mediating Value in Eighteenth- and Nineteenth-Century Britain* (Chicago: University of Chicago Press, 2008).

1
Literary value and the object of Chaucer studies

> The poetry that modern editorial practice assigns to Chaucer may be charming, astute, and, simply, beautiful, but the stable Chaucer whose agency determines this achievement – the Chaucer who serves as a canonical center against whom the marginal voices of vernacular culture have been defined – is more the creation of a Shakespearian-focused textual criticism than a historical medieval reality.
>
> – Tim William Machan[1]

> Few would deny that Chaucer's work has distinctive value.
>
> – Peggy Knapp[2]

As I mentioned in this book's introduction, the ground and provocation of the book's ruminations on literary value, as well as the leash that aims to keep those ruminations manageable, are specific, practical experiences of the study of literature. For this chapter, the provoking experience is an instance of my own pedagogical bad faith. When I first began teaching the *Canterbury Tales* (and to a significant degree as I still do), on the first day of the course I would inevitably cast the work as a wonderfully complex linked set of short stories, wholly conceived as such in all its details – a much more capacious and generically adventurous version of, say, *Dubliners*. Such a characterisation of the *Tales* is of course problematic for numerous reasons, and on that same first day, I would fully admit this. And yet – in the same way that, although Milton continuously reminds his readers that Satan is, well, Satan, we nonetheless remain fascinated by the character – no matter how much I emphasised the unfinished state of the *Tales*, its manuscript messiness, and the variety of objectionable motives behind its canonisation, somehow the work always ended up a Work (by the capitalisation of which I mean, here and throughout this chapter, a putatively unified aesthetic object abstracted from any of its material witnesses). My repeated falling into this temptation may have been merely a personal weakness, but I am arrogant enough to believe that it was, at least in part, a symptom of a more significant critical conundrum, one that was particularly visible around the turn of the century when I began teaching the *Tales*. This conundrum is the result of a conflict between what was then an ascendant trend in scholarship on premodern texts and inherited approaches to Chaucer criticism and pedagogy, a conflict that, as I will argue in this chapter, ultimately pivots on the problem of literary value. To be sure, the felt pressure of this conundrum was already beginning to fade by 2008, when I published the article that serves as the basis of this chapter, and by now in most quarters I suspect that it is not much felt at all. But this change is not due to any resolution of the conundrum. Rather, as I will suggest, it attests to the continuing impact of the problem of literary value, which has ensured the conundrum's sweeping under the rug. The story of the momentary palpability of this conundrum, therefore, provides an apt launching point into this book's inquiry into that problem.

The trend in scholarship to which I refer is that which is evident in the Machan quotation above. Extending well beyond Chaucer studies, it consists of a loose amalgamation of late twentieth-century critiques of authorship, authority and canonicity; historicism and the related, if not entirely coincident, emphasis on material culture in interpretive studies; and the self-consciousness about the theory and practice of textual criticism and editing that arose, in Middle English studies, in the wake of the Athlone *Piers Plowman* and from the prompting of textual critics and bibliographers of other periods and traditions, such as Jerome J. McGann, Bernard Cerquiglini and D. F. McKenzie. It overlaps and has a mutually inspiring relationship with the burgeoning field of book history.[3] Although my impression is that over the last two decades this trend has plateaued, it remains a vital force in the study of late medieval literature as well as in the larger field of literary studies, an approach ever more reflective upon its methodological and theoretical distinctiveness, affinities, provocations and evolutions. (Book history, for example, has been positioned as dovetailing with so-called distant reading.)[4] For convenience, I will call this amalgamation manuscript studies, recognising that this term is used by others both in more specific and more general ways, and that not all scholars who understand themselves to be working under this label would want themselves associated with all (or perhaps any) of the elements of my definition.[5]

The conflict to which I refer is evident in Machan's opposing of the 'beautiful' canonical Chaucer enshrined in the products of 'modern editorial practice' with the Chaucer of 'historical medieval reality'. This conflict, in one sense, was hardly novel. As David Matthews has shown, the beautiful, canonical Chaucer had thrived for centuries (in contrast with the rest of Middle English literature) before colliding with historicism in the form of nineteenth-century philology – a collision that in this instance turned out to be mutually generative, as it inaugurated, under the auspices of the first Chaucer Society, modern Chaucer studies.[6] As Ethan Knapp describes, Chaucer's subsequent eligibility for admission into the university in the late nineteenth century rested on his dual status as a poet 'gifted with visionary insight and universal applicability' (that is, as a proleptic Romantic canonical poet) and as an 'object of analysis for philology and *Textkritik*' (that is, as an object of rigorous, scientific historicism).[7] To an extent complementary, these two apprehensions of Chaucer nevertheless possess antithetical principles, and the tension between them has been felt in various ways throughout the history of Chaucer studies, sometimes in the form of oppositional schools (as in New Criticism versus Exegetics) and sometimes in the work of individual scholars (as in the disjunction between the philological and literary critical work of such Chaucerians as George Lyman Kittredge and John Livingston Lowes).[8]

Knapp goes on to suggest that the critical movements of the last thirty-some years have so shifted the terms of this conflict that we may in some respects have moved beyond it. Yet the ascendance of manuscript studies at the turn of the century revived it in at least one specific, concrete and crucial way: as Machan's remarks indicate, a manuscript-informed historicist scepticism put into question that which had served as both the longstanding product and object of Chaucer studies, the critical edition. The editorial tradition that marked the first phase of modern Chaucer studies – and which later culminated in the collective effort of *The Riverside Chaucer* – had sought, as Stephanie Trigg puts it, to produce critical editions answerable both to 'generalist' and 'specialist' readers. Trigg characterises these audiences as those without and within medieval studies, respectively, but the division also aligns with the Romantic/philological split lying at the origin of modern Chaucer studies. According to Trigg, the generalist reader understands Chaucer's text 'to embody timeless values and perspectives of easy relevance to modernity', which corresponds to the Romantic, canonical understanding of Chaucer; in contrast, the specialist reader insists 'on a discontinuous linguistic and historical past, approachable only through specialist training' – traditionally, philological training.[9] Put simply, the *Riverside*, like all the products of this editorial tradition, seeks to answer to this split by being at once an object of artistic excellence and an object of historical authenticity. But by the turn of the century, the notions of authorship and canonicity that underwrite the notion of artistic excellence had been widely subjected to intense scepticism, and, conversely, commitment to some form of historical authenticity, however provisional, had come to predominate interpretive criticism. The fusion of aims represented by the *Riverside* thus began in some quarters to seem instead conceptual *con*fusion, if not merely an ill-founded, misleading anachronism.

Derek Pearsall conveyed this critique of the Chaucer edition as early as 1985 (while the *Riverside* was still being compiled) in an essay published in a collection edited by McGann. In his characteristically witty fashion, Pearsall compares the 'the sterile operating theater (or terminal intensive care unit) of the modern critical edition' to listening to 'medieval music played on modern instruments'. Nonetheless, he maintains a commitment to the critical edition as a 'practical necessity for the needs of readers and students'.[10] Conceding the rift between generalist and specialist readers later described by Trigg, he suggests that different objects be constituted for each of these audiences. A little over a decade later, Theresa Tinkle, focusing specifically on the importance of manuscript *mise-en-page*, offered a similar account of the liabilities of the critical edition:

> Modern editors adopt a page layout that insists on Chaucer's alienation from medieval annotations and, accordingly, from scholasticism, medieval Catholicism, and Latinity. The page layout pronounces medieval readers and ways of reading at best irrelevant, at worst stodgily wrongheaded. The uncomplicated page also asserts

that the text is immediately accessible, that every reader is sufficient to it. Chaucer's medieval alterity becomes invisible.[11]

Tinkle's comments, with their implication that accessibility to Chaucer's work should give way to his 'medieval alterity', typifies many of the statements on the topic from the time of Pearsall's essay through the turn of the century.[12] As Trigg remarked in 2002, today's 'professional Chaucerians ... seem willing to make it more difficult to read Chaucer',[13] and they were so, as in Tinkle's privileging of 'medieval readers and ways of reading', in the name of historical authenticity unmoored from debunked Romantic notions of authorship and canon.

Tinkle's exceptional study – which, through close examinations of text, gloss and *mise-en-page* across versions of the *Wife of Bath*'s Prologue in different manuscripts, limns the different ways that early readers, editors and scribes apprehended the *Wife of Bath* – represents one possible avenue of literary critical response to the deauthorisation of the critical edition.[14] This response requires the decentring of the critical edition in favour of the medieval manuscript, that is, the elevation of the latter to the status of central object of inquiry, not just for those who have been traditionally concerned with manuscripts (e.g., textual critics, palaeographers) but also for many who fill the departmental ranks of medieval literary hermeneuts.[15] In studies such as Tinkle's, investigators put aside that which used to be the *end* of the labour devoted to manuscripts, the critical edition, in favour of the *means* to this end – or, more specifically, in favour of the material conditions of the production and dissemination of late medieval books, the state of those books and their reception and use by various audiences. This is the sort of work (whether or not Tinkle intends the association) that Stephen Nichols affirms in the introduction to the 1990 'New Philology' issue of *Speculum*, a mode of investigation that he describes as an examination of the 'manuscript matrix' rather than merely the texts represented in editions, 'and of both language and manuscript [in interaction] with the social context and networks they inscribe'.[16] Similarly, in an essay published around the same time, John Dagenais writes,

> I think the first thing we have to do in order to get at this physical text is to free it from relations of representation, that is, from the idea

that it represents, badly, an originary, authentic text. What I would propose as the first level is a simple shift in the unit we study from 'text' to ... the individual, unique, concrete manuscript codex.[17]

Tinkle's article exemplifies the undoubted perspicacity of this approach to medieval literary scholarship, as do many other, subsequent interpretative engagements with Chaucer's 'manuscript matrix', such as Maidie Hilmo's study of the pilgrim portraits in the Ellesmere manuscript, Arthur Bahr's study of the dynamic constellations of *Canterbury Tales* 'threads' (among other medieval texts he examines) and the contributions to a special issue of *ChR* on 'Medieval English Manuscripts: Form, Aesthetics, and the Literary Text', guest edited by Bahr and Alexandra Gillespie.[18] As Mary Carruthers remarked in her 1998 New Chaucer Society Presidential Lecture, '[M]uch of the most innovative and important work in medieval literary study ... has come from material studies of manuscripts and early books, and the greatly sophisticated theorising of editing procedures that these have enabled.'[19]

Given this demonstrated vitality of manuscript studies – along with its neat confluence of the old and new, the empirical and theoretical, and strands of several different widely adopted critical movements – one might fairly have expected it to produce a comprehensive paradigm shift in Chaucer studies. In particular, one might have predicted that the neglect, in published interpretations of Chaucer's poetry, of its formative critique of the critical edition would render those readings retrograde: conservative, naïve, ahistorical, presentist attempts to cover up the conflicts, fix *variance*, reprivilege the canon and just generally bring back the good old days. Yet, in fact, all through the period of manuscript studies' ascendency and up to the present, by far the majority of published interpretations of Chaucer – even the avant-garde, such as Aranye Fradenburg's *Sacrifice Your Love*, and even those in Marion Turner's historicist *tour de force* biography of the poet – generally restrict themselves to the *Riverside*.[20] Despite the prominence of some of the work that I have referenced, a manuscript studies approach to Chaucer was then and remains today the exception to the rule. As inclusive as current Chaucer scholarship may be of a variety of intertexts, for the text itself it usually does not look beyond the *Riverside* and, much less frequently, that edition's textual apparatus. Although Fradenburg, for example, certainly seeks to complicate our reading of Chaucer (as well as our understanding of Chaucer studies), she and most other Chaucer interpreters, then and now, show little interest in locating those complications in the material object of study. Indeed, wondering aloud about this discrepancy back in 2007, the manuscript studies scholar Andrew Taylor issued a call for papers for the 2008 New Chaucer Society conference in which he poses the question of whether 'Middle English manuscript studies and Middle English literary criticism constitute distinct academic cultures'.[21]

Such a distinction between the 'academic cultures' of manuscript studies and literary criticism, insofar as it exists, surely does not derive from mutual ignorance, since studies that call attention to this distinction – such as Trigg's and, more particularly, those of Ralph Hanna cited below – have been widely read in the field. Let us then assume, for the sake of argument, that the critique marshalled by manuscript studies of the aims, methods and ideologies of the Chaucer edition did not languish in obscurity but rather that professional Chaucer interpreters have generally granted its applicability, at least that of the moderate version as voiced by Pearsall. This seems plausible, given that no substantial counterargument to that critique (if not to manuscript studies generally) has to my knowledge been put forward. If this assumption thus holds to any significant degree, then the Chaucer critic's continued use of the edition as the basic material object of study necessarily incurs some amount of bad faith. This situation can lead to awkward moments, not just for the critic but also, as I suggested in this chapter's opening, for the teacher in the undergraduate classroom. As students file in on that first day – students who are unlikely to know much if anything about the late Middle Ages, much less about late medieval literary culture – does one begin by debunking the editions of Chaucer that they have just purchased? In an institutional economy in which study of the Middle Ages has been marginalised and at some institutions (including my prior one) faces the loss of faculty positions, how much ought a teacher emphasise that the *Canterbury Tales*, already in forbidding Middle English, is, as a Work, merely a modern editor's fiction?[22] One obvious solution to this awkwardness, both for teaching and for scholarship, would be the development of textual materials that attest better than does the standard print edition to the historical production, circulation and reception of Chaucer's writings. A marriage of manuscript studies to Chaucer interpretation and teaching might thereby be made on the basis of a replacement of the print edition as the basic material object of Chaucer studies with this other common object of study. But what ought, then, to constitute the latter?

In a 2001 article assessing the implications of the *Canterbury Tales* Project – an ongoing, now over three-decade effort, founded by Peter Robinson and currently led by Barbara Bordalejo, to produce digital editions of Chaucer – Charlotte Morse suggested, with only partial enthusiasm, 'Perhaps we will eventually prefer an electronic text for teaching students struggling with Middle English, a text ... whose parts we could reorder at will, whose text we could modify, leaving in or out, for example ... the Man of Law's Endlink.'[23] In the early 1990s, when the rise of manuscript studies coincided with excitement over the then nascent revolution in the electronic accessibility and digital representation of information, similar suggestions appeared with relatively more degrees of enthusiasm. For Murray McGillivray, for example, a hypertext edition could be 'an editorial vehicle that responds to the real nature of medieval textuality by presenting medieval works in their original state, as series of varying manuscript texts'.[24] Yet, despite the subsequent publications of the *Canterbury Tales* Project and widespread use of the Web as a pedagogical resource, the print edition remains today the basic material object of criticism and teaching. As of this writing, the paper pages of the *Riverside* still constitute the standard scholarly object of study, and, from what I have been informally able to gather, most teachers continue to assign one or more of the print options designed for classroom use, if they do not assign the now hard-to-order *Riverside*.[25] One new complete edition of Chaucer's works – the 2019 *Norton Chaucer* – has been published since the *Riverside*, and two others are in preparation.[26] The *Norton*, a student edition, is available as an eBook that comes equipped with a set of digital learning tools that does realise some of the potential imagined in the 1990s for electronic publications. Nonetheless, this eBook – as well as, say, the Harvard online interlinear translation of the *Tales*, which legions of students now consult as a crib – does not attempt, in the manner that McGillivray and others envisioned, to emulate 'the real nature of medieval textuality'. Nor will, as far as I am aware, the two forthcoming scholarly editions. In 2006, Ethan Knapp was still hopeful that digital editions may 'bring the diversity of manuscript culture into the classroom as never before'.[27] But by 2013, Bella Millet, reflecting on some of the continuing challenges with digital editions (including those of the *Canterbury Tales* Project), concludes, 'But even if electronic editing is not – from an academic point of view at least – a dead end, the way forward for those who use it is by no means clear.' Of the three kinds of challenges that Millet discusses, the most relevant for present purposes is 'impact' – the challenge of getting people to use such editions, 'even specialists in the field', which challenge, as Thorlac Turville-Petre admits in an essay in the same volume, remains daunting, despite his generally more optimistic view.[28] For now and the foreseeable future, therefore, the 'print' edition remains the field's object of study, no matter what its actual means of access.

This persistence, I argue, does not merely reflect the predictable lag between the promise and practicability of new technology, nor does it only derive from legitimate uncertainty about whether a digital edition truly would respond to the 'real nature of medieval textuality' better than a print edition. Rather, it represents, more profoundly, a *resistance* to an edition of Chaucer anything like that which was envisioned in the 1990s, and especially a resistance to such an edition of the *Canterbury Tales*, one that would announce in its very structure its own impossibility. It represents, that is, a resistance to an edition that would admit, it its material realisation, that there really is no *Canterbury Tales*, conceived of as a Work, but instead only eighty-some manuscripts dressed up to look like one.

This resistance is diffuse and largely unvoiced, discernible mostly through Chaucerians' collective decisions or the lack thereof. If it were to be formally articulated, I suspect that it would not be stubbornly traditionalist but rather speculatively interrogative. It would ask why the 'real nature of medieval textuality' ought necessarily to be the most appropriate object of study. It would wonder if the best material realisation of an object of study is necessarily the one that is, in theory, the most historically authentic. And, relatedly, it would ask on what basis ought we to allocate more scholarly and interpretative attention to some objects of study over others.[29] Manuscript studies shook loose these and other practical, foundational questions from their formerly secure institutional underpinnings. Chaucer studies silently responded, it seems, with a nod of the head and a shrug. In retrospect, then, it appears that the provocations of manuscript studies represented a sophisticated evolution of the same mixed motivations that lay behind the original concept and institutionalisation of Chaucer studies, in which Chaucer's texts as objects of timeless literary value sat uncomfortably next to his texts as objects of historical inquiry. The foundational questions shaken loose by manuscript studies, that is, represented a momentarily pronounced confrontation with the continuing operation of literary value in the subfield. Literary value has apparently won this confrontation, thereby demonstrating, among other things, that it still possesses determining force on the nature of the subfield's material object of study.

This victory of literary value has a number of important implications of cascading significance, some of which derive from the fact that that confrontation and subsequent victory went, as I have suggested, mostly unacknowledged outside of manuscript studies. While it is quite evident, as I will discuss below, that a more prominent, cognate confrontation with historicism likely provided cover for this one, that confrontation, too, pivots upon literary value in some essential respects. Literary value thus remains central to Chaucer studies in ways that at the very least call for examination. Moreover, if following that scrutiny we wish to embrace this centrality, in however qualified form, that embrace requires some defence, and a defence not merely for this or that instance of Chaucer study but for the institution of Chaucer studies – and more generally for the field of literary studies for which it constitutes a synecdoche. It is the project of this book as a whole to perform this scrutiny and to consider at least some responses to the problem of literary value, which in some cases will resemble provisional defences of it. In the rest of the present chapter, I will argue that literary value's particular claim on the nature of the material realisations of the object of Chaucer study is neither fully avoidable, nor theoretically indefensible nor wholly undesirable.

To make this case, I have much groundwork to lay. It would seem, for example, that I need to provide at least a skeletal formulation for the concept of literary value. But in fact that task will require deferral until the next chapter, following the ground-clearing efforts of the ensuing three sections of this present one.

In the first of these sections, I take a closer look at the collision between manuscript studies and inherited approaches to Chaucer studies in order to identify the basic conflict involved. In that light, the second section establishes a sort of toe hold for the concept of literary value and proceeds to consider the nature and implications of the basic conflict in its terms. The final section puts forward claims about the conflict's consequences, some of which will provide cues for the theorisation of Chapters 2 and 3. Before moving on, however, I should make plain that in broaching this topic, I am not in any fashion seeking a return, with some Ghost of Criticism Past, to the days when Great Works could simply be studied and taught as Great Works. Rather, I am claiming that the considerable achievements of manuscript studies over the last several decades have exhumed some ghosts that have not really left us: in particular, the ghosts that had informed some central New Critical presuppositions. I aim not to reanimate those ghosts but rather to scrutinise the implications of the continuing influence of one in particular, the ghost of judgement.

New Critical revenant

It is no coincidence that the rise of manuscript studies followed shortly upon the heels of the demise of New Criticism as the dominant ideology and set of practices governing literary studies. Although manuscript studies cannot claim credit for this demise, several of its practitioners make plain that the New Critical hegemony was a hostile environment, one premised on an *a priori* hierarchical disjunction between manuscript studies – in its earlier, edition-oriented formation – and literary criticism. As Machan describes it,

> Within this interpretative framework [of New Criticism], the labors of textual critics of any historical period could only be pedestrian: they provided the texts necessary for serious and sensitive scholars to do serious and sensitive work. The transcendent verbal icon by nature simply is, and so any inquiries about its origin or development are non-questions; indeed, when the New Critics themselves glanced at textual criticism, the attention they manifested was often in essence indifference or ignorance.[30]

Although Machan offers here, for polemical purposes, something of a caricature of New Criticism, he fairly calls attention to New Criticism's notorious emphasis on the autonomy of the literary object and its consequent deemphasising of that object's historically contingent material origins and realisations. Even when formalists and textual scholars were, so to speak, on the same side (as when they were the same individual, e.g., George Kane and E. T. Donaldson), the assumptions regarding the critical utility of such basic categories as intention made the perspectives of the two roles rather different, and hence registered a division of hierarchy between their labours. As Machan notes, to create the 'medieval verbal icon' out of the surviving manuscript evidence, editors relied on 'the supposition that an author's final intentions and an authoritative text lay in the distant but recoverable textual past'.[31] The edition was thus an edifice constructed out of authorial intention, and yet, when that edition subsequently became an object of critical explication, considerations of intention became categorically suspect, if not simply relegated to the realm of fallacy.

In practice, New Criticism – especially as applied to Chaucer – was rarely so categorical, but it nonetheless did maintain the inherited conception of manuscripts as, to put it figuratively, shadows on a cave wall cast by the light of genius shining on a Work. Only with the loosening of New Criticism's grip on the academy – first by poststructuralism and then by historicism and cultural studies – was it possible to undo this conception. What was subsequently accomplished within some quarters of manuscript studies was, as I have described above, akin to Marx's standing of Hegel on his head: the materiality and multiplicity of manuscript matrices became the real, and the edition became a sort of false consciousness. This demystification was largely salutary, and, again, I have no wish to turn the clock back in this regard. Nonetheless, while the number of Chaucerians wholly comfortable with the identity of New Critic likely dwindled to zero over the course of the last third of the twentieth century, key formalist concepts and practices maintained a core influence on Chaucer criticism. In part, this influence consisted of the continuing, if increasingly obscured, legacy of such powerful critics as Donaldson and Charles Muscatine, whose shaping of Chaucer studies in the second half of the twentieth century, particularly in contestation with D. W. Robertson and the exegetical school, has been well documented by Lee Patterson.[32] In part, too, this influence is simply that which was carried forward within some versions of late twentieth-century historicism. As Alan Liu and others have argued, the historicist criticism practiced under the label 'cultural poetics', for example, represented not an abandonment of formalism but a projection of it into the space of history and culture.[33]

For certain types of Middle English texts, such as the lyric, the continuing influence of formalism was scarcely even hidden, as Seth Lerer pointed out in 2003 in 'The Endurance of Formalism in Middle English Studies'. In this essay, Lerer expresses dissatisfaction with New Critical readings of Middle English lyrics that then still held currency (and had led to the genre's relative marginalisation, even in respect to the already marginal subfield of Middle English Studies), and he concludes by calling for a renewed attention to form as a locus of historical contingency.[34] With this exhortation Lerer took a position that had affinity with the growing array of approaches, originally developed in respect to the literatures of other periods, that was beginning to be called New Formalism. As in Lerer's essay, many of those who have embraced this sort of approach (whether or not under that label) understand it to be more of a correction or an expansion of historicism than a rejection. They maintain, for example, that inattention to the specific nature of literary forms, deriving from the historicist suspicion of the autonomy of the art object, had actually circumscribed the analytical reach of historicism.[35] Today, this revitalised, more theoretically nimble and ideologically self-aware concern with form has taken up firm residence within Chaucer studies, as evident in, say, the work of Eleanor Johnson and a recent collection of essays entitled *Chaucer and the Subversion of Form*.[36] Indeed, the very ease with which this approach has secured practitioners constitutes another indication that earlier varieties of formalism had not really been wholly eclipsed.

Like the rise of manuscript studies that preceded it, this trend in scholarship is, I believe, wholly laudable. The distinct historicity of form, as well as its relation to the historicity of other elements of the text and contexts of a work of literature, is surely worth the renewed attention that it is receiving. Moreover, that New Formalism began to be adopted in Chaucer studies amid the ascendency of manuscript studies does not attest to any necessarily agonistic relation between the two. To be sure, the rise of New Formalism was, as I have suggested, plainly part of a more general inclination within the field of literary studies to move beyond historicism,[37] and therefore inasmuch as manuscript studies partook of the latter, the return to form also supplied some cover under which the implications of manuscript studies may be evaded. Without actually seeking any engagement with the critique of the Chaucer edition, that is, New Formalism's revisionary response to historicism has helped to bury that critique. Nonetheless, the two approaches are not *prima facie* mutually exclusive and are not infrequently fruitfully complementary – indeed, the latter view is the overall contention of the aforementioned *Chaucer Review* special issue edited by Bahr and Gillespie, and no few Chaucerians have worked both sides of the aisle.[38]

These new kinds of formalist analyses, however, may still put demands on their objects of study – though not as many or as rigidly as did New Criticism – that manuscript studies would resist. Such resistance, for example, was readily in evidence during the Q&A that followed a 2006 New Chaucer Society conference session dedicated to 'The Value of Close Reading: Theory'. Several times, manuscript studies scholars raised questions about, for example, textual variance, and finally the session organiser and chair, Christopher Cannon, understandably moved the conversation on to other topics.[39] As an illustration of exactly where the resistance lies, let us imagine a New Formalist reading of the *Wife of Bath* that closely examines the forms of her speech habits, against the backdrop of records of actual fourteenth-century women's speech, for evidence of her attitudes toward sexuality. As Tinkle's article shows, variation in the wording of the Wife's speeches on this topic between the Ellesmere and Hengwrt manuscripts makes a determination of these attitudes for *the* Wife of Bath (as distinct from either the Ellesmere or Hengwrt Wife) problematic.[40] Without the mooring of a critical edition and its restriction of variation to a carefully circumscribed apparatus, therefore, any instance of formalist analysis, old or new, may potentially transmogrify into either an epiphenomenon of an editorial debate (such as that of the relative authority of Ellesmere and Hengwrt) or, as in Tinkle's study, analysis of something other than the meaning of a literary text (for example, of that text's reception, rewriting or misunderstanding by a professional reader). And when one extends the scope of formalist analysis beyond lexical detail to structure, the situation may become proportionally more tenuous, especially in regard to the *Canterbury Tales*, with its manuscripts' variation in tale order and links. To be sure, *Tales* manuscripts, especially the earliest ones, share a great deal more than, say, the notoriously variant manuscripts of popular romances, and editors have resolved differences in accidentals and wording, in many cases, with a high degree of likelihood.[41] Moreover, countless formal characteristics, such as Chaucer's use of rime royal for particular tales, are universally attested. Nonetheless, despite the hopes that some may hold for the *Canterbury Tales* Project or, several generations ago, the monumental efforts of J. M. Manly and Edith Rickert to construct a definitive edition from all available witnesses, a single form for the *Tales* will necessarily remain an editorial fiction, and hence the ground of formalist treatments of its text always, to greater and lesser degrees, shaky.[42]

In response to this situation, a manuscript-alert, historically robust formalism might consist of context-saturated studies of the literary forms evident in individual or particular sets of manuscripts – which is in fact more-or-less what Tinkle achieves in her essay, as do some New Formalist studies. But this sort of project takes us back to the position, discussed above, that would make the manuscript, rather than the critical edition, the central object of study. Hence, insofar as this sort of project represents a way forward that reconciles historicism, manuscript studies and emergent formalisms, its shift in the object of study returns us to the basic questions that this chapter seeks to explore, which may now be rephrased as: what rationale remains for *not* giving the manuscript this place of honour? The answer, it appears, is: essentially the same rationale that had been hiding in plain view prior to the twenty-first century renovation of formalism. To see this, we may turn the clock back a few years and revisit a celebrated study published during the apex of the influence of manuscript studies by one of its most prominent practitioners.

In 1996's *Pursuing History*, Ralph Hanna argues that the production of critical editions is still necessary, but only so that the distinct features of individual manuscripts may thereby be cast into relief. He contends that the notion of a stable, authorial text that transcends any of its manuscript witnesses – a postulate that had undergirded the autonomous New Critical verbal icon, the putative unity of which depended upon lexical and structural constancy – still possesses heuristic power, in that it provides access to precisely those materials that the New Critical verbal icon hid:

> History is not to be found initially in 'the genuinely authorial' but only through what is 'inauthentic', 'not genuine'. And erroneous readings only reveal themselves to editorial judgment, to a knowledge of how textual transmission occurs within a manuscript culture. Hence, identifying possibly authorial (or at least archetypal, O^1) readings remains important as allowing a more pervasive historicization, that of medieval literary communities.

The authorial text remains necessary, but primarily for its position within a negative dialectic that yields the 'more pervasive historicization' evident in departures from this text. In Tinkle's study, for example, the critical edition serves as the backdrop for identifying the manuscript variants pertaining to the *Wife of Bath*'s language that constitute the more important object of study. Hanna thus calls for continuation of traditional author-centred editorial activity but only so that we may use the traditional result of this activity – the supposed canonical text – to unearth a more important object, the 'Middle English literary communities the record of whose existence Chaucerian canonical hegemony had by and large suppressed'.[43]

Like other manuscript studies scholars, then, Hanna calls for a shift in the object of study from edition to manuscript, but he also provides a rationale for retaining the edition, albeit a much diminished one. As undeniably fruitful as this approach has been, however, it also puts rather awkward demands on Middle English scholars, as it calls for considerable energy to be devoted to producing editions in whose critical priority (and even authority) we ought no longer to believe.[44] In effect, Hanna calls for the production of two distinct but interdependent material realisations of objects of study – the critical edition and the collection of 'erroneous readings' that carry the history of 'medieval literary communities' – and then asks us to put aside the latter for the former. Yet even if the expertise required for such an enterprise abounded, it is not likely to become widely adopted, as the elapsed years between Hanna's comments and now appear to attest. And the reason for this is in fact evident in Hanna's own account of the origin and outcome of his career-long pursuit of just this enterprise, which provides us with a sort of parable about the inevitability of literary value.

This account requires some close attention, as, for the purposes of this present chapter, it serves as a paradigm for the persistence of literary value, inherited from supposedly discarded critical practices, even among those scholars who consciously devote their work elsewhere. As Hanna describes, his first exposure to Chaucer occurred when he was twelve years old, when his father, reprimanding him for his use of questionable language, made an off-hand comment about Chaucer's use of such language. In response, Hanna developed what may be described as, for lack of a more sophisticated term, a passion: 'But I'd also discovered a poet apparently salty enough for twelve-year-old tastes (and within a week acquired a used Vintage Chaucer at a Guadalupe Street bookstore) and discovered that "in form of speche is change". I was hooked irrevocably, however I tried to wriggle away'. Hanna's experience resembled, precociously, that of many undergraduates in their first encounter with Chaucer: initially attracted by the poet's salacious reputation, they soon are drawn by other aspects of his writing and, in some cases, become 'hooked irrevocably'. And, like many of those who become so hooked that they pursue postgraduate study, Hanna later experienced a demystification of his former passion. As with his initial encounter, this experience was a precocious one, although in this instance (with its anticanonical sensibility) it was so in respect to the history of Chaucer criticism and in particular the rise of manuscript studies:

> I began to realize that what I felt alienated me from Chaucer was, not knowability, but overfamiliarity – not Chaucer's ease, but what modern literary study had made of Chaucer ... the Chaucer we read had come to be conceived of as the ultimate New Critical poetic text ... In this critical context, the notion that Chaucer or his readers had a history and were embroiled in one was largely suppressed. Whatever the effect of such repression upon 'the father', the effect on study of his contemporaries and successors was even more dispiriting. Informatively, the literary canons that privileged Chaucer's Art directed attention from these figures as of interest only 'historically' – but then failed to outline what such a history would be.

Hanna discovered that the object of his initial attraction was a New Critical object, and, as he learned about all that New Criticism had 'largely suppressed', he began a search for an alternative object. The latter object became the local histories of medieval literary communities, as they have been transmitted by the specificities of individual manuscripts:

> I began to wonder whether some aggressive use of the primary evidence for the existence of such [noncanonical] literary figures – the manuscripts themselves – might undo what Chaucer studies had done only too well, return these figures to a historical context and direct research toward a local knowledge that would uncover that context, whatever it was.[45]

No one would dispute that Hanna, in his many publications, has made a remarkable contribution to the 'local knowledge' of the production and dissemination of Middle English texts. And yet, the very book in which these passages occur, which states so clearly in these introductory remarks its anticanonical intentions, makes a major contribution to Chaucer studies.[46] Half of its sixteen chapters take some aspect of one or more of Chaucer's texts as their basic topic, and Chaucer features significantly in several others. Conscious of this potential contradiction, Hanna seeks to explain it as follows:

> The center of the volume in the main takes up Chaucerian problems. This block of six essays consists of studies I should have preferred not to have undertaken, deviations from the major areas of my concern. (All, in fact, began as accidents.) However, writing about the text of Chaucer, the poet's ipsissima verba, may be construed as an inevitability: just as Shakespeare's text has always triggered the most exciting advances in general bibliographic studies, so the canonically central medieval poet demands the attention of anyone involved with Middle English textual dissemination.[47]

As Hanna describes, the return to a canonical author is 'an inevitability', indeed, one that supersedes the will of the scholar. In pursuing what he calls the 'precanonical' history of medieval literary communities in the evidence provided by manuscripts, Hanna is led repeatedly back to the manuscripts of 'the canonically central medieval poet'. The reason for this recursion (other than the 'accidents' that initiated each study) seems to lie in the fact that because so much attention has already been bestowed on the study of Chaucer manuscripts, as in the case of the folios and quartos of Shakespeare, they have become the principal vehicles for reflection on the complexities in the relations between surviving documents and the myriad histories to which they attest. Because Chaucer's canonicity has garnered his texts so much scholarly attention, even studies with anticanonical intentions are drawn into the orbit of that canonicity. As a result, *Pursuing History*, however much it seeks to circumvent Chaucer's value, makes Chaucer's texts one of its principal objects, thereby contributing, against its intentions, to Chaucer's prominence within Middle English studies.[48]

This parable thus begins with a boy drawn to a literary work by qualities that seem intrinsic to it (for example, its saltiness). Later as a young man he realises that whatever qualities the work in fact possesses, its character has been constructed for him by an interpretative heritage (New Criticism) that suppresses the real (local histories). He therefore puts aside intrinsic literary value as an object and sets off in pursuit of the real. The parable concludes with the protagonist as an older man discovering that in this very pursuit, he has returned to the scene of the value that he earlier put aside, albeit in a different interpretative fashion. When extrapolated from the career of one particular scholar, Hanna's experience tells the story of the rise of manuscript studies more generally: at both the beginning and on the horizon of this trend (as well as at the beginnings and ends of many of its individual projects) stands literary value, even when practitioners do not consider such value integral and sometimes – as with Hanna in the introduction to *Pursuing History* – when they depict it as hostile. More specifically, the parable tells the story of the uneasy relation between Middle English manuscript studies and Chaucer's *a priori* literary value, the energies of which manuscript studies both draws upon and at times resists.

The New Critical ghost that haunts the Hanna parable, the one that never left Chaucer studies and with which the rise of manuscript studies provoked confrontation, is thus the ghost of judgement, the assessment of the relative value of a literary work. Of course, judgement, as a task of criticism, was hardly invented by New Critics. Going back at least as far as Aristotle and Plato, the critical imperative of evaluation was, as mentioned above, particularly integral to the establishment of modern Chaucer studies in the nineteenth century, as it was the long history of affirmative judgement of Chaucer's poetry that constituted the enabling companion to 'scientific' philology. Moreover, I do not mean to overemphasise the influence of New Criticism on Chaucer studies. In comparison with, say, the early modern lyric, Chaucer's works (especially the long narratives) were less amenable to the approach, and many scholars, for a variety of reasons (Robertsonianism being one of them), were reluctant to adopt or just outright opposed to it. Insofar as I am addressing the judgement of Chaucer's texts per se, then, my topic necessarily has roots in deeper soil than the shifts in critical approaches over the last three-quarters of a century. Nonetheless, those shifts provide a revealing lens and convenient scope, both because the influence of New Criticism on Chaucer studies – albeit not comprehensive – is unquestionable (as, for example, Hanna's and Machan's negative reactions to it attest) and because judgement was, in comparison to other approaches, so central to New Criticism.

New Criticism's ghost of judgement, however, was in 1996 and remains today easy to ignore for at least two principal reasons. First, it is such an obvious target for both poststructuralist and historicist (and, for that matter, any of the post-New Critical) approaches to literature. Evaluative terms such as 'great', 'better' and 'more valuable' have been justifiability considered cheap ideological Trojan horses, and the most cursory survey of literary history proves characterisations of worth to be among the most evanescent of literary pronouncements. One may thus decisively discredit judgement categorically, without a deeper examination of whether one has in fact thereby evaded it. (By the same token, as I will explore in Chapter 4, one may thus discredit canonicity without actually freeing oneself from it.) Second, New Critics themselves expressed varying degrees of ambivalence towards judgement. Not wishing their method to appear impressionistic like that of so many of their predecessors outside the academy, they typically framed their arguments in terms of explication or understanding, rather than evaluation.[49] The critique of New Criticism marshalled by manuscript studies consequently focused not on judgement but on principles of explication, especially New Criticism's antihistoricism, anti-intentionalism and requirement of a singular, fixed text – that is, all that Machan places together under the label 'transcendent verbal icon'.

Yet, for New Critics, understanding always implied judgement, since explication was a process of disclosing how all the elements of a poem either succeed at contributing to a whole or fail to do so. As W. K. Wimsatt put it, 'our main critical problem is always how to push understanding and value as far as possible in union, or how to make our understanding evaluative'.[50] Indeed, in Wimsatt and Monroe C. Beardsley's famous polemic against the 'intentional fallacy', it is the fundamental category of judgement that makes intention (as well as history) relatively unimportant in critical practice: 'How is he [the critic] to find out what the poet tried to do? If the poet succeeded in doing it, then the poem itself shows what he was trying to do .... Judging a poem is like judging a pudding or a machine. One demands that it work. It is only because an artefact works that we infer the intention of an artificer.'[51] For Wimsatt and Beardsley, and New Criticism generally, the determination of the relative success of a poem – that is, its aesthetic merit – is identical to the process of understanding it. A poem becomes less successful to the extent that appeals to intention or historical context, deemed external, are required for this understanding. Hence, given judgement's foundational role, a critique of New Criticism that does not fully account for literary value leaves itself open to be haunted by what it has supposedly left behind.

In the field of English literary studies generally, and especially in the products of its institutionalisation, the persistent ghost of judgement is not hard to find. In addition to the type of vexing presence evident in Hanna's *Pursuing History*, it makes, pervasively, more straightforward appearances. For example, for all the changes to the *Norton Anthology of English Literature* over the last several editions to bring it in line with changing notions of literary history – the greater variety of texts, the retuned historical introductions to periods, the timelines of texts juxtaposed with contexts, the groups of texts centred around historical and cultural issues such as 'women in power' – the headnotes to authors are so consistently laudatory of aesthetic prowess that most undergraduates must come away with a powerful sense of judgement's role in the discipline. New to the seventh edition (2000), for example, was the offhand value-laden remark, 'Andrew Marvell's finest poems are second to none in this or any other period', and this remark – the opening to Marvell's headnote – has been retained in the most recent (tenth) edition.[52]

Similarly little effort is required to locate offhand remarks of judgement in Middle English criticism. In addition to this chapter's second epigraph, the opening sentence of an article by Peggy Knapp, an example especially resonant with present purposes (although with Langland standing in for Chaucer as the self-evident instance of literary value) appears in Kathryn Kerby-Fulton's response to what she perceives as Hanna's charge, in his negative review of *Iconography and the Professional Reader*, that she and Denise Despres undervalued *Piers Plowman*:

> The particular approach under disapproval here is our reception history. Contrary to what Hanna implies, it is an approach, we feel, that pays Langland the profoundest authorial compliment: we *know* he's a great poet, and we do not feel we have to prove that in every sentence we write. (Previous generations did carry this burden, and established his poetic reputation brilliantly.)[53]

For the celebrated manuscript studies scholar Kerby-Fulton, the value of Langland's poem is irrelevant to her project, not because such evaluative terms as 'great poet' are ideologically freighted or mere historical contingencies, but rather because the value has been so well established it need no longer be of concern. Moreover, she positions her and Despres's critical project neither in opposition, nor even as an alternative, to the activity of judgement. Instead, she suggests that manuscript-based reception study, while not directly evaluative, is in its very existence affirmative of the worth of Langland's poem – since, presumably, only a 'great poet' justifies such extensive critical attention to a single manuscript. Inasmuch as *Iconography and the Professional Reader* succeeds, then, it testifies not only to the historical interest in the Douce *Piers Plowman* but also to the continuing value of the Work *Piers Plowman*. As in the parable of Hanna's *Pursuing History*, once again a manuscript-oriented study begins with value (the already established 'poetic reputation' of Langland) and ends with value (the 'profoundest authorial compliment' the study represents).[54]

It perhaps goes without saying that if we may spot the ghost of judgement within manuscript studies out of the corners of our eyes, so to speak, we may expect its regular appearance in more-or-less full view in the more value-friendly approach of New Formalism. As with New Criticism, however, this ghost usually wears a thin disguise, appearing not as judgement per se but as some sort of aesthetic success brought about through an author's canny deployment of formal devices and, sometimes, reflection on the category of form itself. Quite frequently, the aesthetic success also entails a windfall of some other kind of value (ethical, epistemological, political, etc.), and later in this book I will explore the broader nature and implications of this tendency in literary criticism generally to propagate kinds of value. As just one example for present purposes, I highlight Johnson's contribution to *Chaucer and the Subversion of Form*. In considering how several works of literature, including Chaucer's *House of Fame*, formally enact a 'disavowal of the necessity or even utility of linear causality in human life', Johnson argues that in Chaucer's poem, 'the dreamily rendered antiplot becomes a formal tool for meditating on the unknowables and inscrutables of life'. In this way, the *House of Fame* joins the other works in showing us that 'linear causality has become a distortionary hermeneutic that must be overthrown if the true experience of things – whether those things comprise a quest for good fame, human vulnerability, or political resistance – is to be conveyed'.[55] Not unlike Wimsatt and Beardsley's 'pudding or machine', Johnson plainly tacitly reaffirms Chaucer's literary value by judging the form of the *House of Fame* to be successful, in this instance by its disavowal of linear causality. And she goes further than her New Critical predecessors by understanding this formal success as reaping the reward of some extra-literary value, here 'the true experience of things'. As in New Critical studies, the very inclusion of Chaucer presumes his literary value, which the ensuing analysis goes on to reaffirm, and so literary value stands as both the study's enabling condition and its product.

The object of value

If the ghost of judgement – whether in the form of Langland, Chaucer or some other signifier of literary excellence – thus continues to haunt late medieval English literary studies, then we must ask what the nature of this ghost is and what the consequences of its haunting are. As I have just recalled, for New Critics, that one piece of language could possess more 'greatness' or aesthetic value than another was the preexisting condition that made literary criticism, as a definably distinct intellectual activity, both possible and necessary. Without the assumption that texts possessed relative greatness, the task of criticism (conceived of as, most fundamentally, judgement) was meaningless. Hence, the object of study that both justified the discipline and was its product was the *notional object of literary value*. What was held to constitute this value was theorised in different ways by different groups of formalists (and thus tended to distinguish one from another, for example, the New Critics from the Chicago School). Indeed, as I mentioned in this book's introduction, such theorisation, well before and after the age of New Criticism, has constituted a vast collective enterprise. Inasmuch as a definition of *literary value* requires a definition of *literary*, it raises the questions of the nature of the literary per se and whether and how texts may possess relative amounts of it – questions that go as far back as we can trace the history of meditations on something that we now include in the category of literature and that have received an intimidating array of answers. In the next chapter, I formulate a preliminary theory, not of the literary nor even of literary value, but of literary valu*ing*, a more modest task that has more likelihood of fitting the box to which it is assigned. For present purposes, I will simply emphasise only that which strikes me as a more-or-less self-evident pragmatic given: the *structural role* that literary value plays in the field of Chaucer studies as a *concept* (hence my label 'notional object'), conceiving of that concept first as a placeholder in an institutionalised system of scholarship and teaching, prior to whatever content this placeholder may contain. In Chapter 2, it will be precisely this emphasis on literary value as a placeholder that becomes the basis of this book's preliminary theory of literary valuing.

Literary value, regardless of the relative persuasiveness of the many and various attempts to define it in a tangible sense, was pragmatically extant for New Critics as a collective surmise. If a group of investigators – under the influence of a long tradition of judgement both within and without the academy – assumes that some texts are somehow better than others, then the selection and elucidation of those texts become justifiable scholarly and pedagogical activities. For New Critics, the structural position held by literary value could thus function institutionally as centripetal mission, the notional centre around which the discipline was organised. For individual acts of critical practice, literary value could function as both anchor point (what one looks for in a text) and outcome (what one finds or does not find). The notional centre hence enabled the myriad activities of literary studies and was at the same time (that is, dialectically) confirmed and defined by those activities: the presumed existence of this quality necessarily preceded the act of formalist criticism, and the evidence for its presence, or lack thereof, was that act's product.[56]

New Critics acknowledged other relevant and related objects of study but considered them adjuncts to the object of value and named as 'fallacies' those critical practices that unduly sought to elevate one of those lesser objects. For example, for Wimsatt and Beardsley, a poem is unarguably from one perspective an object of intention: 'A poem does not come into existence by accident. The words of a poem ... come out of a head, not out of a hat.' But, as their immediately subsequent assertion makes plain, a critic errs when making this object the focus of investigation: 'Yet to insist on the designing intellect as a *cause* of a poem is not to grant the design or intention as a *standard* by which the critic is to judge the worth of the poet's performance.'[57] The authors' two emphases in this statement mark two different objects of study, and, for Wimsatt and Beardsley, the second object – the object of 'worth' or value – constitutes the logical apriority that, for poetry, would lend any interest at all to the first, the object of intention.

As I have reviewed, such a hierarchy was also, until the rise of manuscript studies, largely assumed among the scholars who concerned themselves with Chaucer's manuscripts and whose primary aim was the production of editions of Works. Although their more immediate object of study was the object of intention – that is, authorial readings – they readily acknowledged the subordination of this object to the one of value. The search for authorial readings among the manuscripts of the *Canterbury Tales*, for example, proceeded on the assumption that the *Tales*, as a singular literary Work in the very process of being constituted by the editor, *a priori* possessed value, which thereby justified the effort. Putatively cordoned off from consideration until the quasi-scientific work of the editor was complete, this *a priori* object of value in fact not only initiated the effort but also, as many have shown (and as most editors would readily admit), was a determining factor in the minutest editorial decisions, regardless of editorial method – for example, recension, best-text or eclectic.[58] Editors conceived of the completed effort – the edition – as an imperfect reification of the notional object of value, the material substitute upon which critical judgement of value may be exercised, a substitute assumed stable until subsequent editors constituted new, presumably less imperfect reifications.

Given this history, what we have seen to be the persistence of the ghost of judgement subsequent to the rise of manuscript studies – even among those scholars whose work exemplifies that trend – suggests that this New Critical hierarchy of objects has never really been supplanted. But if this is so, it stands in stark contradiction with the many insinuations and no few explicit assertions, sometimes programmatic ones, otherwise. Manuscript studies, as evident in Hanna's emphasis on 'Middle English literary communities', has often (though certainly not always) appeared to subordinate the object of value to, if not wholly replace it with, the object of *cultural significance* (or, less neutrally, the object of ideology). This object, which often goes under the name 'material culture', is also more-or-less the one that historicist approaches have typically sought to put at the centre of inquiry. As Catherine Gallagher and Stephen Greenblatt described in 2000 (in retrospect, at the beginning of the end of historicism's hegemony), while historicism by no means rejects the object of value, it has – under the influence of cultural anthropologists such as Clifford Geertz – subordinated it to the more general 'cultural text', demoting it to the status of just one historical integer among others. This move 'vastly expands the range of objects available to be read and interpreted' and thus in turn entails, to some degree, an attitude 'skeptical, wary, demystifying, critical, and even adversarial' towards the object of value that no longer holds centre stage.[59] It is the move that David Wallace, in his general preface to the 1999 *Cambridge History of Medieval Literature*, describes as especially well suited to the study of the late medieval literatures produced in Britain, and the one that Charlotte Morse in a 1997 essay understands as (among other things) transforming the largely formalist-inspired notion of 'Ricardian poetry' into the project of 'Ricardian studies'.[60] And, to many of those who remain committed to the central position of literary value – even such manuscript-savvy and historically-informed critics as Pearsall and John Burrow – it is a move that therefore threatens the discipline by its failure to distinguish works of lesser and 'greater intrinsic literary significance' and its tendency to push literature 'aside in the quest for socio-political significance'.[61]

Moreover, as many readers will have already recognised, this putative subordination of the object of value to the object of cultural significance by manuscript studies and historicism is one that has obtained more purchase in the more general distinction between the disciplines of literary and cultural studies, the latter being famous for having no particular commitment to literature at all and certainly not to canonical literature.[62] And for the study of medieval literature this distinction is further complicated by the already longstanding distinction between literary studies and the multidisciplinary formation of medieval studies. The multilayered relation between the latter and the sort of cultural studies approaches that emerged in the late twentieth century, however, requires more attention that I can supply here. It will have to suffice to observe that on the one hand, medieval studies traditionally has been very welcoming of the distinctive objects of each of its contributing disciplines, but, on the other hand, under the influence of historicism and cultural studies, its potential as a kind of flagship for medieval cultural studies has garnered some recognition, as, say, the aforementioned essay by Morse suggests. There is hence something of a parallel, albeit a very imperfect one, between the distinction between the objects of literary and cultural studies and the distinction between the objects of Chaucer studies and medieval studies, with manuscript studies (at least that which involves Chaucer) often explicitly aligning itself with the latter even while it maintains a more-or-less subterranean commitment to the former.

The emergence of manuscript studies, as I reviewed above, was related but not reducible to the emergence of historicism and cultural studies – as evident, for example, in the fact that a scholar such as Pearsall was so active in manuscript studies even while taking an adversarial stance toward some historicist approaches. Nonetheless, the apparent subordination of the object of value to the object of cultural significance, which historicism and cultural studies often explicitly trumpeted, provided crucial legitimation for the elevation of the manuscript from means to end. As a key element of the 'cultural text', the physical manuscript for Middle

English investigators became the most important of the vastly expanded 'range of objects to be read and interpreted' described by Gallagher and Greenblatt. Dovetailing with initiatives in the theory of textual criticism (in particular, the demotion of the authorial text), this emphasis blurred the distinction between literary critic and manuscript scholar in a way that is so visible in studies such as Tinkle's or, in a somewhat different vein, Lerer's 1993 *Chaucer and His Readers*.[63] Indeed, in his introduction to a 1999 collection of manuscript studies essays, Thomas Prendergast calls attention to this blurring as such, stating that the collection's 'variety of approaches ... encompass the palaeographical concerns of Hanna and Pearsall, the New Historical approach of Lee Patterson, and some of the bibliographical methods of Greetham and McGann'.[64]

In *Chaucer and His Readers*, Lerer constructs from a codicological study of fifteenth-century manuscripts and early printed books an understanding of how, and to what end, the authority of Chaucer was constituted vis-à-vis the particular time, place and constituency of the producers and audiences of those codices. The cultural significance of such artefacts – to a much greater extent than the timeless literary value of Chaucer's Works – appears to serve for Lerer as the *a priori* notional object of study that dialectically both enables the investigation and is that investigation's product. Indeed, from the perspective of this and similar studies – or from a metacritical perspective such as Trigg's – the object of literary value might well seem an ideological screen to be lifted, the false transmutation of historically contingent, material conditions into a historically transcendent virtue, one that blinds us both to history and to the ideological uses to which literature is put. In short, the object of value may seem everything that the many exposers of the conservative ideologies of New Criticism have accused it of being.[65]

This returns us to the critique of the Chaucer edition put forth by Machan and others. If the Chaucer editions produced under traditional editorial paradigms are reifications of the notional object of value, then the subordination of this notional object in literary critical studies would seem to necessitate a corresponding subordination of that object's material reifications to more suitable ones. And, indeed, it is precisely the persistence of the traditional reifications of value that prompts Machan's complaint recorded in this chapter's first epigraph. In the place of these reifications ought to be, say, reifications of cultural significance (that is, of the complexity of cultural influence and transmission, properly historicised), such as might be achieved by a digital representation of various interlaced manuscript matrices, in which manuscript reproductions are linked rhizomically to each other and hypertextually embedded in myriad informing contexts. For both scholarship and pedagogy, this replacement material realisation of the object of study would correspond to the shift in the central self-justifying task of the field from judgement to, say, something like Hanna's discernment of 'medieval literary communities'.[66]

We have already seen, however, that this shift away from judgement has been far from decisive and, accordingly, that digital editions, at least those designed to convey the complexity of cultural influence and transmission more so than literary value, have not been widely adopted. Further consideration of Hanna's remark about how 'Shakespeare's text has always triggered the most exciting advances in general bibliographic studies' suggests the precise source of this continuing resistance to editions of Chaucer not constructed as objects of value. Hanna's remark reminds us that the presumed value of Shakespeare's Works remains firmly in place despite the considerable attention given to the textual indeterminacy of those Works and their lack of authorial imprimatur. Indeed, as the remark further implies, this very attention has more likely perpetuated this value than diminished it. (In Machan's view, the literary value attributed to Shakespeare's Works has not only determined the entire history of Shakespeare editing but also that of Anglo-American textual criticism generally, so that Chaucer's texts have been edited to accord with the model of value set by the Bard's plays.)[67] Similarly, within the realm of historicist literary criticism, the immense amount of attention given to the culture of early modern England over the last forty years or so has done nothing to displace the centrality of the Bard in either early modern criticism or in British literature curricula. (In this regard, one may observe that many – perhaps most – historicist studies, such as Gallagher and Greenblatt's, do not hesitate to include valorisations of such traditional objects of value as Shakespeare's texts.) Although Chaucer has never possessed literary capital anywhere near the scale of Shakespeare's, his Works nonetheless continue to play an analogous role in the disciplinary economy of Middle English studies.

During the height of historicism's and manuscript studies' influence, as much as, say, the topics of Lollardy, Lancastrian politics and women's literary activities turned critical energies in other, often explicitly noncanonical, directions, Chaucer's Works maintained their prominence in the field. As Nicholas Watson observed, in his response to the 2006 New Chaucer Society conference (and despite what he considered, on the one hand, to be the field's broadening concerns and, on the other, the potential negative consequences of its continued dependence on Chaucer),

> It's obvious that, for many here [at the conference], Chaucer remains simply the most interesting and demanding of all the writers in our field to study and to think with; and that even for those of us whose most passionate attachments are elsewhere [as for Watson], Chaucer is still the place where many of our new intellectual perspectives come from or find their ultimate test (the question 'does it work for Chaucer?' can still make or break in this business), as well as being the bedrock of our medieval teaching.[68]

We may fairly wonder from comments such as these whether the proposal to subordinate the object of value to the object of cultural significance is not only highly unlikely practically but also just contradictory in principle, as we may begin suspect that the object of value actually possesses determining influence over the object of cultural significance. For if cultural significance were indeed to be promoted as the principal object of study, then we would expect that, say, the *Middle English Prose Brut*, with its 181 surviving manuscripts – or even the *Prick of Conscience*, with 117 – would be given equal if not more attention than the surviving manuscripts of the *Canterbury Tales*. Surely the numerous manuscripts of the former works were at least as culturally significant and ideologically powerful in late medieval England as were the manuscripts of the *Tales*, and in fact they strike me as very likely to have been more so. To this observation, an obvious rejoinder is that the *Tales*, unlike the *Brut* or the *Prick of Conscience*, has continued to possess cultural significance. But that argument effectively extends the object of cultural significance through the full history of Chaucer reception and thereby dilutes historical specificity from that object, reducing it to the generality that Chaucer has been significant for particular constituencies in particular times and places. And this generality is simply another way of saying that Chaucer's texts have been regularly construed, by various constituencies for various reasons, as possessing more value than other texts. In effect, the object of cultural significance, at least when posited within the ambit of 'studies in the age of Chaucer', becomes merely a displaced object of value, which, even when obscured, thereby retains its role as the disciplinary centre of gravity. What changes through this displacement, however, is the perception of this object's ownership and the perceived need to assign it stable content. By naming the object cultural significance, we are able define it as someone else's object of value rather than ours, and we may thereby allow the content of that object to be whatever those others needed or desired it to be in their particular historical moments.

Hence, even when projects do not concern Chaucer directly (or another established object of value, such as *Piers Plowman*) and avoid even such aesthetically neutral evaluative terms like 'significance' in favour of a notional object of historical authenticity, they may still depend on a displaced object of value, at some level of indirection. For example, Hanna has declared that 'the ultimate goal of manuscript studies should be the composition of cultural histories ... At every step, one strives to integrate minutiae toward a holistic analysis which reaches beyond books, indeed literature, to society and history.'[69] In this formulation, 'cultural histories', rather than any special significance within them, is the stated object. Yet, as modern historiography has repeatedly taught us, simply to notice something in the past is already to conceive of its value for, and bearing on, the present.[70] A study of, say, the manuscripts of Wycliffite sermons is also an argument for why those manuscripts matter to us. If that study appears in *SAC*, then implicitly that argument must be, in part, that those manuscripts convey a significant aspect of the culture that also included Chaucer, and hence they may (among other functions, of course) help explicate Chaucer's texts. And the only reason that Chaucer's texts require such explication is because they have already been conceived as an object of value.

To be sure, I do not mean to imply that the entire field of late medieval English studies revolves around a Chaucerian star. Moreover, as I have mentioned, I realise that the position of the object of value vis-à-vis manuscript studies depends at some level on the ambiguous relation between Chaucer studies and medieval studies (a relation further blurred by the bridge term, 'studies in the age of Chaucer') – or the relation between the more general (and more contested) formations of literary and cultural studies. Indeed, for the latter's advocates, one of the benefits of the multidisciplinary nature of cultural studies is that it tolerates multiple, competing objects of study (which, of course, is one of its liabilities to its detractors). But the corollary to this point is that inasmuch as Chaucer studies remains part of literary studies (and as long as the term 'literary' remains in any way meaningful), the institutionalisation of Chaucer studies carries with it an inherited commitment to value that we may put at arm's length but which we cannot finally evade.

If we cannot then escape the historically sedimented investments of the institutions in which we first learned about Chaucer, and in which we now teach and produce criticism, one might argue that we should at least seek exactly this arm's length distance – the critical distance that levels of indirection from the object of value may achieve. And, certainly, the substitution of cultural significance, or simply cultural history, for the object of value has served this function in the work of many celebrated Chaucerians. Yet, this critical distance, from another perspective, remains an attempt at evasion. If the object of cultural significance in Chaucer studies ultimately translates into the object of value as perceived by historically distant others, and if this object's cultural significance extends, *mutatis mutandis*, to the present and thus includes us, then we have performed a sort of conceptual sleight of hand. The attribution of the object of value to historically distant others enables our own inherited commitments to that object to remain in some inchoate state – to varying degrees offhand, intuitive, impressionistic and unexamined, if not simply submerged and unacknowledged – even while they continue to structure the field.[71] Moreover, by conceiving of the content of the other's object of value as historically contingent, we exempt ourselves from the responsibility of defining the content of the object of value to which we remain committed – on the argument that to do so would merely reflect our own historical conditioning. Again, as a tactic of critical distance, these evasions have use, but they nonetheless remain evasions, and hence the decisions that we might make on the basis of them bear reexamination.

Reifying the *Canterbury Tales*

One of these potential decisions returns us to the question of whether the best material realisation of an object of study is necessarily the most historically authentic – by which I mean, at this point, whether a reification of the notional object of historical authenticity is necessarily the most desirable material object upon which to practice criticism and pedagogy. As long as the aim of the various tasks involving manuscripts remained the production of a Work in the form of a print edition, the objects of intention, cultural significance and historical authenticity were subordinate to the object of value and hence not thoroughly distinguished from it. But, as the complaint of Machan's recorded in this chapter's first epigraph indicates, reifications of value, inasmuch as they are historically vitiated, would seem to present a mismatch with the aim of investigating cultural histories. As Machan puts it elsewhere, 'All of the modern editions of Chaucer's complete works contain carefully presented, artistically pleasing poetry, but none of them offer genuine examples of works produced within the discourse of Middle English manuscripts, since the Chaucer they imply can only be a projection of postmedieval thinking.'[72] Yet even if we grant the categories that Machan wields here, we nonetheless remain confronted with the question of whether to choose for critical and pedagogical practice 'modern editions' with their 'artistically pleasing poetry' or something that better reifies 'genuine examples of works produced within the discourse of Middle English manuscripts' – perhaps, again, one of the digital editions first imagined in the 1990s.

Machan published the above comments in 1994, at a time when the historicist hegemony and increasing influence of manuscript studies within Chaucer studies would have made the rejection of 'postmedieval thinking' and the embrace of 'genuine examples of … the discourse of Middle English manuscripts' appear wholly salutary and perhaps inevitable, once digital technology made this possible. As we know, however, Chaucer studies has silently pushed this option aside (and, not coincidentally, 'postmedieval' has of course been embraced as the title of a journal in the larger field of medieval studies). As it was the notional object of value that in fact remained the field's central structuring force throughout the historicist hegemony and ascendency of manuscript studies, the necessity to provide a reification of that notional object as the field's fundamental material object could not, in practice, be weakened. Yet this outcome, as I have said, has not been articulated as a matter of principle but rather was more the result of a kind of business-as-usual moving on.

What it would mean to articulate this outcome as a matter of principle is in a sense the project of this book as a whole. For the specific instance of the problem of literary value under consideration here, the principle involved may be provisionally invoked by the question of what the necessary, justifying logic would be for the choice of a rhizomic, dynamically reconfigurable, variant-comprehensive, hypertext edition of the *Canterbury Tales* over, say, the 1975 Donaldson edition, if (and this 'if' is crucial) the latter represents more effectively the object of value and thus more precisely corresponds to the notional object that remains the centre of the field's actual organisation. Upon reflection, one has little basis on which to claim the former as a more legitimate material literary object than the latter. Both are historical composites produced by multiple agents, in essence collaborative projects involving numerous individuals, most of whom are unknown to one another, pursued over the course of hundreds of years. Both lift material from one, uncertain aesthetic context and place it in another, better known but radically different one. Both may be the objects of rigorous and illuminating interpretative practice, although in both cases the interpreter must take care to respect the multiple intentions and contexts constituting the object.

As is well known, Donaldson produced his edition under the New Critical assumption that complex artistic unity is what makes a literary Work valuable, and he manipulated the surviving material record of the *Tales* to create a Work possessing ample amounts of this quality (most strikingly, perhaps, by having the 'Wif of Bathe' disrupt the Host's plan in the Man of Law's Endlink, revealingly defending this decision by simply remarking, 'this gives coherence to the chosen order').[73] This quality is without question 'postmedieval', but this fact alone does not make his version *a priori* any less legitimate as a material literary object. His version is rather simply one produced over time by diverse agents with different motivations. The same description applies in fact to the very earliest witnesses to the *Tales*, such as the Hengwrt and Ellesmere manuscripts.

Although the temporal distances among the several agents responsible for these manuscripts are obviously much smaller than those of any print edition, those agents plainly still possessed diverse motivations, as, say, Hilmo's and Tinkle's studies amply demonstrate. In Tinkle's apt phrasing, the pages of any manuscript reflect a 'hybrid, cumulative authorship'.[74] Hence, even what is arguably the most historically authentic version of the *Tales*, the Hengwrt, is already a historical composite – as indeed is any material literary object in any era. What necessary reason dictates that a less radically composite work (the Hengwrt) be chosen over one that is more so (the Donaldson edition) if – and again this 'if' is crucial – the latter better represents the object of value?[75]

The proposed digital *Canterbury Tales* would also, obviously, be a historical composite, one even more radical than the Donaldson edition, although, in contrast, it would possess the (equally postmedieval) motivation to represent the 'discourse of Middle English manuscripts' with as much authenticity as possible. If one would choose this version of the *Tales* solely because its constitution possesses this motivation, despite finding more literary value in the Donaldson version, then one self-contradictorily abandons the motivation that actually continues to define the field for a motivation that is, at best, an arm-length displacement of the former. One in effect diminishes the 'greatness' of the *Tales*, even while that very quality (whatever it may consist of) remains the reason why any critical energy is expended upon it, in favour of a less 'pleasing' *Tales* that nonetheless ultimately still depends on an idea of greatness for its *raison d'être*. This potential self-contradiction is, then, the principle at stake in the tacit resistance to and ultimate *de facto* casting aside of the manuscript studies argument about the Chaucer edition. However committed Chaucer scholars may be to the idea of historical authenticity – or indeed to any sort of epistemological or ideological position – they are, as an institution, more committed to the object of literary value because that object remains at that institution's centre and indeed provides the rationale for the very presence within Chaucer studies of those other commitments.

An imagined scenario may make this point plainer. Suppose tomorrow someone unearthed incontrovertible evidence that corroborated the speculation that David Lawton made years ago, that Thomas Hoccleve authored some of the linking passages in the *Canterbury Tales*.[76] Say (to make the scenario more extreme) this individual discovered a manuscript – in the attic of an obscure descendent of Adam Pinkhurst – that contained *all* the linking passages, as well their most important revisions, and that concluded with an envoy to Pinkhurst in which Hoccleve pseudo-humbly proclaims his inadequacy to complete the work of his recently deceased master; and all this appears in Hoccleve's hand, dated November 1400. Obviously, scholarly understanding of a number of things would change rather dramatically, but how should this discovery affect editions of the *Canterbury Tales*? Should the linking passages be bracketed, supplied but not lineated, relegated to endnotes or just dropped altogether? In my view, the best choice would be to use the new evidence to maximise aesthetic power – to produce an edition with, say, the tales and links more seamlessly and confidently integrated than previously, with no indication of so-called fragments and the tale order fixed without hesitation in the Ellesmere schema.[77] To choose one of the other options would be, as in the Donaldson edition example, to choose self-contradictorily the motivation of historical authenticity over that of value, thereby diminishing the very quality that continues to sustain critical interest in the *Tales*, the interest that was the very reason to produce a putatively more historically authentic edition in the first place. Figuratively speaking, it would be to set out for the best pizza restaurant in town but then settle begrudgingly for an undressed salad, even while longingly looking over at a neighbour's pizza. My argument is that most Chaucerians, no matter how nutritionally informed, rightly still want the pizza that motivated the trip out in the first place.

Clearly, the key conditional assumption in both of these examples is that one version of the *Tales* better reifies the object of value than another (or, for that matter, that one likes pizza better than an undressed salad). In these examples I have assumed a specific content for the object of value, one rather tendentiously calibrated to my opening admission of teaching the *Tales* as a linked set of short stories. This assumption is mostly heuristic, inasmuch as my aim has been to call attention to the persistence of the structuring power of literary value in Chaucer studies rather than to define the nature of that value. Given this structuring power, however, the obvious implication is that as a conscientiously reflexive postmodern literary critic, one ought to make such assumptions explicit, scrutinise their ideologies, investigate their theoretical bases and – I would add – continue to embrace them to the extent that after this process one still believes in them. I will return to variations of this latter point in the subsequent chapters, since, insofar as this book has any advice to give beyond its reflections on the problem of literary value, this simple point is indeed the essence of that advice. In concluding this opening chapter, I offer the following two related considerations, which in various ways have been hovering throughout and which are precursors to the formulations of the next chapter.

First, literary value in general and that of Chaucer in particular plainly neither originated in, nor is decisively controlled by, the academy. Rather, literary value was one of the enabling conditions of the initial academic institutionalisation of Chaucer studies, and its sustained presence outside the academy is in part what continues to legitimise, shape and perpetuate the subfield. In this regard, Hanna's youthful extracurricular encounter with Chaucer may stand as an illustration of how broadly disseminated and influential extra-institutional literary value may be. Also revealing in this regard is Hanna's comparison of Shakespeare's and Chaucer's roles in their respective bibliographic studies. Clearly, Shakespeare scholarship from the start has been and continues to be pendant on the immense value ascribed outside the academy to the Bard's plays.[78] This consideration suggests that no matter how we within the academy choose to define the content of literary value, we would do well to take into account in some fashion the definitions current outside the academy – a task that, as subsequent chapters will indicate, academics have indeed been pursuing in various ways over the last many years. This consideration also confirms the *de facto* choice of Chaucer studies to stick with editions that are more-or-less reasonable representatives of literary value, since it is as an object of value that anyone outside the academy is likely to pick up an edition in the first place and thereby later become, like Hanna, one of those who sustains the field within the academy. (More typically, of course, one's first exposure to Chaucer will be as a student, that is, as temporary consumer within the academy, for whom the point holds equally if not more so, despite however their professor negotiates Chaucer's value.) If in the future Chaucer studies becomes fully submerged within medieval cultural studies (or any other larger, differently centred formation), then this concern with value may no longer apply. But I do not foresee this submersion occurring until Chaucer no longer possesses literary value outside the academy, at which point it may well occur by default.

The second consideration is that the specific content of the notional object of value – the presumed qualities that define it – is always multiple and potentially unstable, for individual readers as well as among different readers. Attempts to define this content are, as I have suggested, an essential component of reflexive criticism but are also necessarily partial, in both senses of that term. When, for example, Fradenburg, in the final pages of *Sacrifice Your Love*, critiques both John Guillory's adaptation of Pierre Bourdieu's theory of cultural capital and the principles of New Philology as articulated by Stephen Nichols, she does so to promote one content of literary value – 'enjoyment' in the psychoanalytic sense – over others (or, in the case of New Philology, over a different object of study).[79] In this light, the early 2000s agon that occurred within Chaucer studies between psychoanalysis and historicism (an agon that Fradenburg seeks to dispose of as a false dichotomy) may be understood, in my terms, as a debate about the content of literary value. Similarly, the more general conflict between supposedly historically rigorous and supposedly anachronistic theoretical approaches to Chaucer (which is still felt in some quarters, although increasingly less so) dissipates when one understands the latter as performing, however consciously, the necessary definition and critical examination of literary value that justifies the former in the first place. As I will argue in Chapter 5, axiological theorisation, no matter how putatively anachronistic, may function as a mark of literary critical integrity.

If one were to follow these considerations and develop a definition of the notional object of value for the *Canterbury Tales*, ought one then to construct an edition that best corresponds to this definition and proceed to use this edition in one's criticism and teaching? Although this conclusion is practically absurd and conceptually nearly as ridiculous, it is in fact not far from the position taken by eminent textual critic G. Thomas Tanselle many decades ago in his account of an editor's aims and responsibilities – a position that amounts to a more radical version of Pearsall's proposal for different editions for different audiences:

A person of taste and sensitivity, choosing among variant readings on the basis of his own preference and making additional emendations of his own, can be expected to produce a text that is aesthetically satisfying and effective. Whether or not it is what the author wrote is another matter; but editing which does not have as its goal the recovery of the author's words is not necessarily illegitimate – it is creative, rather than scholarly, but not therefore unthinkable ... it is ... obvious that an editor could conceivably produce a version of a work aesthetically superior to the original. In such a case the editor would in effect become a collaborator of the author, in the way that publishers' editors or literary executors sometimes are. So long as one is concerned only with individual aesthetic objects, there can be no objection to the procedure; but if one is interested in the work as part of an author's total career, one must insist on having the words which that author actually wrote.[80]

In effect, Tanselle divides the universe of editions into two – the 'creative' ones that correspond to literary value (in his terms, aesthetic superiority) and the 'scholarly' ones that correspond to historical authenticity (which he equates with 'the recovery of the author's words') – and willingly grants legitimacy to the former.

But, as most editors (including Tanselle) have known all along and as manuscript studies has repeatedly taught us, all existing print editions (not to mention the manuscript witnesses themselves) are to some degree creative. They all are products of one or more individuals of (ideally) 'taste and sensitivity', who have manipulated the evidence according to preconceived notions of aesthetic superiority – precisely because such notions are irrecoverably entangled with those individuals' perceptions of what 'the author's words' might have been. Yet the solution to this situation is not, say, to give up the inevitably value-vitiated activity of editing and, in scholarship and teaching, just to consult facsimiles of one manuscript or another. To do so would be, as I have argued above, a misguided attempt to sever the field from the axiological energies that actually sustain it. Neither, however, is the solution to hold all editions equally worthy objects of study simply because no edition may escape being to some degree 'creative'. Such would be to mistake solipsism for subjectivity. Instead, the solution is to continue to produce value-potent editions that nonetheless recognise in some fashion, both in themselves and in the criticism that takes them as its objects, the constraints of the latest historical and textual findings – for, as I will argue in subsequent chapters, those constraints are actually themselves ascribers of value that necessarily mediate whatever definition of the object of value we may possess. One of the tasks of Chaucer criticism is not just to make its own and its chosen edition's definitions of the object of value explicit but also to shift the axiological grounds in such a way as to highlight the conversation between the creative and the scholarly that has always defined our work.

Notes

1 Tim William Machan, '"I Endowed Thy Purposes": Shakespeare, Editing, and Middle English Literature', *Text*, 13 (2000), 9–25 (23).
2 Peggy A. Knapp, 'Aesthetic Attention and the Chaucerian Text', *ChR*, 39:3 (2005), 241–58 (241).
3 For the especially textual-critical conscious volume of the Athlone *Piers Plowman*, see William Langland, *Piers Plowman: The B Version*, ed. George Kane and E. Talbot Donaldson (London: Athlone Press, 1975). For key works by McGann, Cerquiglini and McKenzie, see Jerome J. McGann, *A Critique of Modern Textual Criticism* (Chicago: University of Chicago Press, 1983); Bernard Cerquiglini, *In Praise of the Variant: A Critical History of Philology*, trans. Betsy Wing (Baltimore: Johns Hopkins University Press, 1999); and D. F. McKenzie, *Bibliography and the Sociology of Texts* (Cambridge: Cambridge University Press, 1999). For a couple of additional representatives of late twentieth-century textual-critical theoretical ruminations, see Philip G. Cohen (ed.), *Devils and Angels: Textual Editing and Literary Theory* (Charlottesville: University Press of Virginia, 1991); and Joseph Grigely, *Textualterity: Art, Theory, and Textual Criticism* (Ann Arbor: University of Michigan Press, 1995). For an excellent survey of the field of book history, see Alexandra Gillespie, 'The History of the Book', *New Medieval Literatures*, 9 (2007), 245–77.
4 See, e.g., Leah Price, 'From The History of a Book to a "History of the Book"', *Representations*, 108:1 (2009), 120–38, as well as the comments in this regard by the guest editors of this special issue of *Representations*, Stephen Best and Sharon Marcus, 'Surface Reading: An Introduction', 1–21. I cite below several instances of

Middle English literary scholarship that take a manuscript studies approach. For three examples of relatively recent collections that exemplify this approach and, to varying degrees, also reflect on it, see Orietta Da Rold and Elaine Treharne (eds), *Textual Cultures: Cultural Texts* (Cambridge: D. S. Brewer, 2010); Kathryn Kerby-Fulton, Maidie Hilmo and Linda Olson, *Opening Up Middle English Manuscripts: Literary and Visual Approaches* (Ithaca: Cornell University Press, 2012); and Michael Johnston and Michael Van Dussen (eds), *The Medieval Manuscript Book: Cultural Approaches* (Cambridge: Cambridge University Press, 2015).

5 Machan, for example – at least in 'Shakespeare, Editing' – seeks to disassociate his position from 'relativism, post-modernism, and other perceived threats to the integrity of the subject, whether that of the author, the critic, or the society' (p. 25), even though his historicism is plainly the product of the age in which those threats became literary critical commonplaces.

6 See David Matthews, *The Making of Middle English, 1765–1910* (Minneapolis: University of Minnesota Press, 1999), pp. 162–86.

7 Ethan Knapp, 'Chaucer Criticism and Its Legacies', in Seth Lerer (ed.), *The Yale Companion to Chaucer* (New Haven: Yale University Press, 2006), pp. 324–56 (322).

8 For these oppositions, see – in addition to Knapp, 'Chaucer Criticism' – the influential account of the history of Chaucer studies in Lee Patterson, *Negotiating the Past: The Historical Understanding of Medieval Literature* (Madison: University of Wisconsin Press, 1987), pp. 3–39. For Patterson's final views on the topic, and for his thoughts on manuscript studies that anticipate some of those that I express here, see Lee Patterson, *Temporal Circumstances: Form and History in the* Canterbury Tales (Basingstoke: Palgrave Macmillan, 2006), pp. 1–18, 20–25. For the broader history of the nineteenth-century emergence of literary study under the auspices of philology, see James Turner, *Philology: The Forgotten Origins of the Modern Humanities* (Princeton: Princeton University Press, 2014), esp. pp. 254–73. Turner observes that the tension between the antithetical principles involved was not particularly felt until the twentieth century.

9 Stephanie Trigg, *Congenial Souls: Reading Chaucer from Medieval to Postmodern* (Minneapolis: University of Minnesota Press, 2002), p. 11.

10 Derek Pearsall, 'Editing Medieval Texts: Some Developments and Some Problems', in Jerome J. McGann (ed.), *Textual Criticism and Literary Interpretation* (Chicago: University of Chicago Press, 1985),

pp. 92–106 (105, 106). Pearsall's suggestion reflects his well-known commitments, if sometimes inscrutably harmonised ones, to the ideas of both artistic excellence and historical authenticity.

11 Theresa Tinkle, 'The Wife of Bath's Textual/Sexual Lives', in George Bornstein and Theresa Tinkle (eds), *The Iconic Page in Manuscript, Print, and Digital Culture* (Ann Arbor: The University of Michigan Press, 1998), pp. 55–88 (74). Tinkle traces this treatment of Chaucer all the way back to the William Thynne's 1532 *Works*. See also Elizabeth Scala, *Absent Narratives, Manuscript Textuality, and Literary Structure in Late Medieval England* (New York: Palgrave Macmillan, 2002), especially the introduction (pp. 1–36), which covers in some detail the critique that I am summarising.

12 For two of many possible examples, see the pair of consecutive articles published in *Text*, 7 (1994): Murray McGillivray, 'Towards a Post-Critical Edition: Theory, Hypertext, and the Presentation of Middle English Works', 175–99; and Daniel W. Mosser, 'Reading and Editing the *Canterbury Tales*: Past, Present, and Future (?)', 201–32. Helen Cooper, 'Averting Chaucer's Prophecies: Miswriting, Mismetering, and Misunderstanding', in Vincent P. McCarren and Douglas Moffat (eds), *A Guide to Editing Middle English* (Ann Arbor: University of Michigan Press, 1998), 79–93, offers a similar but more moderate conclusion: 'Editions of Chaucer … are not safe as a basis for certain kinds of critical work, and it may be impossible to tell when one crosses the boundary into danger' (p. 86).

13 Trigg, *Congenial Souls*, p. 14.

14 See also Theresa Tinkle, *Gender and Power in Medieval Exegesis* (New York: Palgrave Macmillan, 2010), pp. 101–16, in which Tinkle revisits the manuscripts of the *Wife of Bath*'s Prologue, in this case focusing especially on the implications of the glosses.

15 For a wonderfully personalised account of this shift in the central object of inquiry, see Derek Pearsall, 'The Value/s of Manuscript Study: A Personal Retrospect', *Journal of the Early Book Society*, 3 (2000), pp. 167–81.

16 Stephen G. Nichols, 'Introduction: Philology in a Manuscript Culture', *Speculum* 65:1 (1990), 1–10 (9). Although New Philology, as a label, never achieved widespread currency, and this special issue of *Speculum* represented an observation of an ongoing and diverse shift in scholarship rather than a point of origin, Nichols's articulation of this shift remains influential. See, for example, Siân Echard and Stephen Partridge, 'Introduction: Varieties of Editing: History, Theory, and Technology', in Siân Echard and Stephen Partridge (eds), *The Book Unbound: Editing and Reading Medieval Manuscripts and*

Texts (Toronto: University of Toronto Press, 2004), pp. xi–xxi, which characterises New Philological ideas as a 'formative influence' (p. xii) on the anthology's contributions. Matthews, too, explicitly registers his sympathy with these ideas, although in *The Making of Middle English* he adapts them 'in a way that does not privilege manuscript culture over copy technology' (p. xxi). And Carol Symes, 'Manuscript Matrix, Modern Canon', in Paul Strohm (ed.), *Middle English* (Oxford: Oxford University Press, 2007), pp. 7–22, in reproaching a Bloomian approach to literary criticism, offers more-or-less the same argument as Nichols.

17 John Dagenais, 'That Bothersome Residue: Toward a Theory of the Physical Text', in A. N. Doane and Carol Braun Pasternack (eds), *Vox Intexta: Orality and Textuality in the Middle Ages* (Madison: University of Wisconsin Press, 1991), pp. 246–59 (252).

18 Maidie Hilmo, *Medieval Images, Icons, and Illustrated English Literary Texts: From Ruthwell Cross to the Ellesmere Chaucer* (Aldershot: Ashgate, 2004), pp. 160–99; Arthur Bahr, *Fragments and Assemblages: Forming Compilations of Medieval London* (Chicago: University of Chicago Press, 2013); and Arthur Bahr and Alexandra Gillespie (eds), 'Medieval English Manuscripts: Form, Aesthetics, and Literary Text', *ChR*, 47:4 (2013). For other examples (among many) of interpretive work on Chaucer that follow a manuscript studies approach, see the essays collected in Seth Lerer (ed), *Reading from the Margins: Textual Studies, Chaucer, and Medieval Literature* (San Marino: Huntington Library Press, 1996); and Thomas A. Prendergast and Barbara Kline (eds), *Rewriting Chaucer: Culture, Authority, and the Idea of the Authentic Text, 1400–1602* (Columbus: Ohio State University Press, 1999).

19 Mary Carruthers, '"Micrological Aggregates": Is the New Chaucer Society Speaking in Tongues?', *SAC*, 21 (1999), 1–26 (18–19). Carruthers, however, then seeks to steer the efforts of Chaucerians in another (or an additional) direction.

20 L. O. Aranye Fradenburg, *Sacrifice Your Love: Psychoanalysis, Historicism, Chaucer* (Minneapolis: University of Minnesota Press, 2002); Marion Turner, *Chaucer: A European Life* (Princeton: Princeton University Press, 2019). One need only browse through the last several volumes of *SAC* and *ChR* to confirm this point.

21 Andrew Taylor, 'Session 3 (Papers): "In Praise of the Middle English Variant"', *The New Chaucer Society Newsletter*, 29:1 (2007), 2. The call resulted in three separate sessions.

22 Erick Kelemen, 'Critical Editing and Close Reading in the Undergraduate Classroom', *Pedagogy: Critical Approaches to Teaching Literature,*

Language, Composition, and Culture, 12:1 (2012), 121–38, partly in response to the initial published version of this chapter, has described ways in which the problematising of the edition may indeed be pedagogically valuable, and, anecdotally, I am aware that other teachers of Chaucer successfully include some sort of exercise along these lines. I am not so confident, though, that this strategy, however sound pedagogically, serves to broaden, or even sustain, interest in medieval literature. Revealingly, more frequently debated in published discussions of Chaucer pedagogy than how best to respect late medieval manuscript culture is whether nor not to discard the Middle English edition in favour of a modern English translation. See, for example, the essays collected by Christine M. Rose for the symposium 'Teaching Chaucer in the Nineties', *Exemplaria*, 8:2 (1996); and those in Gail Ashton and Louise Sylvester, *Teaching Chaucer* (Basingstoke: Palgrave Macmillan, 2007).

23 Charlotte C. Morse, 'What the Clerk's Tale Suggests about Manly and Rickert's Edition – and the *Canterbury Tales* Project', in A. J. Minnis (ed.), *Middle English Poetry: Texts and Traditions: Essays in Honour of Derek Pearsall* (Woodbridge: York Medieval Press, 2001), pp. 41–56 (42). Morse sees this idea as a technologically more sophisticated version of the proposal of Pearsall, 'Editing Medieval Texts', for an edition of the *Tales* packaged as a partially bound book containing 'a set of fragments in folders, with the incomplete information as to their nature and placement fully displayed' (p. 23). Timothy Miller has since developed a website that accomplishes digitally something of what Pearsall imagined: Timothy S. Miller, 'Hyper Chaucer', www.thefishinprison.com/hyper-chaucer.html (accessed 17 October 2021). For an overview of the *Canterbury Tales* Project, see its website, www.canterburytalesproject.org, and Peter Robinson, 'The History, Discoveries, and Aims of the *Canterbury Tales* Project', *ChR*, 38:2 (2003), 126–39.

24 McGillivray, 'Towards a Post-Critical Edition', p. 192. See also Mosser, 'Reading and Editing'; and Tim William Machan, 'Chaucer's Poetry, Versioning, and Hypertext', *Philological Quarterly*, 73:3 (1994), 299–316, who, after painting a picture of an ideal hypertext edition of the *Canterbury Tales*, offers a more sober assessment of its potential.

25 See Ruth Evans, 'An Interim Report on the Standard Edition(s) of The Works of Geoffrey Chaucer', *The Chaucer Blog*, https://chaucerblog.net/2017/10/an-interim-report-on-the-standard-editions-of-the-works-of-geoffrey-chaucer/ (2017; accessed 9 January 2022).

26 *The Norton Chaucer*, ed. David Lawton (New York: W. W. Norton, 2019). The forthcoming omnibus editions are one from Oxford edited by Christopher Cannon and James Simpson, and one from Cambridge edited by a team headed by Julia Boffey and A. S. G. Edwards.
27 Knapp, 'Chaucer Criticism', p. 355 n. 73.
28 Bella Millett, 'What Happened to Electronic Editing?', in Vincent Gillespie and Anne Hudson (eds), *Probable Truth: Editing Medieval Texts from Britain in the Twenty-First Century* (Turnhout: Brepols, 2013), pp. 39–54 (54, 36); Thorlac Turville-Petre, 'Editing Electronic Texts', in the same volume, pp. 55–70. For an account of some of the practical problems that have stymied the *Canterbury Tales* Project, see Peter Robinson, 'Response to Roger Bagnall Paper: Integrating Digital Papyrology', in Jerome J. McGann (ed.), *Online Humanities Scholarship: The Shape of Things to Come* (Houston: Rice University Press, 2010), pp. 99–108.
29 As these were questions that I did actually voice in 2008, I obviously cannot say that they went entirely unarticulated. But, then and now, the questions represent just my own attempt to capture some of the deeper issues that underlie most Chaucerians' apparent complacency with the print edition.
30 Tim William Machan, 'Middle English Text Production and Modern Textual Criticism', in A. J. Minnis and Charlotte Brewer (eds), *Crux and Controversy in Middle English Textual Criticism* (Cambridge: D. S. Brewer, 1992), pp. 1–18 (8).
31 Machan, 'Middle English Text Production', p. 10.
32 For Patterson's study, see note 8 above. For an assessment of Donaldson's influence in particular, see *ChR* 41:3 (2007), a special issue devoted to his legacy.
33 Alan Liu, 'The Power of Formalism: The New Historicism', *ELH*, 56:4 (1989), 721–71.
34 Seth Lerer, 'The Endurance of Formalism in Middle English Studies', *Literature Compass*, 1 (2003), 1–15.
35 Early examples of this sort of work include Ellen Rooney, 'Form and Contentment', *MLQ*, 61:1 (2000), 17–40; and Stephen Cohen, 'Between Form and Culture: New Historicism and the Promise of a Historical Formalism', in Mark David Rasmussen (ed.), *Renaissance Literature and Its Formal Engagements* (New York: Palgrave, 2002), pp. 17–41, as well as the other essays collected in these volumes (Rooney's article appears in a special issue of *MLQ* devoted to formalism). The seminal reflection on New Formalism as an emergent trend is Marjorie Levinson, 'What Is New Formalism', *PMLA*,

122:2 (2007), 558–69. See also Verena Theile and Linda Tredennick (eds), *New Formalisms and Literary Theory* (Basingstoke: Palgrave Macmillan, 2013), several contributions to which directly take up the relations among New Formalism, New Historicism and New Criticism. The trend achieved a certain apotheosis in Caroline Levine, *Forms: Whole, Rhythm, Hierarchy, Network* (Princeton: Princeton University Press, 2015).

36 Eleanor Johnson, *Practicing Literary Theory in the Middle Ages: Ethics and the Mixed Form in Chaucer, Gower, Usk, and Hoccleve* (Chicago: University of Chicago Press, 2013); Thomas A. Prendergast and Jessica Rosenfeld (eds), *Chaucer and the Subversion of Form* (Cambridge: Cambridge University Press, 2018). See also the volume of essays that I edited with Catherine Sanok: *The Medieval Literary: Beyond Form* (Cambridge: D. S. Brewer, 2018).

37 For this general inclination within medieval studies, see, e.g., Elizabeth Scala and Sylvia Federico (eds), *The Post-Historical Middle Ages* (New York: Palgrave Macmillan, 2009).

38 As with, for example, Prendergast's role as coeditor for both the 1999 manuscript studies and the 2018 New Formalist collections cited above. See also Helen Marshall and Peter Buchanan, 'New Formalism and the Forms of Middle English Literary Texts', *Literature Compass*, 8:4 (2011), 164–72.

39 I confess to being one of those stubbornly raising this question, although I was (and am) as much attracted to formalism as I am to manuscript studies. Another questioner was Wendy Scase.

40 See Tinkle, 'Textual/Sexual', p. 64.

41 For *variance* and the popular romance, see, *inter alia*, Jennifer Fellows, 'Author, Author, Author …: An Apology for Parallel Texts', in McCarren and Moffat (eds), *A Guide to Editing Middle English*, pp. 15–24.

42 As Peter Robinson avers, 'the notion that we can, in textual situations of any complexity, reconstruct the "original form" of the text, or what Chaucer actually wrote or intended to write, is obviously absurd and always was' ('The History', p. 135). Yet, in the same article, Robinson defines 'the single most important issue in Chaucer textual scholarship' to be the understanding of the nature of Chaucer's 'lost set of originals' (p. 133). Machan, while recognising the potential of the project, accuses it of still possessing 'early modern objectives', by which he means the traditional, author-centric aims of textual criticism ('Shakespeare, Editing', p. 21). For a recent (qualified) affirmation of the *Canterbury Tales* Project, see Thomas J. Farrell, 'The Value of the *Canterbury Tales* Project, and Textual Evidence in the

Emendation of *Canterbury Tales* III.117', *JEGP*, 120:1 (2021), 93–129. For one explanation for why the *Tales* cannot be reduced to a single form, see Derek Pearsall, 'Authorial Revision in Some Late-Medieval English Texts', in Minnis and Brewer (eds), *Crux and Controversy*, pp. 39–48. For another, see Stephen Knight, 'Textual Variants: Textual Variance', *Southern Review*, 16:1 (1983), 44–54. I address the instability of the structure of the *Canterbury Tales*, or lack thereof, in 'Abandon the Fragments', *SAC*, 35 (2013), 47–83. For Manly and Rickert's project, see John M. Manly and Edith Rickert, *The Text of the Canterbury Tales: Studied on the Basis of All Known Manuscripts*, 8 vols (Chicago: University of Chicago Press, 1940).
43 Ralph Hanna, *Pursuing History: Middle English Manuscripts and Their Texts* (Stanford: Stanford University Press, 1996), pp. 11, 7.
44 I do not mean to imply that Hanna's views in this regard stand for the consensus of practitioners of manuscript studies or, more narrowly, textual critics. In fact, how much and what kind of a role the project of discerning the authorial text still possesses are matters of some debate. See, for example, the essays collected in McCarren and Moffat (eds), *A Guide to Editing Middle English*, especially those in the first section, 'Author, Scribe, and Editor'.
45 Hanna, *Pursuing History*, pp. 1, 2–3, 3.
46 Or, to be more precise, the book represents the major contribution to Chaucer studies that Hanna, at this juncture in his career, had already made, since only two of the sixteen chapters are entirely new.
47 Hanna, *Pursuing History*, pp. 14–15.
48 In this light, one might understand Hanna's follow-up book, *London Literature, 1300–1380* (Cambridge: Cambridge University Press, 2005), as a less diverted culmination of his project, in that it steadfastly focuses on 'local knowledge' of the literary communities extant in London before Chaucer's major productions. Indeed, in the preface to this book, Hanna contrasts his project with those of historicist critics Richard Firth Green and David Wallace, whom he claims ultimately underwrite Chaucer's traditional canonicity.
49 See Gerald Graff, *Professing Literature: An Institutional History* (Chicago: University of Chicago Press, 1987), esp. pp. 121–61.
50 W. K. Wimsatt with Monroe C. Beardsley, *The Verbal Icon: Studies in the Meaning of Poetry* (Lexington: University of Kentucky Press, 1954), p. 251. Cf. René Wellek and Austin Warren, *Theory of Literature* (New York: Harcourt Brace, 1949): 'To spend time and attention on a poet or poem is already a judgment of value … "Understanding poetry" passes readily into "judging poetry", only

judging it in detail and judging it while analyzing, instead of making the judgment a pronouncement in the final paragraph' (p. 262).
51 Wimsatt, *Verbal Icon*, p. 4.
52 M. H. Abrams and Stephen Greenblatt (eds), *The Norton Anthology of English Literature*, 7th edn, 2 vols (New York: W. W. Norton, 2000), p. 1:1684. Stephen Greenblatt (ed.), *The Norton Anthology of English Literature*, 10th edn, 6 vols (New York: W. W. Norton, 2018), p. 2:1339.
53 Kathryn Kerby-Fulton with Denise Despres, 'Fabricating Failure: The Professional Reader as Textual Terrorist', *The Yearbook of Langland Studies*, 13 (1999), 193–206 (194), emphasis in original. Hanna's review directly precedes in the same volume: '*Piers Plowman* and the Radically Chic', 179–92.
54 One may also consider in this regard that while the study of Middle English documents by literary scholars has expanded aggressively into the arena of the non-literary, perhaps the most celebrated work of this sort over the last couple of decades – Linne Mooney's use of documentary records to identify Adam Pinkhurst as the scribe of Hengwrt and Ellesmere – is plainly invested in the value that we continue to ascribe to the *Canterbury Tales*. See Linne R. Mooney, 'Chaucer's Scribe', *Speculum*, 81:1 (2006), 97–138.
55 Eleanor Johnson, 'Against Order: Medieval, Modern, and Contemporary Critiques of Causality', in Prendergast and Rosenfeld (eds), *Chaucer and the Subversion of Form*, pp. 61–82 (79, 80).
56 That this sort of critical activity thus possessed a marked logical circularity – as its conclusions ('the poem succeeds') are more or less restatements of its assumptions ('the poem is an object of value') – has been argued well and often. For a trenchant, early articulation of this point, see Stanley Fish, 'Interpreting the Variorum', *Critical Inquiry*, 2:3 (1976), 465–85.
57 Wimsatt, *Verbal Icon*, p. 4.
58 For Middle English studies, the editors/critics Donaldson and Kane have been especially vocal in their insistence on the role of subjective judgement in all methods of editorial work. For the former's views on this topic, see 'The Psychology of Editors of Middle English Texts' in E. Talbot Donaldson, *Speaking of Chaucer* (London: Athlone Press, 1970), pp. 102–18. For a consideration of the affiliations between New Criticism and Kane's and Donaldson's editing practices, see Patterson, *Negotiating the Past*, pp. 77–113. For this view in respect to English literature more generally, see G. Thomas Tanselle, *Textual Criticism and Scholarly Editing* (Charlottesville: University Press

of Virginia, 1990), who argues the point throughout this collection of essays – e.g., 'In scholarly editing the role of literary judgment is vital to all decisions – those concerning accidentals as well as those concerning substantives' (pp. 329–30).
59 Catherine Gallagher and Stephen Greenblatt, *Practicing New Historicism* (Chicago: University of Chicago Press, 2000), p. 9.
60 David Wallace (ed.), *The Cambridge History of Medieval English Literature* (Cambridge: Cambridge University Press, 1999), pp. xi–xxiii; Charlotte C. Morse, 'From "Ricardian Poetry" to Ricardian Studies', in A. J. Minnis, Charlotte C. Morse and Thorlac Turville-Petre (eds), *Essays on Ricardian Literature: In Honour of J. A. Burrow* (Oxford: Clarendon Press, 1997), pp. 316–44.
61 Derek Pearsall, 'Medieval Literature and Historical Enquiry', *The Modern Language Review*, 99:4 (2004), xxxi–xlii at xl and xxxvii. In the first quotation, Pearsall refers specifically to James Simpson, *Reform and Cultural Revolution* (Oxford: Oxford University Press, 2002); and, in the second, to Lee Patterson, *Chaucer and the Subject of History* (Madison: University of Wisconsin Press, 1991). Pearsall follows, with some qualifications, the disciplinary diagnosis of J. A. Burrow, 'Should We Leave Medieval Literature to the Medievalists?', *Essays in Criticism*, 53:3 (2003), 278–83, but adduces different causes.
62 See, e.g., Easthope, *Literary into Cultural Studies*.
63 Seth Lerer, *Chaucer and His Readers: Imagining the Author in Late-Medieval England* (Princeton: Princeton University Press, 1993).
64 Thomas A. Prendergast, 'Introduction: Writing, Authenticity, and the Fabrication of the Chaucerian Text', in Prendergast and Kline (eds), *Rewriting Chaucer*, pp. 1–9 (2). Cf. the statement of aims in Siân Echard and Stephen Partridge, 'Introduction: Varieties of Editing: History, Theory, and Technology', in Echard and Partridge (eds), *The Book Unbound*, pp. xi–xxi.
65 See, for example, Terry Eagleton, *Literary Theory: An Introduction* (Minneapolis: University of Minnesota Press, 1983), pp. 17–53.
66 Part of Turville-Petre's argument for the virtues of the digital edition suggests a rationale along these lines, although I do not think that he would subscribe to this shift in literary study's self-justifying task; see 'Editing Electronic Texts', p. 56.
67 This is the basic argument of Machan, 'Shakespeare, Editing'.
68 Nicholas Watson, 'Response to the New Chaucer Society Conference, New York, July 27–31, 2006', *The New Chaucer Society Newsletter*, 28:2 (2006), 1–5 (2).
69 Ralph Hanna, 'Analytical Survey 4: Middle English Manuscripts and the Study of Literature', *New Medieval Literatures*, 4 (2001), 243–64 (255–6).

70 This basic historiographical position will serve as one of the points of departure for Chapter 5.
71 In this regard, it is to Pearsall's credit that in his defence of Chaucer's literary value in 'Medieval Literature', he offers what one rarely encountered in Chaucer criticism through the period of historicist hegemony: an explicit attempt to define poetic literary value generally and to demonstrate its presence in Chaucer's verse. That this demonstration seems so much like a formalist exercise is striking.
72 Tim William Machan, *Textual Criticism and Middle English Texts* (Charlottesville: University Press of Virginia, 1994), p. 181.
73 *Chaucer's Poetry: An Anthology for the Modern Reader*, ed. E. T. Donaldson, 2nd edn (New York: Ronald Press, 1975), p. 1074.
74 Tinkle, 'Textual/Sexual', p. 76.
75 In raising this question, I echo arguments made to somewhat different ends by Michelle R. Warren, 'Post-Philology', in Patricia Clare Ingham and Michelle R. Warren (eds), *Postcolonial Moves: Medieval Through Modern* (New York: Palgrave Macmillan, 2003), pp. 19–45.
76 See David Lawton, *Chaucer's Narrators* (Cambridge: D. S. Brewer, 1985), pp. 127–9. If the more recent contention of Simon Horobin, 'Thomas Hoccleve: Chaucer's First Editor?', *ChR*, 50:3–4 (2015), 228–50, that Hoccleve served as 'editor' of both Hengwrt and Ellesmere is correct, Lawton's speculation is perhaps a little less farfetched.
77 Representation of the *Tales* as a collection of fragments is, in any event, not even historically authentic. See my 'Abandon the Fragments'. I offer this whimsical thought exercise of Hoccleve's coauthorship, rather than one of the actual debates about how the *Tales* ought to be represented, to avoid digression into textual controversies. But readers may easily see how the debate about, say, the status of the penitential treatise and so-called *Retractions* that stand at the end of the *Tales* (whether, that is, they belong in the *Tales* at all) depends not just on textual questions but also on the inertia of the literary value attributed to the current configuration of the *Tales* and the likelihood that a new configuration (ending with the *Parson's* Prologue) would possess more. For the argument that the *Parson's Tale* and *Retractions* are a scribal appendage, see Charles A. Owen, 'The Canterbury Tales: Beginnings (3) and Endings (2 + 1)', *Chaucer Yearbook*, 1 (1992), 189–211; and, more extensively, Míceál F. Vaughan, 'Creating Comfortable Boundaries: Scribes, Editors, and the Invention of the Parson's Tale', in Prendergast and Kline (eds), *Rewriting Chaucer*, pp. 45–90.
78 For a general consideration of how literary canonicity is not nearly as much a function of the academy as academics tend to believe, see

E. Dean Kolbas, *Critical Theory and the Literary Canon* (Boulder: Westview Press, 2001).
79 Fradenburg, *Sacrifice Your Love*, pp. 243–52. Knight is similarly forthcoming about his (rather different) sense of the literary value of Chaucer's texts when he frankly admits, in respect to his work as an editor, 'when faced by equally possible variants I will print the one which has the maximum possible historical tension, the reading which loads the text most strongly with ideology' ('Textual Variants', p. 49).
80 Tanselle, *Textual Criticism*, p. 329.

2
A preliminary theory of literary valuing

In the preceding chapter, I argued that literary value – in the guise of the 'ghost of judgment' – continues to serve as the structuring centre of Chaucer studies. But rather than offer an explanation for what constitutes literary value in that context, I suspended the question in favour of the pragmatic option of conceiving literary value 'first as a placeholder in an institutionalised system of scholarship and teaching, prior to whatever content this placeholder may contain'. This was in fact a strategic suspension of the question in addition to a merely convenient one. For I will argue in this chapter that this manner of approaching the problem of literary value, with some elaboration, provides an alternative to the dialectical pingpong match between the antithetical (which is to say, complementary) approaches that, as I mentioned in this book's introduction, characterises much of the Anglo-American treatment of the problem over the last several decades. After describing these approaches with some additional detail, I will suggest – without thereby derogating them – what both exclude and hence the rationale for developing an alternative. I will then attempt a systematic definition of this alternative, a theory of literary valuing that I call 'preliminary' because the relatively scanty definition that I provide is rather more along the lines of a schema than a full-blown theory. But it will serve, I hope, to anchor the chapters that follow and connect them back to the first chapter's initial pedagogical conundrum and the issues that it raises.

To summarise this preliminary theory succinctly, if at this point necessarily with some obscurity, this approach to the problem of literary value is pragmatic in orientation and takes as its basis the evident, pervasive valuing of literature that occurs – as recognised at the end of the previous chapter – both inside and outside of the academy. It understands literary value as emerging by means of an activity coextensive with its conception as a quality, an activity performed by actors within a network that shapes all individual instances and an activity that is a social fact integral to the phenomenon of the literary and yet – as also recognised at the end of the previous chapter – neither singular nor necessarily stable in character. This approach seeks to offer a middle way of conceptualising literary value that escapes some of the difficulties of existing approaches and that may also, as I will explore in the next chapter, eventuate in a framework for the study of literature – of any historical period, in any of its myriad facets – that recognises the centrality of value but does not in itself predetermine a specific attitude toward value, even though some such attitude is in practice ultimately inevitable.

Such an inclusive framework will necessarily be a rather abstract one, and thus much of what follows may seem far removed from the sort of actual critical and pedagogical practices that informed the preceding chapter. To help clarify this framework's application here at the outset, then, let me briefly situate it in relation to an example of my own critical practice, which will serve as an illustration of one of the common stumbles provoked by literary value. In particular, as I argued in Chapter 1, the continued operation of literary value within critical approaches that otherwise disclaim or simply ignore it may manifest as conceptual lacunae. One such lacuna resides within my 2007 study of fifteenth-century English poetry, *Poets and Power from Chaucer to Wyatt*. Presented as an exploration of how a commingling of poetry and politics altered the form, transmission and conception of English literature at the very moment in which a self-conscious tradition of this literature was emergent, this study – as typical of historicist approaches – seeks to adopt a kind of aesthetic agnosticism about its subject poems. Yet the book is nonetheless manifestly a reclamation project of the most aesthetically denigrated poetry in English literary history, and consequently it is rife with such crypto-evaluative assertions as 'mid-century Lydgatean poets are not opportunistic mindless imitators, but rather discover ... a powerful strategy with which (or against which) to position themselves in respect to their particular historical circumstances'.[1] That there is an implicit argument about literary value in such statements, one which never receives full articulation, is evident in some of the reviews of the book, which find precisely this implicit – and hence undefended – argument the most difficult aspect of it to accept.[2] By not articulating the evaluative assumptions upon which, despite its putative historicist neutrality, the book depends, I left myself open to critique on traditional aesthetic grounds for which I offered no replacement.

As with my pedagogical bad faith that prompted the preceding chapter, I am vain enough to believe that this conceptual and methodological gap is not merely the result of my own incompetence but rather more generally symptomatic of the problematic status of literary value in the field. This chapter, then, along with the next, seeks to provide a framework for understanding and responding to this gap. The previous chapter, in 'conceiving' of value as a 'placeholder', insinuated a fuller account of literary value, one that would take exactly this suspension of 'content' as its point of departure. In this chapter, I will seek to elucidate how content is an effect of action: acts of valuing are the condition of an actor's registering of a text as literary, whether that actor is a critic, an edition, a poet or any number of other mediators of value. The next chapter will explore, among other things, how a specification of the relations among such valuing actors is what may both fill the evaluative lacunae in studies like *Poetry and Power* and reconcile disparate literary critical efforts.

Ontology and genealogy

In this book's introduction, I described how, since about the mid-1990s, numerous studies have been devoted toward countering what they perceive as diminishment within the field of literary studies of the emphasis, or even merely attention, given to a distinctive literary, to literary value or to the aesthetic. To cite just one relatively recent example, Charles Altieri positions his 2015 book-length study against those who 'tried to align literary studies with the disciplinary focus of various social sciences', thereby seeking to preserve 'some of the discipline's traditional emphases on close reading but focus those skills on practical rather than aesthetic concerns'. He claims, 'One would be hard pressed to find in elite programs of literary study even two younger critics concentrating on aesthetic values or even the importance of the plural, contemplative sympathies traditionally characteristic of aesthetic attitudes.' In contradistinction, Altieri's book builds a case – primarily by way of Wittgenstein – for the value of a distinctive literary, one that answers such questions as, 'How can we treat literature as both a distinctive cultural enterprise and one that is arguably central to the quality of social life for everyone, or at least potentially central for enough people that this would make a substantial difference in the quality of collective life?'[3] And in his final chapter, 'Appreciating Appreciation', this emphasis on the value of literature as a category entails prescriptive reflections on the value of valuing particular literary works.

What advocates for literary value such as Altieri, those mentioned in my introduction and many others share – despite sometimes stark differences in theoretical affiliation and sophistication, generic and period focus, nature of argument and intended readership – is the tendency to conceive of value as some kind of historical constant, even if – as for those influenced by Adorno's *Aesthetic Theory* – that constant is in fact the multi-temporal dynamic of history itself. From his reading of Adorno, for example, E. Dean Kolbas concludes that the value of literature (and art in general) resides in its 'unique cognitive content, its capacity for being a valid form of *knowledge*, revealing certain historical truths about this world that other forms of knowledge, such as scientific or empirical forms, either inherently cannot provide or would approach in qualitatively different ways'.[4] Derek Attridge, guided more by Derrida and Levinas than the Frankfurt School, arrives at a similar conclusion:

> the revelation [provoked by the introduction of 'otherness into the field of the same' by literature or art in general] of the hidden costs of a culture's stability, the bringing to fruitfulness of seeds that had lain dormant, the opening-up of possibilities that had remained closed, is – however risky – a good in itself, particularly when the process is a continuous one, allowing no permanent settling of norms and habits, and therefore no single structure of dominance and exclusion.[5]

In all such views, literary value – whether conceived of as a quality of a text or, more commonly, of the experience of apprehending a text – maintains a basic character regardless of its specific contexts. Although it would be an overstatement thus to denote this entire diverse body of advocacy as essentialist or universalist (despite some instances that are indeed one or both of these), as a whole it does display a tendency in this direction. For convenience, therefore, I will group these studies together under the label *ontological*, by which I do not mean to connote any specific philosophical orientation but simply to indicate their common tendency to focus on what the value of literature *is* more so than how it has been *made*.

The converse, antithetical or complementary tendency to this one, as I described in the introduction, is that which initially emerged in the aftermath of the 1970s canon debates as a critique of the presumed literary value of canonical texts and that persists in various forms to the present, sometimes in direct confrontation with the ontological tendency. For example, in a 2005 essay John Frow asserts,

> Any attempt now to define the literary as a universal or unitary phenomenon necessarily fails to account for the particular institutional conditions of existence which underpin its assumptions, and falls thereby into the fetishism of a culture of social distinction and of the marketing regime which it supports.[6]

What studies such as Frow's share with later and earlier ones[7] is an anti-essentialist orientation to literary value and an interest in disclosing the elements with which and mechanisms by which value is constructed. As different as their focuses, methods and conclusions may be, as a group they emphasise the constructedness, relativity and instrumentality of literary value. Despite these studies' diversity (and, indeed, outright antagonism in some cases), I name their common tendency *genealogical*, by which I do not so much mean to invoke Foucault as simply to signal an emphasis on how literary value is *made* prior to considering what it *is*.

This characterisation of these two tendencies in treatments of literary value is likely familiar, as what I have denominated *ontological* and *genealogical* correspond in general ways to more elaborated and theorised label pairs proposed in surveys covering similar critical terrain. They more-or-less align, for example, with Steven Connor's *absolutist* and *relativist*, Peter McDonald's *enchanted anti-essentialist* and *skeptical anti-essentialist*, Rita Felski's *theological* and *ideological* and John Fekete's 'post-Marxist, post-Existentialist' and 'neopragmatist post-liberal'.[8] Indeed, at the most reductive level, one may see in the tension within each pair the ancient debate between the claims of the timeless and the time-bound – and this point underscores what I hope has been evident in my description of the ontological and genealogical approaches as *tendencies* rather than separate pigeon holes into which studies may be sorted *in extenso*.[9] For inasmuch as all accounts concern themselves in some fashion with both the timeless and the time-bound, they display both tendencies, albeit (obviously) to varying degrees. Hence, for example, George Levine, in an appreciative response to a nuanced ontological case put forward by Satya Mohanty, reluctantly demurs from full acceptance, remaining 'in the bind of constructionism, relativism, skepticism'. Yet he concludes by advocating a kind of semi-disenchanted Kantianism, a valorisation of 'the particular and embattled but disinterested space that art and the beautiful occupy in our cultures'.[10] And to formulate this position, Levine draws on the conclusion of the otherwise thoroughgoing genealogical account of value in John Guillory's *Cultural Capital*.[11] In the latter, after completing his trenchant demystifying analysis of literary value's historical determinations, Guillory somewhat surprisingly concludes his study by allowing for a specific, irreducible aesthetic experience, albeit one never occurring in a pure state within existing socioeconomic conditions.

However, the very proximity between Guillory's and Levine's positions, as well as the manoeuvres that each scholar undertakes to arrive at his, makes evident that ontological and genealogical approaches, while very frequently cohabiting, remain distinguishable, both in comparisons of different studies and in respect to any individual study's internal argumentative development.[12] Indeed, for Connor it is precisely the ceaseless dialectical pivoting between these positions – what I named pinging-ponging in my introduction – that marks the limits of axiological discourse itself: 'As in all paradoxes (rather than contradictions), the absolute opposites of absolutism and relativism both follow from and are implied by each other.'[13] Partly for this reason Connor has more recently called for the abandonment of the discourse of aesthetic value altogether (if not necessarily also that of the more specific discourse of literary value).[14] Yet, whatever the benefits of the particularist, object-oriented approach that he recommends instead, the ontological and genealogical positions, however much locked in a ceaseless dialectical wrestling match (to vary my game metaphors), remain important, ongoing literary theoretical projects. Ontological articulations of literary value serve as salutary efforts towards supplying the field of literary studies with some measure of conceptual cohesiveness, even if faltering and partial, and at the very least enable the authorship of such practically needed documents as the MLA 'Report to the Teagle Foundation on the Undergraduate Major in Language and Literature' (or departmental mission statements) to proceed in something approximating good faith. Conversely, analyses of the genealogy and instrumentality of value help to dispel our inevitable self-justifying self-delusions, assisting us in the ceaseless process of aligning our critical practices with our intentions. Nonetheless, both positions have conceptual and practical limits, which have been rehearsed at length in the publications defending one against the other, and which have hampered their efficacy.

Here I will just mention, for ontological approaches, the limits of definitional scope and practical demonstration.[15] By definitional scope, I mean the conundrum that these approaches face – as famously in the case of Sir Philip Sidney's *Defence of Poesy* – when the value that they define *for* literature turns out to be not much in evidence in many of the texts that in actual literary history have been defined *as* literature, resulting in an account of value that becomes unaccountably narrow. Conversely, the value of literature may be defined so broadly that it ceases to be legible as specifically literary value. By practical demonstration, I mean the difficulty ontological accounts face in demonstrating that a work of literature in fact possesses the value so ascribed to it in anything more than an idiosyncratic instance of experiencing it (typically that of the study's author). Hence, for example, in his book *Literary Interest* Steven Knapp accepts as a distinctive quality of literary texts something close to what Attridge describes, and yet, as Knapp observes, 'The trouble … is that it isn't obvious why bringing thoughts, values, and objects into new relations, which are therefore unlike the ones they had before, should be thought to enhance our knowledge of these matters as they obtain outside the literary representation.' This quality of literature may 'enhance our knowledge' in this fashion, but whether the history of responses to literature testifies to this effect in fact and – more problematically – in general, remains an open question. Knapp comes to a largely negative conclusion: 'Whatever may be the specific benefits of particular literary works in particular social contexts, the right conclusion to draw about the ethical and political benefits of literary interest *in general and as such* seems to be, so far, that there may not be any.'[16]

In contrast, genealogical accounts of value are often quite persuasive in their application to the actual history of literature and its reception. Indeed, a principal problem that they face is with the consequences of this very success. For most genealogical accounts compel us to accept, in some fashion, that many of those who value literature – in some accounts the vast majority of such valuers, except for a few literary theorists – turn out to be, in some way and to some degree, mystified. Frow, for example, offers a striking contrast between his anti-essentialist conception of value (e.g., 'no object, no text, no cultural practice has an intrinsic or necessary meaning or value or function') and that which is 'alive and flourishing in the great world':

> In the café culture of upmarket bookshops, in the cultural promotion apparatus of festivals and chat-shows and prizes, and in Hollywood's version of the art movie, Literature remains a timeless product of genius and feeling, directly apprehended in the heart by the empathetic reader.[17]

While perhaps many within the academy would be comfortable enough with this charge of mystification in respect to the sort of readers whom Frow describes, the position becomes more awkward in respect to authors. For even the most tortured, self-doubting writers will, when pressed, usually grudgingly confirm at least a provisional value for literature generally, while the majority, when asked, are typically willing to assert this value in the strongest, most absolute terms.[18] As Jan Mukařovský long ago observed, '[E]very struggle for a new aesthetic value in art [by artists], just as every counterattack against it, is organised in the name of an objective and lasting value.'[19] For Pierre Bourdieu and the many literary scholars whom he has influenced, such struggles necessarily entail the artists' misrecognition of the full nature of artistic value in order to sustain the very belief in the 'objective and lasting value' that constitutes the field of cultural production.[20] Hence, while genealogical accounts may provide convincing explanations for the diversity of literary history, they must assume some degree of authorial mystification to explain the existence of literary history per se.

In respect to authors, therefore, genealogical literary analysts are thus cast into a position uncomfortably like that of nineteenth-century ethnologists. To make matters more awkward, in this case the 'primitives', with their beliefs in literary magic, reside alongside us in ever-burgeoning creative writing programs, in which a basic premise is, obviously, that authors may somehow make their writing *better*. At the very least, this analogy suggests that the genealogical approach possesses a blind spot in respect to its own categories of belief and the unacknowledged assumptions of historically constant values that may undergird them. Connor succinctly describes one instance of this familiar analytical boomerang effect: 'it is impossible to choose plurality without making a non-contingent commitment to the value of plurality'.[21] Moreover, if authors and the public at large somehow did all become thoroughly convinced by, say, Guillory's argument about value, we may wonder what – in lieu of the Utopic socioeconomic transformation he imagines – such universal demystification would entail. Perhaps, since the successful operation of cultural capital requires some degree of misrecognition, literary value, once fully recognised, would cease to be of any value. And indeed some commentators have suggested that academic literary study's very success at self-demystification is, at least in part, responsible for its institutional decline, a line of argument that, as I indicated in this book's introduction, I find overblown.[22]

There are of course within both approaches various strategies to overcome these problems. I seek here only to make the point that, as Connor has observed, each position in its very limits tends to implicate the other: some ontological conception of literary value seems necessary for there to be literature at all, while any such conception, in consideration of the actual history of literature in all its breadth, tends to falter. As I have suggested, the consequent ping-ponging between positions does not decrease their importance. They remain urgent literary critical projects. Yet their dialectical self-containment does point to a conceptual and practical limit that they share, which is that both have normative force. Simply put, both positions specify how we *ought* to understand the nature of literary value and hence also, at least implicitly, how we ought to value literature (if at all). This observation perhaps goes without saying for ontological approaches, but it may raise some eyebrows among the genealogically inclined, who may understand their projects as socially and historically descriptive and hence precisely not normative. Yet, when, say, Frow asserts, 'Literary criticism remains an important part of a marketing system and of a highbrow taste culture which it blindly serves', and that 'literary studies ... has become lost in irrelevance', he is clearly accusing literary scholars of an improper understanding of the nature of literary value (as evident in, e.g., the 'negative theology in deconstruction'), one which ought to be corrected.[23]

As antithetical orientations towards their subject, therefore, the two positions predictably produce one another, but in their shared normative self-containment, they together *a priori* eliminate consideration of a vast array of manners in which literature has been, in fact, valued, especially outside the research domain of the academy. For, regardless of what the real nature of literary value may be, literature has always been valued by diverse actors for diverse reasons: by journalists, middle-school students, book-club members, mystery writers, dialectologists, executives of large publishing houses, politicians running for positions on state legislatures, copyeditors, rare book collectors, independent bookstore owners and others, *ad infinitum*; or, looking backward toward the Middle Ages, by professional scribes, royal patrons, abbots, and so on. In regard to these actors' perceptions of literary value, both ontological and genealogical accounts imply that inasmuch their perceptions do not correspond to the nature of value specified by the account, they must somehow be mistaken. They either fail to appreciate the primary value of literature (as defined by ontological accounts), whether for appropriate or inappropriate reasons, or they misrecognise the manner in which value is determined and functions (as defined by genealogical accounts), perhaps thereby enabling value's continued operation. Construed with such normative force, both positions *a priori* place under the heading *error* a great proportion of the actual valuing of literature – that is, much, if not most, of the collective experience of literature in any given society (including, of course, that of many academics when not concerned with issuing critical accounts of value).

This presumptive move is typically more implied than articulated, since in the age of cultural studies academics have become rightfully self-conscious of the elitism that attends accusations of philistinism. Hence, we rarely encounter a comment as unguarded as one of Mukařovský's in his mid-1930s *Aesthetic Function, Norm and Value as Social Fact*, which presciently anticipates many strands of both ontological and genealogical arguments current today.[24] Pausing briefly to consider those who 'value the novel only insofar as it is educational or arouses the emotions', he remarks dismissively, 'Their view of art is inadequate and cannot constitute the norm' – even if, presumably, their view *was* the norm, demographically.[25] Nonetheless, as suggested by Frow's remarks about 'café culture' – or, for ontological accounts, by Attridge's comment, 'We rightly value the works belonging to the tradition of literature for a number of different things they are capable of being and doing, most of them not strictly literary' – such exclusionary normative sentiments in accounts of value persist, however formulated and however much explicitly articulated.[26] As Rita Felski explains, it is precisely this persistent critical normativity that motivates her *Uses of Literature*, an 'un-manifesto' in which she takes to task both 'theological' and 'ideological' literary critical styles of reading. The literary critical establishment, Felski argues, needs to take seriously how literature is valued outside its gates: 'There is no compelling reason why the practice of theory requires us to go behind the backs of ordinary persons in order to expose their beliefs as deluded or delinquent.'[27] Rather than (only) serving as mystifications, such beliefs, such experiences of literary value in all their diversity, may collectively – or, as I will shortly propose, in their abstract totality – contribute to a more capacious account of literary value than the ones provided by the ontological and genealogical dialectical pair alone, as compelling as many of those have been.

The network of valuing

As alternatives to the academy's styles of reading, Felski proposes four 'modes of textual engagement' that she believes are widespread – common ways that literature is experienced as valuable. Through what she calls her hybrid phenomenological description of these modes,[28] she in effect offers accounts of four non-prescriptive norms of literary value that have social currency in contemporary Western culture, positioning herself in respect to these not as Victorian ethnographer but instead as participant-observer. While one might readily extend this important project by including additional socially current (or formerly current) norms, in the remainder of this chapter I will instead push the motivating idea of Felski's study to its furthest reach and consider how a comprehensive set of such norms, for any particular society in any particular time, might operate. That is, I will consider the operation of the abstract totality of the ways in which literature is valued.

As is evident in my initial formulation for this operation below, the description that emerges at this high-altitude level of abstraction resembles the seminal demystifying 1980s accounts by Stanley Fish, Terry Eagleton and Barbara Herrnstein Smith. But in addition to the formulation's important differences from these accounts in wording and subsequent development, it differs in its basic purpose, in that it is not a critique. It neither argues for one view of the nature of literary value against others nor seeks to disabuse mystified readers and writers. Instead, it is an attempt at a pragmatic description of how literary value is socially operative, regardless of what literary value may actually be or how it is actually determined. In its focus on how value is operative at any particular moment and place, it neither precludes nor depends on ontological or genealogical claims, but rather brackets them (to adapt that useful phenomenological term).

Readers will notice that this initial formulation appears especially to echo Eagleton's well-known 1983 definition of literature as any 'highly valued kind of writing' (although in fact my stronger influence is Smith).[29] As in Eagleton's phrasing, it does not offer a definition of literary value per se but rather a repositioning of value as an activity prior to a quality, or as 'a process and not a state', as Mukařovský puts it.[30] In this way it offers most basically just a reversal of the common conception of literary value as a function of the nature of the literary, proposing instead that the category of the literary is a function of the activity of valuing (thereby making literature, in John Dewey's terms, a *valuable*).[31] I first give the formulation in the simplest terms possible, and then I will develop it by excavating those terms' underlying complications:

> We register a text as literary when we ascribe value to some aspect of its perceived manner.

To begin with potentially the most misleading term, by the pronoun *we* I do not mean an implied consensus or ideal or typical reader, but rather any specific actor, human or nonhuman, individual or collective, in temporally discrete acts of registration and value ascription as well is in more durable forms of agency, such as English department curricula or critical editions. Moreover, the two instances of *we*, along with the third instance implied by the past participle *perceived*, do not necessarily refer to the same actor. Hence, for example, the first *we* may register a text as literary because some other *we* has ascribed a specific value to an aspect of its manner, an aspect that has been perceived and transmitted by a third *we*. This situation may actually be highly typical, as in the undergraduate classroom in which a student registers a text as literary because the instructor (or an anthology) has ascribed value to an aspect of its manner, an aspect that the tradition of literary criticism has delineated and transmitted to the instructor in graduate school. All three actors participate in what is thus both a temporally discrete and distributed activity of valuing, but they do so at different, inter-implicated relations to the text at hand.

By the phrase *register a text as literary*, I mean the social act of recognition or discovery considered pragmatically. Thus I am claiming that the practical experience of the literary as such requires an act of value ascription, but as indicated above I am not also claiming – ontologically – that such acts form, or are even necessarily relevant to, the actual essence of the literary, whatever that may be. Nor am I claiming that an act of value ascription necessarily entails registration of a text as literary but rather that whenever we do register a text as literary, we are ascribing value to its manner. (In other words, ascribing value to manner is a necessary but not sufficient condition for registering a text as literary, and thus ascribing value to manner may in some cases result in registration of the text as something else than literary.) I am claiming, however, that this operation of registering a text as literary is transhistorical, encompassing the whole array of past, present and future constructions of the category. Hence, in respect to periods prior to the currency of the term *literary* as we commonly understand it, I am implicitly referring to whatever cognate categories were then current (for Chaucer, for example, the categories of *makyng* and *poesye*).[32] These cognates were of course neither conceptually nor empirically identical to our *literary*, but their social registration, I claim, was nonetheless likewise tied to an ascription of value to manner.

By the phrase *ascribe value* I mean an activity that is distributed across a network of actors that extends indefinitely through time and space, and furthermore an activity that is both among and within actors always multiple, various and potentially contradictory. It is also an activity of relative degree, and hence, unlike in Eagleton's formulation of 'highly valued kind of writing', an ascription of little – or even negative – value may be just as efficacious as an ascription of great value in registering a text as literary.[33]

My notion of network, as my terminology has already betrayed, follows loosely that of Actor-Network Theory (ANT) as it has been developed by Bruno Latour, possessing its pragmatic basis, dynamism, simultaneously diachronic and synchronic extension, resistance to subject/object and human/nonhuman dichotomisation, and its aim to describe, rather than to diagnose or unmask, the fabrications that we name facts and essences. (Given the schematic nature of my theory, there will be no need to incorporate a fuller ANT apparatus, or to follow Latour's ramification of networks into 'modes of existence'.)[34] Within this network, individual ascriptions of literary value are always performed in some relation to (or, in Latour's terms, as translations or mediations of) some number of other actors' ascriptions of literary value. These relations extend in multiple directions, encompassing first those other actors most proximate (whether synchronically or diachronically) in the specific situation of valuing and stretching outward indefinitely to those that are indirectly implicated at potentially many levels of remove. Moreover, the particular constellation of relations and hence the character of individual value ascriptions are shaped by their institutional and systemic conditions – social, economic, political, racial, sexual, cultural, ecological, psychological, physiological, and so on – which, in other terminology, might be described as a complex set of overlapping institutional and material contexts. But since 'contexts' implies a false duality between internal and external relations, these contexts are better recognised as networks of other kinds of value (e.g., economic, social, spiritual, etc.), interlinked with the network of literary value and thereby themselves part of the armature of value mediation, forming, altogether, the valuing actor's infinitely receding axiological environment.[35] Admittedly, this notion of interlinked networks puts pressure on the metaphor, given, say, the murky difference between linked networks and just one bigger network. As with Smith's similar idea of 'the continuous interplay among multiply configurable systems', the attempt here is to recognise, heuristically rather than categorically, the practical encounter with values in some relation to each other that nonetheless register as different kinds and that, as such, appear to have distinguishably different channels of determination.[36] (The next chapter, digging a bit deeper into value theory, will revisit this metaphor and its murkiness.)

The network of literary valuing does not comprise a fixed system of definite, stable relationships. Although portions of it may have more-or-less temporal persistence, the network is constituted dynamically by the ascriptions of value performed by the actors themselves. Because these ascriptions occur in mediating relation to the ascriptions of other actors, they are in ANT terms 'translations' or 'displacements through other actors whose mediation is indispensable for any action to occur'.[37] They are also reciprocal, in that an ascription of value forges a mediating relation between actors that potentially affects both. At any given moment in any given place, the network consists of the collective traces of such mediations, which demarcate 'associations of mediators' within which there is always potential for 'discontinuity, invention, supplementarity, creativity'.[38] There is no necessary centre, beginning or end to the network, and no certain structure, although one's own position within it, and the institutional (or inter-network) constraints upon that position, will usually entail some sense of hierarchy, order and stability.

As an illustration of one sliver of one such network, taking for its initial point of consideration the author as actor (an arbitrary choice for the purposes of the illustration, but obviously not an insignificant one), we may imagine the situation of a lyric poet with a day job as an hourly-contracted web programmer.[39] To produce any verse at all, this poet must, however consciously, ascribe some sort of value to that verse, in the very act of choosing to write rather than not. This ascription of value will emerge as mediations of other ascriptions of literary value – say, for the particular chapbook with which the poet is currently occupied, mediations of Keats's negative capability, which she had just encountered as marginal notes

A preliminary theory of literary valuing 85

in a writing group friend's college edition of Keats; her publisher's desire for something more straightforwardly confessional; and the writing group friend's own recent chapbook, which she finds rather shallow. These mediations will in turn be interlinked with mediations of ascriptions of other kinds of value – of, say, racial justice in relation to the recent removal of a Confederate monument and of the core beliefs of her Unitarian upbringing, which shape some of the themes and forms of the poems; of her sense of duty toward her pet kitten and to the environment (in the form of walking rather than driving to the supermarket), both of which she neglects while writing; and, perhaps most practically, of the time and energy that the poet chooses not to devote to her income-producing activity. This dynamic, even volatile blend of mediations of the ascriptions of other actors, human and nonhuman, and of literary and other-than-literary values, then receives is own translation (in the ANT sense) in the empirical object of the chapbook that the poet completes, itself subsequently to serve as actor within the network of literary valuing.

By the verb *ascribe* I mean to connote potential for doubt, indirection and indeterminacy, in that the value we ascribe may be one that we have more-or-less faith in, are more-or-less responsible for and are more-or-less conscious of ascribing; and that has more-or-less clarity in its pragmatic situation. The classroom situation again provides a ready illustration for this point, as well as for those of the preceding paragraphs. The undergraduate student might at first neither understand nor be responsible for the values ascribed to aspects of a text's manner. But nonetheless – through the mediation of the textbook's, teacher's and English major curriculum's ascriptions of value – she might register that those values have been so ascribed, and so accept the text as, say, canonical literature (that is, she ascribes the value of cultural authority). Later, the student might ascribe the value of pleasure to an aspect of the text's manner (say, to its use of lavish descriptive passages). In this case, she might enact her ascription through the mediation not of her teacher but of, say, an animated film adaptation. In turn, the makers of this adaptation might enact their ascription of value through the mediation of an illustrated version of the text adapted for children, which had been marketed as an expensive boutique item to upper-middle-class families, part of a 'great books for tots' series – thereby extending the network of literary value into the network of economic value, among others.[40]

By the tricky, intentionally vague term *manner* I mean any aspect of a text that an actor may apprehend or convey in something other than a strictly communicative fashion (i.e., as other than the *matter* or *sense* of a text). By choosing *manner* to denote this idea rather than the more typical term *form*, I seek to encompass a broader category than the latter is sometimes felt to convey, one that includes all that falls under the rubrics *style* and *mode*, for example, as well as paratextual, bibliographical and codicological features – for the preprint era, everything that falls under the umbrella of the 'manuscript matrix', such as illumination, rubrication, *mise-en-page*, organisation of texts in a miscellany, and so on.[41] And, crucially, manner also includes aspects of what might otherwise be thought of as content or meaning, when the latter is apprehended as a distinctive referential effect, what Attridge has termed a 'mobilization of meanings' or 'the events of meaning: their sequentiality, interplay, and changing intensity, their patterns of expectation and satisfaction or tension and release, their precision or diffuseness'.[42] In this regard, much of what we call *theme*, at least in our more complicated applications of the term, may be understood as aspects of manner.

Finally, the adjective *perceived* indicates that aspects of manner are necessarily activated by ascribers in the dynamic process suggested by such terms as Attridge's *mobilisation*, his more general *staging*, Knapp's *literary interest* or Fish's (and many others') *framing*, to name just a few. And because I take material instances of texts, such as critical editions, as just other value-ascribing actors, I hope to avoid – following Latour – the dichotomisation between subject and object that may infect the verb *perceive*. I hope to avoid, that is, the dichotomy between what Antony Easthope, in a response to Steven Connor, terms 'textual realism' (the text has these inherent features) and textual constructionism (now you see them, now you don't, as the interpretive community decides)'.[43] This is, of course, one of the foundational problems that Russian Formalism and its heirs introduced into literary theory, if it had not already been a source of trouble ever since Plato and Aristotle.[44] My notion of manner, inasmuch as it overlaps with that of form, inherits this problem,

A preliminary theory of literary valuing

which I will return to in Chapter 5. For now, I will attempt to square the circle by recognising, on the one hand, that material instances of texts possess features independent of any reader, that that these features follow – just like readers do – representational protocols for ascribing value and that these protocols are actors in the network of literary valuing; while, on other hand, also recognising that the value ascribed by these protocols only enters circulation in the act of reading – which is also an act of value translation – and that the protocols do not prescribe exactly how they enter circulation, or even whether they do so enter.

Crucially – and in distinction with the above-mentioned accounts by other theorists – recognition of manner is a dynamic process that is coextensive with the activity of literary valuing, as some aspect of manner must necessarily be apprehended as such, to some degree, in the moment in which an actor ascribes value to it. In other words, we do not notice manner *as manner* unless we are ascribing value (whether positive or negative, great or small) to it, and, when we do so, we have effectively isolated manner from matter to some degree, which accomplishes the framing effect – which is to say that in this isolation manner is loosened from its role in the text's strictly communicative function.[45] This point, which may seem to put the value ascription cart before the manner-recognition horse, is merely to grasp literary apprehension as a motivated activity, in which there can be no fact/value dichotomy, even if the value ascribed is one of disinterest: in literary apprehension, to notice manner is to ascribe value to it, and vice-versa. Thus, when, say, Fish defines literature as 'language around which we have drawn a frame' and then conceives of literary value as an effect of the 'framing process', in which the 'formal signals' that trigger this process 'are also evaluative criteria', he astutely identifies the centrality of valuing in the recognition of the literary but misleadingly suggests a logical priority.[46] Instead, an actor's evaluation (or ascription of value) is inseparable from her recognition of 'formal signals' (or aspects of manner), and therefore the 'framing process' is a reflex of her mediation of literary value. To put this in simple semiotic terms, an aspect of manner is in effect a signifier of literary value, and thus just as signifiers are imperceptible as such absent their significations, to recognise manner as such is also to perform an ascription of value. For this reason, the very phrase 'literary value' is in fact a redundancy, since 'value' is inextricable from that which 'literary' denotes.

To consider just one specific textual example, as long as we perceive the Declaration of Independence solely as, say, an act of rebellion, we apprehend it in a communicative fashion. We ascribe value to the *matter* of its political statement (which, if considered in its material documentary singularity, may seem, fetish-like, to carry the value of the nation that it imagines, as the 2004 film *National Treasure* rather crassly dramatises). But the moment that we also appreciate, say, its rhetorical elegance or its imaginative scope, and thereby ascribe value to its *manner*, we have apprehended it also as literary, framing its language in such a way that it would no longer be odd to place the document alongside other examples of such elegance or scope, regardless of their matter, or indeed of their historical actuality as documents. It would no longer be odd, that is, to regard the Declaration as to some degree an exhibition of its manner, and hence suitably placed in a catalogue of texts with like manners rather than like matters.[47]

As this example makes evident, and as literary history has made obvious, an actor may ascribe literary value to virtually any text, regardless of the intentions of its original producers or the specific characteristics of its manner. Yet this open-endedness hardly means that the categories of literature and literary merely reflect the whims of the valuing actor. For all activities of valuing occur, as I have described, within a network that enables that activity but also, by that same token, constrains it – in the sense that any specific activity occurs only as a mediation of other activities, whose character therefore prompts and shapes it, although not in any definitely determining fashion. Moreover, since valuing actors may be, say, critical editions, in practice the activity of valuing may seem to have an objective character. For example, as the preceding chapter observed, *The Riverside Chaucer* follows representational protocols that ascribe value to the manner of Chaucer's poetry.[48] Inasmuch as readers recognise such protocols, their own ascriptions of value to the manner of Chaucer's poetry – while not identical to those of the edition – are predictable, so much so that they may appear to be a quality of the object itself. This example also indicates (as book historians have for some decades been pointing out) that there is no text outside of its set of variable and imperfect material reproductions. Thus, when we ascribe value to the manner of a text, we are translating (among other mediations) the value ascribed by the agency of a particular material instance of that text. Our translations may resist this agency, but they are nonetheless influenced by it. Of course, it is possible for the representational protocols of a material instance of a text not to be legible as such to a reader, in which case the translation may not occur at all, and hence, for that reader, the text would not be literary, unless value ascribed to manner is in some other way mediated. In sum, according to this chapter's preliminary theory, literary value, produced and maintained within a network comprising human and nonhuman actors, in pragmatic practice inheres neither in reader nor text, but in activities of mediation among these and other actors.[49]

Among the objections that this theory of literary valuing may provoke, three strike me as particularly urgent, and hence I conclude this chapter with brief responses to them, which will also supply pointers to topics in Chapter 3. First, as genealogically oriented critics especially may complain, my rather bloodless, highly abstract account of value appears to have exiled the realities of power, authority, gender, sexuality, race, ability, class, and so on that attend any experience of literature. In short, it lacks a consideration of the politics and ideology of valuing. To some degree, the latter may be less immediate in my account because my theoretical touchstone for value is (as I discuss in the next chapter) Georg Simmel rather than, say, Marx. But the primary culprits are my abstraction from the specifics of place and time, my apparent focus on the value ascriptions of individual actors rather than of trans-actorial institutions and my underdeveloped consideration of the relation of literary value to other kinds of value. In fact, the latter two culprits are, as I will consider in the next chapter, ultimately the same, and in that chapter I will seek to fill out somewhat this portion of my theory. But however highly distilled my account of literary valuing remains, I maintain that that does not make it irrelevant or useless, given the nature of the project at hand. I have sought to expose a kind of skeletal schema of the network of literary valuing in order to provide a basic orientation to this network's features and operation. It will be from this position that in later chapters we will descend to consider more flesh-and-blood instances of the problem of literary value, reassessing the stakes and dynamics of them in the light of this framework.

The second objection, conversely, is one that I imagine may be strongly felt by those who take on ontological approach to literary value. Such readers may find that my account is not of literary value at all but simply of the relativism of such value. I might respond that such charges of relativism, as Smith has pointed out, are typically levelled from the vantage point of essentialism, but this would be overcompensating, since my approach is not in fact relativist. While it does not itself define a specific value for literature, it does not preclude the possibility that the nature of literary value may be so specific. I have emphasised the fact that actors ascribe different kinds of value to textual manner for different reasons, and I have argued that such ascriptions make texts socially registerable as to some degree literary. The question of whether the value that some actors ascribe to manner is more truly literary than that of other ascriptions is a normative one that I have bracketed – as I have the normative (genealogical) question of the actual nature of the value that actors, in a particular time and place, perhaps mistakenly take to be literary. My schema is thus neither affirmative nor demystifying. It leaves room for the believer, the atheist and the agnostic. As with ANT, it allows the ascriptions of actors to stand as they are, without necessarily endorsing them. Whether and how such bracketing of normative questions may be critically useful is another one of the topics that the next chapter, and indeed the remainder of the book, take up.

Finally, readers of any stripe may still object that my approach leaves literary value a curiously empty category. They may point out that despite my attempt at theorisation, literary value remains the placeholder of Chapter 1, which I have merely elaborated in order to develop an account of valuing as distributed across a network. Even if they grant the pragmatic utility of my avoidance of a single determination of literary value, they may suggest, as I earlier gestured, that I should have considered a range of specific kinds of literary value in the manner of Felski's identifications of recognition, enchantment, knowledge and shock. I may have considered, say, complex formal unity, cultural exemplification, rhetorical mastery, *jouissance*, cultural capital, commodity fetish, ideological resistance, empathy with the Other, escape from instrumentality, alterity, hybridity, misprision, defamiliarisation, creative reconception of social codes, disinterest, the sublime, beauty, truth or Chaucer's version of *dulce et utile*, 'best sentence and moost solaas'.[50] I may have then, following Felski's lead, described the (nonexclusive) experiences of literature that these kinds of literary value condition. Yet the sheer extent of even this very partial list of possibilities for literary value reaffirms one of my basic motivations: the recognition that literary value has been, in practice, an unusually flexible category. Its emptiness in my account of its pragmatic operation is thus merely another way of denoting this practical flexibility. From the perspective of its pragmatic operation, literary value has no stable nature. This conclusion seems safely uncontroversial, even a truism. Yet it points us towards what has been a historically characteristic (if neither unique nor mandatory) feature of the activity of literary valuing, one that the chapter that follows will explore.

Notes

1 Robert J. Meyer-Lee, *Poets and Power from Chaucer to Wyatt* (Cambridge: Cambridge University Press, 2007), 131.

2 See, for example, Richard Firth Green, 'Rev. of *Poets and Power from Chaucer to Wyatt*, by Robert J. Meyer-Lee', *SAC*, 30 (2009), 387–9.

3 Charles Altieri, *Reckoning with the Imagination: Wittgenstein and the Aesthetics of Literary Experience* (Ithaca: Cornell University Press, 2015), pp. 2, 15, 1–2.

4 E. Dean Kolbas, *Critical Theory and the Literary Canon* (Boulder: Westview Press, 2001), p. 86, emphasis in original.

5 Derek Attridge, *The Singularity of Literature* (London: Routledge, 2004), pp. 136, 137. Attridge has subsequently published a second book-length elaboration of these ideas: *The Work of Literature* (Oxford: Oxford University Press, 2015).

6 John Frow, 'On Literature in Cultural Studies', in Michael Bérubé (ed.), *The Aesthetics of Cultural Studies* (Malden: Blackwell, 2005),

pp. 44–57. This study builds on Frow's earlier *Cultural Studies and Cultural Value* (Oxford: Clarendon Press, 1995).

7 For an example of each, see, respectively, Günter Leypoldt, 'Singularity and the Literary Market', *NLH*, 45:1 (2014), 71–88; and Ian Hunter, *Culture and Government: The Emergence of Literary Education* (Basingstoke: Macmillan Press, 1988).

8 Steven Connor, *Theory and Cultural Value* (Oxford: Blackwell, 1992); Peter D. McDonald, 'Ideas of the Book and Histories of Literature: After Theory?', *PMLA*, 121:1 (2006), 214–28; Rita Felski, *Uses of Literature* (Malden: Blackwell, 2008); John Fekete, 'Introductory Notes for a Postmodern Value Agenda', in John Fekete (ed.), *Life after Postmodernism: Essays on Value and Culture* (New York: St. Martin's Press, 1987), pp. i–xix (xiv).

9 I also hope that it is clear that I am not claiming that these two tendencies comprise all the scholarship on literary value. For example, among other approaches with some prominence in the field, there is that which is sometimes referred to as the New Economic Criticism, which is concerned with how the forms and concepts of economic value appear within literature, or, conversely, with how the forms and concepts of aesthetic value appear within economics.

10 George Levine, 'Saving Disinterest: Aesthetics, Contingency, and Mixed Conditions', *NLH*, 32:4 (2001), 907–31 (921, 929); Satya P. Mohanty, 'Can Our Values Be Objective? On Ethics, Aesthetics, and Progressive Politics', *NLH*, 32:4 (2001), 803–33.

11 John Guillory, *Cultural Capital: The Problem of Literary Canon Formation* (Chicago: University of Chicago Press, 1993).

12 The studies that I am concerned with here are those that are explicitly focused on the question of literary value, but plainly the tendencies that I have identified are implicitly present (whether separately or together) in a much broader swath of research. A study of, say, the ethical implications of Chaucer's *Franklin's Tale* may well be grounded on an ontological account of literary value, while a study of Chaucer's early modern construction as a proto-Protestant may rest upon a genealogical account. How these might all be gathered under one umbrella is a question that I address in the next chapter. Also, in the recent debates about reading methods, ontological and genealogical accounts of value are often in evidence, although there is no necessary correspondence between, say, the general categories of 'surface reading' or 'distant reading' and one account of value or another. Rather, while the problem of value is both prompting of and integral to these debates, its relation to them is oblique and various. I will return to this relation briefly in Chapter 5.

13 Connor, *Theory and Cultural Value*, 32. Forming neat exemplifications of Connor's view, some studies of value achieve a virtually exact inner balance between ontological and genealogical perspectives, which are nonetheless each distinctly voiced. See, for example, the otherwise quite different accounts in John Carey, *What Good Are the Arts?* (Oxford: Oxford University Press, 2006); and Regenia Gagnier, *The Insatiability of Human Wants: Economics and Aesthetics in Market Society* (Chicago: University of Chicago Press, 2000).
14 Steven Connor, 'Doing without Art', *NLH*, 42:1 (2011), 53–69.
15 I draw on Connor, 'Doing without Art', 58–9, for some of the following points, although the criticisms are common ones.
16 Steven Knapp, *Literary Interest: The Limits of Anti-Formalism* (Cambridge, MA: Harvard University Press, 1993), pp. 89, 97–8, emphasis in original.
17 Frow, 'On Literature', pp. 54, 50. Looking back on his own work in 'On Midlevel Concepts', *NLH*, 41:2 (2010), 237–52, however, Frow voices the very limit of this approach that I point out below.
18 In a micro-survey, I can attest that two talented self-doubting poets, David Dodd Lee and Benjamin Balthaser, have grudgingly confirmed this.
19 Jan Mukařovský, *Aesethetic Function, Norm and Value as Social Facts*, trans. Mark E. Suino (Ann Arbor: University of Michigan, 1970), pp. 68–9.
20 Mukařovský, in fact, anticipates the general shape of Bourdieu's well-known account of the relation of artistic value and belief and the position of the analyst in respect to these. For Bourdieu, as he explains in *The Field of Cultural Production*, ed. Randal Johnson (New York: Columbia University Press, 1993), the field-constituting belief in the value of artistic works is a product of forces and struggles specific to the semi-autonomous field of cultural production but also of the relations between that field and others, especially the enclosing fields of power and social class, which relations are necessarily misrecognised by cultural producers. Hence, the analyst must be on guard to avoid the mystification of belief, even while recognising that the mystification is sociologically essential.
21 Connor, *Theory and Cultural Value*, p. 32. For an account of this general problem as it pertains to the social sciences, see the discussion of 'Relativization' in Luc Boltanski and Laurent Thévenot, *On Justification: Economies of Worth*, trans. Catherine Porter (Princeton: Princeton University Press, 2006), pp. 336–46.
22 But for a particularly nuanced and qualified consideration of this view, see James F. English, 'Literary Studies', in Tony Bennett and John Frow

(eds), *The SAGE Handbook of Cultural Analysis* (London: SAGE, 2008), pp. 126–44.
23 Frow, 'On Literature in Cultural Studies', pp. 50, 55.
24 For an appreciation of this prescience, see Michael Bérubé, 'Introduction: Engaging the Aesthetic', in Michael Bérubé (ed.), *The Aesthetics of Cultural Studies* (Malden: Blackwell, 2005), pp. 1–27. Bérubé calls for a 'fresh reading' (p. 15) of Mukařovský, one cognisant of but not predetermined by Raymond Williams's mediation of his work in *Marxism and Literature* (New York: Oxford University Press, 1977).
25 Mukařovský, *Aesthetic Function*, p. 8 n. 5.
26 Attridge, *The Singularity of Literature*, p. 4. Attridge goes on to mention such 'not strictly literary' values as giving 'comfort', providing 'a rich source of historical information', being 'instructive in the art of moral living' and 'ameliorating the lives of many individuals in unhappy circumstances' (p. 4). Although not simply dismissive like Mukařovský and Frow, Attridge must exclude these values *a priori* as 'not strictly literary' because non-instrumentality is crucial to his normative definition of literary value.
27 Felski, *Uses of Literature*, p. 13. For an effort to recalibrate the evaluative criteria of the novel in order to bridge exactly this gap between the literary predilections of academics and 'ordinary persons', see Cecelia Konchar Farr, *The Ulysses Delusion: Rethinking Standards of Literary Merit* (Basingstoke: Palgrave Macmillan, 2016), although Konchar Farr's argument is also ultimately normative. For cautionary reflections on this trend of elevating the 'lay reader', see Tobias Skiveren, 'Postcritique and the Problem of the Lay Reader', *NLH*, 53:1 (2022), 161–80.
28 Felski, *Uses of Literature*, p. 17.
29 Terry Eagleton, *Literary Theory: An Introduction* (Minneapolis: University of Minnesota Press, 1983), p. 10.
30 Mukařovský, *Aesthetic Function*, p. 64.
31 John Dewey, *Theory of Valuation* (Chicago: University of Chicago Press, 1939), p. 4.
32 For the meaning of and distinction between these terms, see Glending Olson, 'Making and Poetry in the Age of Chaucer', *Comparative Literature*, 31 (1979), 272–90.
33 Eagleton later recognised the overly restrictive effect of 'highly' in his definition, and in *The Event of Literature* (New Haven: Yale University Press, 2012), he includes 'highly valued' as just one of five common 'family resemblance' (p. 25) features of literature (albeit one cutting across the others).

34 For ANT, I have drawn on Bruno Latour, *Pandora's Hope: Essays on the Reality of Science Studies* (Cambridge, MA: Harvard University Press, 1999); Latour, *Reassembling the Social: An Introduction to Actor-Network-Theory* (Oxford: Oxford University Press, 2005); and Latour, 'An Attempt at a Compositionist Manifesto', *NLH*, 41:3 (2010), 471–90. See also Latour, *An Inquiry into Modes of Existence: An Anthropology of the Moderns* (Cambridge, MA: Harvard University Press, 2018); and, for a personalised account of the influence of pragmatism on ANT, Antoine Hennion, 'From ANT to Pragmatism: A Journey with Bruno Latour at the CSI', in Rita Felski and Stephen Muecke (eds), *Latour and the Humanities*, trans. Muecke (Baltimore: Johns Hopkins University Press, 2020), pp. 52–75. By taking my concept of network from Latour, I do not mean to insist that ANT is the only viable model for such relations. Other candidates include Bourdieu's apparatus of fields and capital (to cite one that Latour deems antithetical to his own), the refinements of Bourdieu's model evident in Frow's 'regimes of reading' (for which, see Frow, *The Practice of Value: Essays on Literature in Cultural Studies* (Crawley: University of Western Australia, 2013)), Hans Robert Jauss's horizons of expectation, or Pascale Casanova's 'world literary space' (for which, see Casanova, *The World Republic of Letters*, trans. Malcolm DeBevoise (Cambridge, MA: Harvard University Press, 2004)). But ANT, because of the features that I have indicated, lends itself more directly and robustly to the abstract totality that I seek to describe, and to my noncritical (but rather 'compositionist', to use Latour's term) motivations in doing so. It also more easily coordinates with Georg Simmel's theory of value, whose bearing on my formulations I take up in the next chapter. For a (friendly) critique of Latour, see, *inter alia*, Graham Harman, 'Entanglement and Relation: A Response to Bruno Latour and Ian Hodder', *NLH*, 45:1 (2014), 37–49. Felski has been among the most vocal proponents of ANT's usefulness for literary study. See e.g., Felski, 'Latour and Literary Studies', *PMLA*, 130:3 (2015), 737–42; and her introduction to Felski and Muecke (eds), *Latour and the Humanities*, 1–27.

35 The Latour-inspired suspicion of the notion of context I have taken from Felski, '"Context Stinks!"', *NLH*, 42:4 (2011), 573–91; see also Felski's elaboration in *The Limits of Critique* (Chicago: University of Chicago Press, 2015).

36 Barbara Herrnstein Smith, *Contingencies of Value: Alternative Perspectives for Critical Theory* (Cambridge, MA: Harvard University Press, 1988), 31.

37 Latour, *Pandora's Hope*, p. 311.

38 Latour, 'An Attempt', p. 483.
39 This example I have elaborated from my first airing of it in *Literary Value and Social Identity in the* Canterbury Tales (Cambridge: Cambridge University Press, 2019), a book that considers the role of Chaucer's 'day jobs' in his ascriptions of literary value. The example came to me after meeting a poet with exactly the above described day job, although I do not intend definite reference to anyone. For a sociological consideration of the relays between days jobs and literary production that focuses on modern French writers, see Bernard Lahire, *La Condition littéraire: la double vie des écrivains* (Paris: Découverte, 2006), a translated excerpt of which appears in 'The Double Life of Writers', trans. Gwendolyn Wells, *NLH*, 41:2 (2010), 443–65. Lahire supplies a corrective to Bourdieu's field and habitus theory by recognising that actors are almost always simultaneously active in multiple fields, an idea that I have incorporated into my schema as interlinked networks. For elaboration, see Bernard Lahire, *The Plural Actor*, trans. David Fernbach (Cambridge: Polity, 2011). It is beyond the scope of my purposes to account in any theoretically elaborated way for the details of the processes of value mediation for any given kind of actor. There is, of course, a rich, diverse and very long philosophical tradition on this topic for the human actor. For just one example, see Agnes Callard, *Aspiration: The Agency of Becoming* (New York: Oxford University Press, 2018), a reference I owe to Sarah Buss.
40 As evident in this example, the way in which the value of same work shifts according to its material instantiation and the situations in which it is encountered resembles what Lucien Karpik has described as the market of singularities, especially what he calls the 'originality model' of singularity. See Lucien Karpik, *Valuing the Unique*, trans. Nora Scott (Princeton: Princeton University Press, 2010), pp. 17–19. For an especially vivid example that is consonant with my understanding of the mobility of literary value, see his fictional anecdote of shopping for a recording of Beethoven's Ninth Symphony (pp. 80–86). For a study that draws on Karpik's theory to consider the value mobility of particular works, see Günter Leypoldt, 'Degrees of Public Relevance: Walter Scott and Toni Morrison', *MLQ*, 77:3 (2016), 369–93.
41 See Stephen G. Nichols, 'Introduction: Philology in a Manuscript Culture', *Speculum*, 65:1 (1990), 1–10. Obviously, therefore, I am not using *manner* in the narrow sense, evident in the art historical term *mannerism*, of a sort of hyperbole of a specific kind of style.
42 Attridge, *The Singularity of Literature*, 109.

43 Antony Easthope, 'Literary Value Again: A Reply to Steven Connor', *Textual Practice*, 5:3 (1991), 334–6 (335).
44 See, e.g., English, 'Literary Studies'; and Tony Bennett, *Formalism and Marxism* (London: Methuen, 1979).
45 For the formalists, this loosening has of course been most often described as a kind of self-referentiality or autotelic valence, with form conceived as a sort of force-field that turns external reference back inward, producing, say, the New Critical 'verbal icon'. New Formalists, in contrast, have found this view of the text semiotically impoverished, arguing that self-referential significance most often, if not always, depends on the continued viability of reference in general. Nonetheless, what Eagleton asserts about poetry continues to have traction in the field as a theory of the literary: 'Poetry is language in which the signified or meaning is *the whole process of signification itself*. It is thus always at some level language which is about itself.' Eagleton, *How to Read a Poem* (Malden: Wiley-Blackwell, 2007), p. 21, emphasis in original. I will revisit this topic in the next chapter in light of the work of Mukařovský.
46 Fish, *Is There a Text*, pp. 108–9. One advantage of identifying framing with valuing is that it sidesteps some of the theoretical conundrums of the relation between frame and enframed famously explored by Jacques Derrida, *The Truth in Painting*, trans. Geoffrey Bennington and Ian McLeod (Chicago: University of Chicago Press, 1987). Frow's designation of framing as performed by literary regimes is similar to what I am attempting to describe, albeit his account is less abstract and more Bourdieuian; see 'On Literature in Cultural Studies', p. 52.
47 The somewhat farcical tenor of this illustration belies the often illuminating and rigorous – and, over the last four decades or so, various and voluminous – research that takes as a point of departure this very notice of manner in texts normatively categorised as nonliterary. See, for just one recent example, Jennifer Jahner, *Literature and Law in the Era of Magna Carta* (Oxford: Oxford University Press, 2019).
48 *The Riverside Chaucer*, gen. ed. Larry D. Benson, 3rd edn (Boston: Houghton Mifflin, 1987). McDonald supplies an especially lucid account of the general agency of an edition in this regard: 'each edition tends ... also to identify the text as *Literature* in a strongly normative sense. It does so by associating the text with the publisher's reputation, project, and promotional strategies; by inserting it in a particular series or backlist, which functions as a cotextual (as opposed

to a paratextual) frame ... Depending on the categories available at the time, these various factors ... set it on a particular trajectory through the next series of cultural guardians, including booksellers, reviewers, prize judges, librarians, and academics, who then confirm, contest, or revise its identity in their own ways' ('Ideas of the Book', pp. 224–5).
49 Cf. Smith's formulation: 'For, like all value, literary value is not the property of an object *or* of a subject but, rather, *the product of the dynamics of a system*' (*Contingencies of Value*, p. 15, emphasis in the original).
50 *Canterbury Tales* I.798.

3

Loose binding and its affordances

The skeletal theory of literary valuing of the preceding chapter beckons fleshing out in a number of ways. The primary aim of this chapter is to address two principle needs in this regard and, in the course of their elaboration, to consider several other related issues. Across its first five sections, the chapter elucidates a feature of literary valuing – loose binding, as I term it – that has very often characterised the activity and examines some of its implications. Along with the preceding chapter's formulations, these additional considerations comprise the theoretical contribution of this book and also form the conceptual basis for the next two chapters. Then, more briefly in the final section (and to some degree also in the penultimate one), the chapter offers the book's initial explanation of how its theory may be of some use in the field of literary studies.

In the first five sections, the chapter continues the preceding chapter's project of seeking an alternative to ontological and genealogical approaches to literary value, but here this alternative may seem more like the very alternating ping-ponging that I have observed of others, a pivoting between claiming and disclaiming aspects of both of those approaches. In particular, with the concept of loose binding, I introduce a feature of literary valuing that has in one fashion or another served as the basis for many an ontological theory of literary value. Then, by insisting nonetheless that this feature is neither essential nor defining but historically contingent, I may seem to be casting a genealogical eye on this supposedly ontological quality. But as in Chapter 2, my aim is to bracket ontology and genealogy rather than to claim or disclaim them. To say that loose binding is in practice historically contingent will not necessarily prohibit it from also being the essence of the truly literary; and, conversely, to say that it has broadly characterised literary valuing will not require that it must do so for that valuing to be truly literary. The second clause of each of those preceding statements begs a normative question that I am not entertaining, one way or another. With this caveat in place, let us now dig a bit deeper into my preliminary theory.

Differential value

To this point in this book, I have been using the term *value* as if it were only the qualifier *literary* that complicated its denotation, but of course a number of rather different theories of value, with potentially large ideological stakes, may lurk within that everyday word. I cannot hope to enter in any significant way into this vast tradition of debate, which spans several branches of philosophy, economics, political economy, anthropology and sociology, not to mention aesthetics and literary theory. But the preliminary theory of literary valuing that I developed in the preceding chapter requires that I at least account for the operative understanding of value that it rests upon. With that understanding on the table, moreover, further dimensions of the theory will come into clearer view.

As has been evident, if not fully explained, this book takes an axiological approach to value, by which I mean an approach that is interested in the relations among what may seem very different kinds of value – an approach interested in how, say, moral, economic and aesthetic values differ but also, more importantly, in what they share. For this purpose, my ultimate conceptual touchstone is Georg Simmel's turn-of-the-century *Philosophy of Money*, which I have read as refracted through the lens of such later accounts of value as Barbara Herrnstein Smith's *Contingencies of Value*.[1] Although the title of Simmel's sprawling *magnum opus* may give the impression of axiological narrowness – and indeed the work is best known for its penetrating reflections on the pervasive effects of the money economy on society, culture and consciousness – this methodologically idiosyncratic book, as its commentators have pointed out, has an ambitiously far-reaching scope. Disciplinarily anomalous, *The Philosophy of Money* today is perhaps most read by sociologists, even though Simmel understood himself as writing philosophy, with his primary interlocutors including Kant, Nietzsche and Marx (although the latter most often silently). As Elizabeth S. Goodstein observes, '*The Philosophy of Money* asks, not what money is, but rather what the (historical, cultural) phenomenon of money reveals about human existence and the conditions of reflection on that existence.' In this way, Goodstein perspicaciously argues, the work is best understood as 'modernist philosophy' that 'is a crucial point of origin for that modern mode of reflection that has come to be called theory'.[2]

In brief, Simmel understands value as inhering neither in object nor subject but rather emerging in the relation between subject and object, in further relation to other subject-object value relations.[3] At one juncture, Simmel makes use of a geometrical analogy to explain this point:

> from the relationship between us and objects develops the imperative to pass a certain judgment, the content of which, however, does not reside in the things themselves. The same is true in judging length; the objects themselves require that we judge them, but the quality of length is not given by the objects and can only be realized by an act within ourselves. We are not aware of the fact that length is established only by a process of comparison and is not inherent in the individual object on which length depends.[4]

As this analogy clarifies, value emerges in 'a process of comparison', which means that it is inseparable from an activity that involves not only a relation among objects (here in respect to relative lengths) but also a relation between subject and object (in the act of comparing), as well as between one subject/object relation and others (in establishing and recognising length as an evaluative category). In the language of classical economics that Simmel, along with Marx, inherited and problematised, all value is thus, in effect, exchange value, even when – as in most situations, and as the analogy suggests – no physical exchange is involved. Rather, physical exchange stands synecdochically for the broader relation of contingency, which is to say that all ascriptions of value, all judgements, are realised only in relation to other ascriptions from which they somehow differ.

Thus, while the notion of exchange lies at the heart of Simmel's thinking, the term *exchange value* has minimal purchase for him, implying as it may that value may be otherwise realised – as, say, use value or labour value, categories that Simmel puts aside. As evident in his geometrical analogy, for Simmel the value of anything, including labour, is no more and no less than whatever in any particular situation it is being compared to, and so, strictly speaking, the term *value* needs no qualification. For these reasons, Natàlia Cantó Milà has named Simmel's account a wholly relational theory of value. But as my summary has already begun to suggest, we might just as well name it differential. For while Simmel does not, of course, explain his theory by way of Saussurean linguistics, passages such as those quoted above suggest that he would have agreed that value has no positive terms but rather emerges within a system in which equivalence can only be conceived (that is, birthed as well as thought) through difference.[5] The parallel with Saussure, moreover, signals that this theory of value does not entail ontological claims. In the same way that to theorise the differential nature of the signifier and signified is to make no assumptions, one way or another, about the referent, Simmel's description of value's contingency – at least for my limited ambitions – is a pragmatic one that does not necessarily preclude arguments that have their basis outside of that contingency. Such a pragmatic account of value, moreover, slides quite smoothly into the loose adaptation of ANT that I introduced in the preceding chapter. Put in those terms, value of all kinds emerges within a network of mediations among value-ascribing actors.[6] The principal emendation required is that what Simmel calls subject and object are in ANT both just actors in a network, albeit ones potentially of different types. (Hence, here and throughout, when I use the Simmel's terminology of subject and object, I do so merely heuristically in respect to the immediate pragmatic situation of an act of valuing.)

Loose binding

According to this relational, contingent, differential account of value, one which puts aside the notion of use value, virtually any kind of value may in principle be ascribed to anything by anyone (or anything). Yet obviously in practice there are limits to those ascriptions, often very constrained ones. We do not usually ascribe to pizza, say, the spiritual value of access to the divine. *Contra* Simmel's theory of value, most of us instead perceive pizza to possess a definite, straightforwardly identifiable use value. But this case is easily explicable – and generalisable – as the effect of a constellation of value ascription relations having achieved some amount of temporal persistence, a sort of hardening of a portion of the network, in the form of historically specific systems of production and consumption. The impression that pizza has the use value of, say, satisfaction of hunger is the effect of a specific set of mediations of value ascriptions across a network of actors – say, bakers, sellers, advertisers, buyers, eaters, dough, sauce, cheese, and so on (some of which already ascribe a different value to pizza) – that has achieved enough stability so as to seem an effect, rather than the fabricating process, of that value. But at any moment the constellation may shift in a way that alters the impression of a centrally determining use value. Whimsically, we might imagine a supremely successful marketing effort that convinces an ageing but still irony-loving Generation X that using frozen pizza as Frisbees is the next great suburban American pastime. More seriously, we might imagine low-carb diets becoming the norm and thus pizza coming to carry less the value of food and more that of a reactionary ideological statement.[7] In general, however, in very many cases, a stable, persistent constellation of value ascriptions has the pragmatic effect of making some objects appear to us as more tightly associated with some kinds of value than they are with others, so much so that their value strikes us as indeed inherent and self-evident, requiring no explanation or defence. Thus, pragmatically, we may say that pizza, within the networks of valuing in which it is usually produced and consumed, is relatively *tightly bound* with the value of hunger satisfaction, and that, over a long stretch of time and wide swath of space, this tight binding has been stable enough to appear objective.

In contrast, the value of, say, a brick is considerably more mutable. Across actors or even for the same actor, it may have value as home construction material, a piece of garden landscaping, a campfire barrier, part of a tire-changing toolkit, a paper weight, a weapon, and so on. Unless an actor's daily activities involve valuing bricks in a specific fashion, the actor is likely regularly to ascribe various values to them and sometimes find no value in them at all. In contradistinction with pizza, then, the variety of different network constellations involving bricks, the diversity within a single constellation and the relative instability of some or all constellations mean that any one value ascribed to bricks may pragmatically strike us as *loosely bound* – less self-evident, more in need of explanation, not inherent, potentially improper. (Thus, while the value as construction material may in most situations remain self-evident, that of, say, water conservation [by placing a brick in your toilet tank] may not be.) This is not an ontological distinction but rather a pragmatic and socially and historically contingent one. Today's pizzas may be tomorrow's bricks, and vice-versa. Nonetheless, in practice the distinction may be quite consequential, since stable constellations and their tightly bound values tend to provide one sort of constraints and prompts to actors within the network, whereas unstable and loosely bound values tend to provide a different sort. The axiological 'careers' of pizza and bricks are on different paths, shaping their axiological directions and destinies.[8]

As we have seen repeatedly in this book, literature, despite seemingly sharing with pizza the evaluative category of taste, has in practice more often been like bricks in the variety of different values ascribed to it and in the mutability of those ascriptions across time and place. Smith makes a similar comparison in respect to value understood as 'functional explanations', stating that for the 'labels' 'art' and 'literature', 'The particular functions that may be endorsed by these labels ... are, unlike those of "doorsteps" and "clocks", neither narrowly confined nor readily specifiable but, on the contrary, exceptionally heterogeneous, mutable, and elusive.' Any stabilisation of these explanations is the effect of 'the normative activities of various institutions'.[9] Put in my terms, over the course of the history of literature, the kinds of value ascribed to literature have had neither singular nor stable tight binding (though, to be sure, some values, such as pleasure, have been more stable than others), and it has been the endeavours of 'the normative activities' occurring through various, often competing portions of the network of literary valuing that have realised whatever provisional stability there has been. And at a finer-grained level, in respect to the previous chapter's formulation for literary valuing – that is, 'we register a text as literary when we ascribe value to some aspect of its perceived manner' – history attests to a habitual loose binding between particular aspects of manner and the particular values ascribed to them. This, indeed, is a common enough feature of the activity of literary valuing, collectively considered, that we may fairly call it characteristic, albeit keeping in mind that 'characteristic' here does not mean either necessary or distinguishing. It is certainly possible for other kinds of valuing (as with bricks) to be similarly loose, and it is certainly possible for literary valuing not to be loose (as in the case of many individual ascribers of literary value, such as, say, Harold Bloom). Nonetheless, in the history of literary valuing collectively considered, it seems uncontroversial to observe that specific aspects of manner have been relatively unmoored to specific values.[10]

Indeed, as the opening pages of this book suggested, this very instability is one of the engines behind the history of literary theory, driving arguments and counter-arguments for the value of literature from Plato and Aristotle, through Sidney and Shelley, to Martha Nussbaum and John Guillory. It is also one of the reasons why the academic field of literary studies so often – and especially at present – not only has had to defend its value as *field* of study, as do many other fields, but also to defend the value of its *object* of study, which is less typical of, say, oceanography, economics or history. To cite just one example – which I encountered while flipping through what was, at time of this writing, the most recent issue of *SAC* – in the conclusion of a thought-provoking study of how late medieval literature grapples with philosophical dialetheism, or 'the existence of true contradictions', Laura Ashe states,

> No one disputes ... that life as it is lived can seem overwhelmed by them [true contradictions]. I have argued that medieval literature is supremely attentive to their felt ubiquity, and I think that this gives us, now, access to some useful modes of understanding.[11]

Ashe asserts that the study of literature (and specifically medieval literature) is valuable because literature itself is valuable – to us 'now' – in the particular moral sense that she has identified, and she does so, presumably, because the value of literature for us today is not self-evident or even in doubt.

Yet more telling than such in-house self-justifying claims (which are in one sense just a reflex of our scholarly habitus) is the everyday difficulty many of us experience in answering the simple question of why we think a particular text holds (more-or-less, or any) literary value in a way that will convince those who do not already agree with us. For those of us who have at hand a ready vocabulary for features of textual manner, this difficulty is not in the identification of specific features that we find of merit. Rather, the difficulty is in constructing a convincing argument for why those features necessarily carry the particular values that we are ascribing to them. Thus, to recall an example from the previous chapter, while some may point to the mini-narrative of nation foundation and unfoundation in the Declaration of Independence as evidence of its imaginative scope, others may see in this part of the document only its means of argument or matter, and remain unconvinced by claims for the merits of its manner. In this instance, we would win most of the battle if our opponent admits that it has even poor imaginative scope, for, as I have mentioned, low valuation of manner still registers the literary. The greater obstacle is convincing someone prone to see otherwise that the question of literary value is even relevant. (Readers will readily recognise cognate, actual instances of this challenge in the disdainful response from some quarters to the introduction of science fiction, comic books, and so on, into the English curricula.)

In contrast, when the material instance of a text ascribes value to manner with a high degree of social legibility (as in, say, an edition of Shakespeare), the hurdle of recognition is usually easily crossed. In these cases, the challenge that we face (and by the first-person plural pronoun here I mean specifically scholars and teachers of literature) is convincing someone that any particular feature of manner necessarily carries any particular kind of literary value – for example, that the fluid structure of Iago's soliloquies has the value of disclosing a psychological truth in an especially accessible way, say, the truth of the abyssal structure of interiority. While our interlocutor might grudgingly agree that literature in general might sometimes disclose psychological truths, and even do so in a way that other kinds of discourse do not, she may simply not agree that these particular soliloquies disclose that particular truth. This sort of difficulty plainly constitutes one of the reasons why the academic field of literary studies has so often faced charges of subjectivism, charges that have led the field at different times in the converse directions of seeking to diminish the importance of value to its critical discourse (as with cultural studies) or to ground claims of value in quasi-empirical accounts of language (as in some varieties of twentieth-century formalism and, in later decades, stylistics).

The history of literary criticism over the last century has shown that both of these responses, while they have greatly enriched and expanded the field, inevitably falter. As I observed in Chapter 1 and will explore further in Chapter 4, attempts to diminish the importance of value, as the last several decades have especially attested, are impossible to sustain as long as the field continues to embrace the category of the literary. And, as I will review in Chapter 5, attempts to ground claims in empirical accounts of language (often by producing dazzlingly intricate portraits of textual manner) eventually wind up highlighting the very gap between manner and value that they seek surmount. Yet what has troubled the theory of literary value has also been what has enabled this value in everyday practice, both inside and outside the academy, to thrive. Looseness in association between manner and value has enabled the literary to hold countless values for countless ascribing actors with relatively little sense of contradiction. Hence, I might wholly agree with Ashe's claims for late medieval literature, while arguing for its very different value. More generally, one actor's, say, disinterested beauty may be another actor's expansion of empathetic breadth, and indeed this actor may be the same one at different times with different texts, or even at the same time with the same text.

Let me reiterate, however, that my point is not to claim (ontologically) that this looseness is an essential quality of the literary. Rather, I am claiming no more and no less than in the pragmatic registration of the literary, this looseness has been common and persistent enough to seem to many, in some fashion or another, characteristic. And this observation in turn puts us in better position than we were in Chapter 2 to account for the role of other kinds of value in the network of literary valuing.

Interlinked networks and other metaphors

In a brief, practically oriented argument for the value of literature – a contribution to a *PMLA* forum providing answers to the question, 'Why Major in Literature – What Do We Tell Our Students?' – Azade Seyhan writes,

> As literature professors and major advisers, we have all along impressed on our students the role of literature in understanding the human condition and its predicaments. We present literature as a powerful alternative way of knowledge; we read it as a social document, as stories of lives that history forgot to record, and as a guide to moral agency and responsibility. Literature brings into focus and clarifies – in historical, cultural, social, and psychological terms – what is distant in time and geography ... Literary texts offer alternative or novel insights into history, generate an awareness of fundamental human predicaments, record or recover silenced voices ... The study of literature engenders a passion for knowledge and compassion for those who do not necessarily share our views.[12]

I have selected this passage because I believe that some or all of its claims are ones that many literature faculty do indeed make about the value of literature (though perhaps less publically and more guardedly), and because it typifies how many of those claims are for values that are not, in a strict sense, literary. For example, while literature certainly does 'record or recover silenced voices', just as surely it is not the only medium that does so, and hence, by itself, this value cannot be said to be a distinctively literary one. Various lexical cues in the passage, however, point to the usual way that these values are joined with the idea of the literary. With '*alternative* way of knowledge' for example, the implication is that literature possesses a distinctive quality that makes it in some fashion more, or somehow uniquely, efficacious in realising these values. Such ascriptions of distinctive qualities, as I have argued, ultimately rest upon narrower ascriptions of value to textual manner. Although it is not Seyhan's purpose to specify the latter, an example might be that a particular novel's use of interior monologue records 'silenced voices' in a richer, deeper and more memorable way than is achievable by other means.

Seyhan's comments illustrate how the characteristic loose binding of literary value both facilitates and, by that same token, demands linkage to other-than-literary values. On the one hand, if her mostly tacit ascriptions of value to textual manner are what underlie its grander claims for what literature does for us, it is the loose binding between value and features of manner that enables those ascriptions to carry that weight, since, in contrast with a tightly bound situation such as pizza, the value of those features does not seem immediately self-evident and hence constrained. As Seyhan's comments display, the very ambiguity deriving from loose binding as to what constitutes *the* value of literature enables literature, functioning rather like a lint roller, to lap up an array of different values without apparent contradiction or incoherence. On the other hand, that so much of this 'lint' is not in fact strictly literary suggests how the lack of self-evident value at the level of feature of manner is, from another perspective, a weak link: it does not so much 'carry' the weight of grander claims of value as it appeals to them, because in that way it appears strengthened, tightened, more necessary. To continue the above example, the ascription of the values rich, deep and compelling to a specific instance of interior monologue may be confirmed by an appeal to the weightier and more urgent value ascription that sees that instance as the successful recording of a silenced voice. The (circular) logic, that is, is that the interior monologue must be rich, deep and compelling because those qualities are what entail the success of its recording of a silenced voice. Or, to cite an actual example, Ashe, considering a moment in Thomas of Britain's *Tristan* in which the titular character reflects on a moral double-bind, ascribes to its literary mode of fiction the value of that which 'imagines others as whole individuals with inner lives, capable of incurring complex obligations to one another'. And she continues, 'Fiction, then, is the justified falsehood, itself inherently contradictory … a full attention to the contradiction, to the incommensurable and unknowable but nonetheless absolutely real suffering of others, is the basis of a moral existence.'[13] What thus ultimately confirms for Ashe the success of *Tristan*'s rendering of 'whole individuals with inner lives' is an appeal to literary fiction as providing nothing less than a 'basis of moral existence'. Such sheer acceleration of value ascription elevation is by no means unusual but will rather be familiar to any regular reader of certain varieties of literary criticism. Ashe's essay, in this respect, is just a particularly adroit example of how the recognition of literary value can so seamlessly seem to necessitate recognition of a linked other-than-literary value.

In general, then, in the activity of literary valuing, loose binding tends to provoke appeals to other kinds of value as a kind of tightening, strengthening or propping of literary value ascriptions. As my examples have suggested, such tightening is often realised by positioning literary value as serving or leading to other kinds of value perceived as possessing greater weight and urgency. This tightening acts as a sort of axiological ballast, giving an ascription of literary value to a feature of textual manner stronger motivation, if not actually greater necessity. Moreover, one such appeal easily provokes further ones. Thus, for example, the value of vividness ascribed to a novel's rendering of character may serve the value of empathy with the other, which may in turn serve the values of intercultural understanding and geopolitical peace. In this case, the literary value of vividness gains weight by means of its linkage to empathy, which in turn gains weight from the linkage to the value of peace, and together these linkages have greatly tightened the association between the novelistic feature of character description and the particular literary value of vividness. Moreover, in this series of linkages empathy and peace may come to be apprehended not just as possible candidates for the greater values made available by means of a literary value but also as kinds of literary value themselves, because of the way that the narrower literary value has mediated them. That is, literature, by way of its quality of vivid rendering of character, may be understood as providing distinctive, unique access to the values of empathy and peace.

Admittedly, however, the very multiplication of metaphors in the preceding discussion (e.g., propping, serving, etc.), along with their uncertain relation to the metaphor of interlinked networks of value introduced in the preceding chapter, suggests some further clarifications are in order. One pressing question pertains to the presumed difference between literary and other kinds of value on which metaphors such as propping and interlinked depend. Given this book's limited theoretical ambitions, as well as its pragmatic, differential and axiological approach to value, I must put aside any categorical considerations of kinds of value, without thereby denying that some such distinctions might ultimately hold between, say, beauty and justice. Rather, in my approach, what distinguishes an ascription of literary value from an ascription of some other kind of value is simply the relative notional proximity of that ascription to textual manner as practically encountered in any given activity of valuing. Typically, say, the value of a sense of deep immersion into someone else's consciousness will strike actors as 'closer' to the device of interior monologue than the value of global egalitarian politics, and thus these values may manifest as the former literary one being propped by the latter other-than-literary one. In comparison, the aforementioned value of empathy might manifest as either literary or other-than-literary, depending on what other values are most immediately in play in the activity of valuing.

This shifting status of perceived kind of value based on relative notional proximity to textual manner is in fact just a corollary to the Simmelian general theory of value as differential. Since values emerge only in relation to other values, relative notional proximity to one thing or another, as one vector of difference between values, is both a condition and an effect of the axiological network. The differences that a differential network requires are also the kinds of differences that it produces and around which it is organised, however provisionally and dynamically.[14] In this respect, what I have been terming a network *constellation* I can now more precisely define as a set of mutually mediating value ascriptions that share a salient notional proximity to a particular vector of difference, thereby evoking a sense of other-than value ascriptions in respect to that vector that are increasingly less directly relevant or just wholly unrelated. In a tightly bound situation like that of pizza, the constellation in effect has more distinct borders. Within the pizza constellation, the value of, say, economic justice – in comparison to the apparently more immediately relevant values of hunger satisfaction and gustatory pleasure – will strike many actors as marginally relevant at best, even though in a larger view of the network economic justice still plays a mediating role in relation to those latter values. In contrast, in a loosely bound situation, the constellation's borders are considerably more porous. The immediate values of a brick as, say, sturdy, hard, heavy and inexpensive are more easily linked to the other-than-brickly values of, say, gardening, aquarium embellishment or self-defence.[15]

The various metaphors that I have offered for this porousness underscore different aspects of it. The metaphor of interlinked networks emphasises the salience of differences between constellations. The metaphor of propping emphasises how, in any given ascription of literary value, an ascription of an other-than-literary value may play a role so immediately directive that the two ascriptions may strike us as at once distinguishable and yet inseparable. Propping also suggests what is more plainly emphasised in the metaphors of strengthening and axiological ballast: that linkage to other-than-literary values provides an expanded axiological scope, which is one and the same as a measure of importance, thereby increasing the sense of weight and urgency of the literary value ascription. Finally, the metaphor of tightening emphasises how the weight and urgency accomplished by the expanded axiological scope may make ascriptions of value to manner seem more necessary because of the perceived stakes of what they entail.

Boccaccio's genealogical ontology

A more extended consideration of an instance of literary valuing, in the form of a direct commentary on the nature of literary value, may be helpful at this point, in order further to illustrate some of the ideas rather abstractly presented above and in the preceding chapter. Among the vast number of possibilities, I have chosen for this purpose Boccaccio's *Trattatello in laude di Dante* [*Short Treatise in Praise of Dante*], given my period focus and the literary historical significance suggested by the fact that two of the five entries in *The Norton Anthology of Theory and Criticism* falling between the years 500 and 1500 are by Dante and Boccaccio, respectively.[16] This piece is roughly equivalent in aims and in actual function to a modern introduction to an edition of a canonical author's works, combining as it does information about the author and his social and political contexts with commentary on his works and their value. Yet because Boccaccio himself was a writer of grand ambition, with much of his career still before him (he completed the first recension of the *Trattatello* between 1351 and 1355), the piece also functions as a defence of the literary author's calling, as exemplarily embodied in Dante. In particular, the piece formulates a defence of that calling as a defence of the value of poetry, which it argues to be, on the one the one hand, the antidote to the mercenary values of Florentine commercial society (as Boccaccio frequently characterises them)[17] and, on the other, as equal to – or even essentially the same as – the indisputably supreme spiritual value of theology.

While the antagonism between commerce and poetry is felt throughout the *Trattatello*, Boccaccio considers the relation to theology mostly in a single, substantial digression. At the outset of this section, he describes an instinctive spiritual impulse among 'ancient people', who recognise the existence of a transcendental 'supreme power above all others', and then he locates the origin of poetry in a primordial moment in which language is fashioned into an instrument suitable for worship of this power:

> To avoid worshipping this great power in silence or with almost mute rites, they wanted to pray to it with noble-sounding words so that it would be propitious to their needs. And since they believed that this being exceeded all others in nobility, they were eager to use words removed from all plebeian or common styles of speech, which would be worthy to be uttered in the presence of the deity to which they offered sacred prayers. Furthermore, in order that these words might appear to be more effective, they wanted them to be arranged according to laws of fixed rhythm, so that their sweetness would eliminate harshness and boredom. Certainly all this could not be done in a vulgar or ordinary form of speech, but in a way that was artistic, elaborate, and novel. The Greeks called this form 'poetic', and whatever was composed in it was called 'poetry', and those who created or used this style of speech were called 'poets'.[18]

Here we encounter a veritable inventory of evaluative terms pertaining to textual manner, from 'noble-sounding', to 'arranged according to laws of fixed rhythm', to 'artistic, elaborate, and novel'. Although the terms are vague (a habit of many theorisers of literary value, both before and long after Boccaccio), the sort of propping that I described above is plainly evident. For instance, the value of 'sweetness' pertaining to an arrangement of words is depicted as wholly in service to the other-than-literary spiritual value of the 'great power', as indeed in practice it no doubt actually was, and continues to be, in such ritual situations.

Boccaccio insists, moreover, that this 'great power', at least for some of the best of the ancient poets, was in fact the Christian God, as would only later be fully revealed. It is the ancients' necessarily partial knowledge in this respect that leads him to the literary features of fictionality, allegory and figuration:

> the ancient poets have followed, as far as the human mind can, the trail of the Holy Spirit, which (we see from Divine Scripture) revealed through many mouths its profound mysteries to those who were to come, inspiring them to utter in a veiled way what in due time it

intended to unveil through open deeds ... the poets in their work, which we call poetry – sometimes using various fictional gods, sometimes changing men into different imaginative forms and sometimes convincing us with the persuasive argument of their creations – show us the origins of things, the effects of virtues and of vices, what we should avoid and what we should follow, so that we can come, by acting virtuously, to that goal which they, who had no real knowledge of the true God, regarded as the highest blessedness ... [for example,] poets portray the beauty of the Elysian Fields, which I interpret to be the sweetness of Paradise, and the darkness of Dis, which I take to mean the bitterness of Hell. Our poets did this so that, enticed by the joy of the one and frightened by the anguish of the other, we should follow the virtues that will lead us into Elysium and avoid the vices that might make us be precipitated into Hell.[19]

In comparison with 'noble-sounding words', these literary devices – which Boccaccio claims possess the more specifically literary value of giving 'comfort to the minds of the simple' (that is, pleasure)[20] – are not only suitable for worshipping the divine but further provide a means of human access to knowledge about Christian truths, even before the Christian era. Pulling out his trump card, then, Boccaccio observes that Christian scripture itself uses these same devices for the same purposes. In this way he arrives at the most grandiose claim that in his day could be made for the value of literature: 'I say that theology and poetry can be considered almost identical when their subjects are identical. In fact, I will go even further and decree that theology is nothing less than the poetry of God.'[21] Literary value here is linked with spiritual value so securely as to be virtually indistinguishable from it. And since for Boccaccio God encompasses the entirety of the axiological network in all its countless constellations, at once its centre and its circumference, literary value is elevated to the pinnacle of all earthly values.

And yet, the five-word qualification within Boccaccio's grand claim – 'when their subjects are identical' (six in the original: 'dove uno medesimo sia il suggetto') – holds great import, in effect undoing much of what the rest of the statement asserts. In its immediate context, the qualification refers to the referential gulf between Christian and pagan writing that Boccaccio acknowledges a few paragraphs before, namely, that '[s]acred theology is concerned with divine truth, while ancient poetry deals primarily with pagan gods and heroes ... obviously false, erroneous, and contrary to the Christian religion'.[22] Hence, while the value of the aforementioned aspects of textual manner, even in pre-Christian texts, could be in service to Christian spiritual value, they could just as well be in service to some other 'obviously false, erroneous' spiritual value. This situation highlights how the tightening of literary value ascriptions achieved through appeals to other sorts of value is in fact just that, rather than, say, an infused manifestation of some greater value uniquely available via literary manner, as in some ontological accounts of literary value. The secure link between literary and spiritual value turns out to be a pro forma one, belying an underlying looseness in which 'true' and 'false' versions of the latter value are interchangeable.

But the situation for literary value is in fact even direr than this, as that five-word qualification ultimately reaches back to the comments that bridge Boccaccio's initial claims about poetic language and his later ones about fiction and figuration. There he extends his account of the primordial origin of poetry through the emergence of polytheism and animism up to the initial establishment of polities around deity-kings, who were originally men who 'began to devise clever schemes or other designs that would make themselves masters of the ignorant masses of their regions'. One of these 'clever schemes' was to leverage the spiritual practices presumably already in place: 'they used faith to instill fear into their subjects and to insure by oaths the obedience of those whom they could not subjugate by force'. For this purpose, the poets were instrumental:

> These things could not have been easily done without the collaboration of the poets, who, in order to extend their own fame, as well as to win the favor of the princes, delight their subjects, and persuade everyone to act virtuously (which actually ran contrary to their true intentions), made the people believe what the princes wanted by masterfully contriving various fictions that are wrongly understood by the uneducated today, to say nothing of that earlier time. The poets employed ... exactly the same style that the first people used to praise only the one true God.[23]

Here we see the same aspects of textual manner ('exactly the same style') that had been linked to authentic spiritual value ('the one true God'), linked instead to a collection of rather less lofty values: worldly renown ('their own fame'), political patronage ('the favor of the princes', which presumably entailed economic benefits) and what might be termed, roughly and anachronistically, the propagandistic utility of a sort of false consciousness, the power to make 'the people believe what the princes wanted' with 'fictions' that encourage the people 'to act virtuously' when the real intent of poets is otherwise, presumably that of keeping the people in line. Colloquially, we might say that the poets have sold out: that is, they have redirected literary value (e.g., 'artistic, elaborate, and novel' forms of speech) away from its original, authentic and true spiritual value to a set of worldly, politically dubious and self-serving values. It turns out, therefore, that almost from its very origin, poetry has served something akin to the very mercenary values that so vex Boccaccio's about his contemporary Florence. While he most often depicts the latter values as the antithesis of and indeed outright antagonist to Dante's poetic accomplishments, here his own argument prompts him to acknowledge the continuing possibility of poetic complicity, as the celebration of deity-hero-kings 'still is today ... the duty and function of the poet'.[24]

In less judgemental language, we may say that this passage, in the context of the whole digression on poetry, underscores the capaciousness and flexibility of literary value's characteristic loose binding. Boccaccio's account of the origin and uses of poetry, however fancifully speculative in some respects, is in several others wholly plausible and even in some points historically demonstrable. While I have for the sake of illustration called attention to apparent self-contradictions in this account, Boccaccio presumably would see none, and he would be justified in doing so. Poetry may be close to a verbal sacrament, as in Dante's case, or it may be an instrument of tyranny wielded by artistic mercenaries (a role that, as we know, Boccaccio sometimes felt his friend Petrarch too readily accepted). Ascriptions of value to textual manner do not demand mediation of any specific other kind of value, which is to say that they may plausibly mediate a range of rather different or even antithetical values, without contradiction or incoherence. Moreover, with its non-contradictory antitheses, Boccaccio's digression on poetry also illustrates how genealogical accounts of literary value (here, the story of how it becomes an instrument for instilling false consciousness by pretending to be one value while actually being another) may not only accompany ontological accounts (here, the relation between literary value and Christian truth), but even how the latter accounts prompt the former, and vice-versa. From this perspective we see again how ontological and genealogical accounts, however rhetorically opposed, are in fact complementary. They collectively seek to cover the axiological territory annexed by way of loose binding and are simply exploring different regions of the same domain.

Defamiliarisation revisited

While Boccaccio's meditation upon literary value in the *Trattatello* may illustrate aspects and consequences of loose binding in an especially cogent fashion, it is certainly far from unusual in what it reveals. I will cite just two of many possible other examples. Looking backward several centuries, one might notice that the Old English poem *Widsith* conveys dramatically a similar simultaneity of idealisation and demystification of literary value, likewise ultimately prompted by loose binding. In this poem, a first-person Christian poet/narrator depicts the activities and accomplishments of a pagan counterpart, conveying in poetry to a presumably monastic audience how the titular pagan *scop* creates encomiastic poems for politically powerful patrons in exchange for gifts, sometimes celebrating them simply for that very gift-giving.[25] Looking forward several centuries, one might see in Walter Benjamin's famously ambivalent and ambiguous comments on aura, which are prompted by the differences in manner between art of the past and the technologically reproduced art of his present, a compact formulation of the two sides of the axiological coin. Reproducing in a single idea the formulations that *Widsith* and Boccaccio divide between Christian and pagan, aura encompasses the values of uniqueness, authenticity and artistic tradition, and simultaneously serves as a cultic instrument of mystification that, as Benjamin's editors put it, helps to 'reinforce the larger claims to political power of the ... ruling class'.[26]

Revealingly, what all these instances of meta-axiological accounts of literary value share is a tendency to follow mediations of literary value ascriptions through the axiological network to notionally totalising kinds of value – ones that seem to comprehend all others and serve as the ultimate motivation and measure of human action. Each of these kinds of value, however different or even antithetical they may seem in respect to one another, appears at once all-pervasive in human experience and yet also intangible – a presence that is also, at a more basic level, an absence. For Boccaccio, as we have seen, these totalising kinds of value are spiritual and political, as manifested in the Christian God and in the power of rulers. Both of these were obviously everywhere present in some fashion in the actions, institutions and human self-knowledge of Boccaccio's lived experience, but they were also, as attested by voluminous medieval writings on the topics, fundamental aspects of reality that remained in some essential way immaterial (and were thus not surprisingly frequently linked to one another).[27] Although my sample size of meta-axiological accounts is of course exceedingly minimal, from those cited elsewhere in this book, or just from a passing familiarity with the genre, it seems fair to conclude that literary value's characteristic loose binding lends itself to extension not just to other-than-literary kinds of value but especially to these totalising, intangible kinds of value. And inasmuch as what Boccaccio, *Widsith* and Benjamin describe corresponds in some fashion to actual practices of literary production and consumption, we may further conclude that this sort of extension may (at times) characterise the ascriptions of literary value that occur within those practices themselves. This is all just to say – in a vaguer though much simpler, more typical way – that literature often claims to disclose the truth, whatever that may be, and that no small number of literary theorists have sought to elucidate how it in fact does so.

In ontological accounts of literary value, this sort of extension to totalising values is usually understood as categorically defining, with literary practices that do not exhibit such extension taken to be inferior examples of the literary or just not truly literary at all. In contrast, from the axiological perspective that I have sought to develop, this sort of extension is one of the affordances of loose binding, which is itself not a categorical feature but rather, as I have said, widely but not universally characteristic of literary valuing. In the history of literary theory, and especially the stage of that history inaugurated by twentieth-century formalism, this affordance has often proven pivotal, connecting, as it seems to do, discrete aspects of textual manner with a range of possible totalising kinds of value. Since formalism has been one of my regular interlocutors in this book, a brief consideration of my preliminary theory of literary valuing in respect to formalism's use of this affordance will help further to elucidate that theory and its differences from formalism, old and new. More importantly, it will lead to a specification of one of ways that my approach to the problem of literary value might help to navigate that problem.

From the perspective of my preliminary theory, what is crucial to notice in the example of Boccaccio's digression is not just the extension of literary values to totalising values but also the extension to different kinds of totalising values that are mutually defining through their antagonism. This observation returns us to the Simmelian differential nature of value, in which one kind of value emerges only in relation to others. The axiological ballast obtained through the weighting of literary value ascriptions with other-than-literary value comes at the 'cost' of alternative other-than-literary values that in fact make that weighting possible through their difference from the weighting value, that is, through their status as, in a sense, rejected options. By that same token, moreover, the very requirement that some options must be rejected for the choice to occur affords the possibility that the choice will bring into view the rejected alternatives, making unusually salient what is always actually the case: that our axiological paths are defined by those not taken. To put this point simply, for Boccaccio, Dante was a great theological poet precisely because he was not a mercenary one, and this difference brings into sharp relief, as we saw in the digression, the relation between spiritual value on the one hand and economic and political values on the other, a relation (among others) that differentially determines each kind of value.

In some contexts, therefore, loose binding in literary value ascriptions may afford not only an extension to totalising values but also a kind of bird's-eye perspective on a portion of one's axiological environment. The activity of literary valuing may disclose perspectives on some of the myriad interconnected networks of value that are always operative in our day-to-day experience. And this particular affordance, in turn, may easily be understood as itself the most defining value of literature. That is, it may be identified not merely, as I understand it, as a historically available possibility for any situation of loose binding – which is itself a historically available possibility for any activity of valuing – but rather as the essence of the literary. It is precisely in relation to these points that my approach to literary valuing converges with and diverges from formalism.

As I argued in the previous chapter, the ascription of value to textual manner necessarily effects some degree of notional decoupling of manner from matter, as that ascription requires (and so produces) some degree of a recognition of manner as such. This decoupling may in turn be understood as itself a feature of textual manner. For formalism, because the decoupling puts referentiality into a kind of frame, it constitutes the quintessential formal effect of self-referential staging, of an act of communication that calls attention to its own features. And because this effect is understood as a feature of manner, ascriptions of value to it, like all loosely bound ascriptions, may produce the secondary effect of the axiological bird's-eye view. This disclosure of one's enmeshment within axiological networks, ultimately deriving from loosely bound ascriptions of value to the textual feature of literary staging, is what formalists have long recognised as defamiliarisation. I wholeheartedly affirm defamiliarisation, therefore, as something that engagement with literature may accomplish. In my approach, though, it is just that: simply a possibility and neither necessary, nor categorical, nor normative.[28] To construe it as any of the latter would be to step into one of the pitfalls of ontological approaches that I summarised in the previous chapter. Nevertheless, defamiliarisation does constitute a distinctive effect, one that may be of help in our inevitable negotiations with the problem of literary value.

Particularly resonant with my approach is the account of defamiliarisation by Prague School formalist Jan Mukařovský. Writing about the absorption of the reader by a novel such as *Crime and Punishment*, Mukařovský argues,

> The change which the material relationship of the work – the sign – has undergone is thus simultaneously its weakening and strengthening. It is weakened in the sense that the work does not refer to the reality which it directly depicts, and strengthened in that the work of art as a sign acquires an indirect (figurative) tie with realities which are vitally important to the perceiver, and through them to the entire universe of the perceiver as a collection of values. Thus the work of art

acquires the ability to refer to a reality which is totally different from the one which it depicts, and to systems of values other than the one from which it arose and on which it is founded.[29]

In my terms, the 'weakening' of the sign occurs when the decoupling of manner from matter, necessary for value ascription, is itself perceived as a feature of textual manner, underscoring a self-referential staging that entails 'that the work does not refer to the reality which it directly depicts'. The 'strengthening' of the sign occurs when this feature is valued as such (and, as Mukařovský states, the weakening and strengthening are simultaneous, since to perceive the feature is to value it), with the accompanying loosely bound ascriptions of value prompting a salient movement outward through interlinked networks, tying the value of the feature to 'realities which are vitally important to the perceiver, and through them to the entire universe of the perceiver as a collection of values' – what I have called a bird's-eye view of an actor's axiological environment.

For Mukařovský the value of the literary (or, more generally, of the 'aesthetic function') resides in this ability to disclose the 'systems of values' underlying the reader's concrete social existence, systems that may thereby 'experimentally crystallise into a new configuration and dissolve an old one, [and may] adapt to the development of the social situation and to new creative facts of reality, or at least seek the possibility of such adaptation'.[30] These systems of values are – as they were in Boccaccio – totalising ones, and they are unrelated to literary value except inasmuch as the latter is their point of access:

> The material components of the artistic artifact [i.e., features of textual manner], and the manner in which they are used as artistic means [i.e., the values ascribed to those features], assume the role of mere conductors of energies introduced by extra-aesthetic values. If we ask ourselves at this point what has happened to aesthetic value, it appears that it has dissolved into individual extra-aesthetic values, and is really nothing but a general term for the dynamic totality of their mutual interrelationships.[31]

In the terms of this account, Boccaccio's 'noble-sounding words' are 'mere conductors of energies introduced by' the ultimate 'extra-aesthetic' value of an omnipotent spiritual power, and so the 'aesthetic value' of those words becomes an index of the Christian understanding of God as encompassing 'the dynamic totality of [the whole set of extra-aesthetic values'] mutual interrelationships'. Mukařovský has in effect formulated a precise, technically elaborated, secular, Marxist version of Boccaccio's digression – one that, in its wider applicability, supplies a satisfyingly detailed account of how the activity of literary valuing may lead to disclosure of a some crucial portion of an actor's axiological environment.

For Mukařovský, the availability of this disclosure is categorical and normative: it describes the ultimate, defining value of the most truly literary of literary texts when readers value them for the right reasons and not, for example, 'only insofar as [a text] is educational or arouses the emotions'.[32] Yet to dismiss those latter sorts of ascriptions of value in favour of the single one that Mukařovský has identified is – as discussed in the preceding chapter in relation to Rita Felski's work – to present an impoverished, elitist, historically blinkered and dubiously ontological theory of literary value. Instead, we may pause here with my preliminary theory of literary value and place a more contingent, pragmatic concept of defamiliarisation in our pocket, so to speak, as one possible means for literary scholars and teachers to navigate the problem of literary value.

A big tent

The next two chapters take up the problem of literary value in relation to canonicity and interpretation, thinking through in light my preliminary theory of literary valuing the practical challenges of that problem as they manifest in those regards. But with my theory (such as it is) now in place, before turning to those particular arenas of literary scholarship and teaching it will be helpful to consider what the theory may have to offer more generally to the field of literary studies beyond a rather diminished version of defamiliarisation.

As I noted in this book's introduction, over the past several decades the question of what actually makes the field of literary studies a distinctive academic discipline has garnered no small amount of debate, polemic and professional angst, and at least according to some commentators the resulting disarray has damaged the field's public's perception. To recall Carlos J. Alonso's observation from 2002, '[T]here is no longer a consensus on the object of literary studies or on the justifications for pursuing this field as an intellectual project ... we are confronted with the weakness that arises from our dismantling of our own house.'[33] As James F. English summarised this view in 2012, the field, having lost its claim on a 'central and anchoring position among the disciplines',

> adopted a strategy of multiple positions, fostering a proliferation of new methods, materials, and constituencies, but, in the eyes of some, splintering itself across too broad an array of incompatible subfields, from book history to television studies, subcultural ethnography, and the poetics of race – squandering its disciplinary coherence and thereby further undermining its academic legitimacy.[34]

In light of this conundrum, one contribution my preliminary theory might make is to provide for the field – *in situ*, without any necessary other alterations – a unifying framework, one that reveals 'an array of incompatible subfields' to be instead an exhilaratingly rich and diverse area of study that is nonetheless held together by a definite centre of gravity. For if, as I have said, *literary value* is a redundant phrase because *literary* is necessarily already a value-laden adjective, then we can readily understand the label *literary study* as the exploration of that value-laden condition. More precisely, it is an exploration of actors' mediations of other actors' ascriptions of value to textual manner, and of their mediations of ascriptions of other kinds of value that are interlinked with (or serve as props for) the former ascriptions. In these terms, any particular literary research project may be understood as exploring one portion of the axiological network by tracing the mediations of one such set of actors. What then distinguishes one project from another are its starting set of actors, the relative capaciousness and granularity of the examination of mediations, and the scholar's self-positioning (whether implicit or explicit) in relation to the delineated portion of the network.

Although this language may seem quite alien to how literary scholarship of whatever stripe understands itself, it actually quite straightforwardly encompasses the whole breadth of that scholarship, at least as far as I am familiar with it. It encompasses, say, both a twenty-first-century scholar's ideological critique of the relation between the text of advertisements and the qualities of superheroes in 1950s Marvel comics, and a 1950s scholar's appreciation of the timeless virtue of nobility in Othello's final speech. In the first instance, the scholar positions herself as critically examining a network of other actors' value ascriptions (those of the readers and producers of the comics, as well as those of the advertisers, among others); that is, she positions their ascriptions at some implied distance from her own. Her project may involve a large archive of comic books, which she analyses according to some taxonomy of manner (say, the topoi of superhuman attributes), being less interested in any particular comic and more in the axiological links between mid-century US capitalism and this form of popular culture. In the second instance, the scholar positions himself directly alongside of Shakespeare's ascriptions of value, implicitly proposing that his ascriptions overlap with Shakespeare's in more and less significant ways. This enables him to understand the text as an intricate record of directly intuitable authorial value ascriptions, leading him to minute explorations of the linkages between specific features of manner and the totalising values that he understands as ones organising both his and Shakespeare's cultures. The differences between these approaches obviously afford different kinds of tracings of the axiological network, with different kinds of results. But both are no more and no less than such tracings, and together they provide a fuller account of the axiological network than either approach would separately.

To consider an actual example, we may return to the work of Tim William Machan that constituted an important interlocutor in Chapter 1. Taking a manuscript studies approach to Chaucer, Machan fashions a critique of modern Chaucer editions on the basis of their imposition of anachronistic aesthetic categories on Middle English poetry. In the language of my axiological framework, Machan's project takes one or more of those modern editions as an entry point into the axiological network and follows traces of mediations to proximate actors such as precedent editions and editorial traditions, and established models of literary and epochal history; and to proximate other kinds of value, such as ideological, cultural and social. Machan scrutinises aspects of manner of those modern editions but positions himself at a critical distance from their ascriptions of value. In contrast, my own rather different sort of historicist project, *Poets and Power from Chaucer to Wyatt* (to return to an example broached in Chapter 2), begins with the much more traditional network entry point of authors' ascriptions of value, in this case, those of the so-called fifteenth-century Chaucerians. Retrospectively, I may now characterise that project as tracing the mediations of value ascriptions among authors, literary predecessors, political and religious patrons, and so on, and assessing the nature and historical significance of the reciprocal relays among the different kinds of values involved. At those times when the study leans toward a reclamation effort for this period's oft-denigrated poetry, my axiological distance shrinks, with my own ascriptions of value overlapping in some ways with those of some of the actors I describe.

Thus, the typical literary research triumvirate of author, text and reader, and the sometimes radically different kinds of studies that a focus on one or the other engenders, are subsumable into my framework as different entry points into the axiological network. Moreover, any of the current kinds of literary study, even when they move beyond this triumvirate, may just as easily be rearticulated in the terms of this framework. So, to list just some of these kinds (most of which are of course nonexclusive of others), distant reading, descriptive reading, ethical approaches, critical race theory approaches, ecofeminist approaches, object-oriented approaches, animal studies approaches, some versions of cultural studies and media studies approaches, cognitive poetics, LGBTQ+ approaches, affect theory approaches and New Formalism may all be rearticulated as some form of exploration of the axiological network, since they all manifestly consider ascriptions of value, whatever their own positioning in respect to those ascriptions. (In the following chapters, the several examples of literary study that I consider in the terminology of my theory provide further illustrations of this rearticulation.) Even research that scarcely considers literary texts, as strictly defined, constitutes an inquiry into some portion of the network of literary valuing if the adjective *literary* is in any way operative.

Such a rearticulation of the array of approaches to literary scholarship, however schematically and informally performed, would constitute more than just superficial substitutions of one set of terms for another. It would have the potential to serve as a big tent for the field of literary studies that all of us within the field might recognise as such. An explicitly articulated axiological framework may make visible the coherence that the field actually already possesses, emphasising the remarkable breadth and depth of the complementary ways that myriad subfields and approaches account for literary valuing. David J. Alworth, in a review of how ANT has been and might further be adapted to literary studies, advocates for a criticism that 'heeds Latour's call to "follow the actors", whoever or whatever they are and wherever they lead'; what I am claiming is that in the diversity of our existing approaches, we are already doing this rather capaciously.[35] Moreover, I believe that the axiological framework, if shorn of its specialist language, has the potential effectively to communicate that coherence to crucial external audiences, in the form of, say, department mission statements that characterise what we do as explorations of the way that the world, in all its dimensions, becomes value-laden.

I will leave these activities of translation for internal and external audiences to another day and, I can only hope, to some of those who have found any of these ideas persuasive. More humbly, let me instead acknowledge that I have no expectation that literature departments will someday rename themselves, say, departments of literary axiology, or that literary researchers of any significant number will begin explicitly incorporating an axiological framework into their projects. If, as I have imagined above, literary scholars and teachers were simply to recognise in some way the relevance of this framework to what they do – which, I admit, is already an extravagantly ambitious surmise – that recognition by itself could have powerful effects and would not require those scholars and teachers to alter what they do on a day-to-day basis. I am not therefore calling for a dramatic rethinking of the field of literary studies, as does, say, Felski in *The Limits of Critique*, as sympathetic as I am to that study and the way that it draws on Latour to propose an alternative mode of literary inquiry.[36] Nonetheless, I do believe that the axiological framework, if it were to be explicitly drawn upon in particular scholarly projects, could have some potential benefits. I will mention just three.

First, the framework helps to draw our attention to our own positionality within the network whose mediations we are tracing and so encourages us to include in that tracing the mediations of value that lead from the initial set of actors to ourselves. In the light of these latter mediations, otherwise obscure aspects of our own axiological environments may emerge, and hence our accounts of other actors' value ascriptions may be enriched, or some of our own blind spots uncovered, by way of this dimension of critical reflexivity. An explicit axiological framework would help us neither to privilege, obscure, nor deny any particular ascription of value, including our own. So, for example, for my *Poets and Power*, the framework would have encouraged me to provide a more explicit argument for the literary value that I implicitly ascribe to the fifteenth-century Chaucerians. Rather than just locating the latter's value ascriptions firmly in the past, I might have also identified the continuities and contrasts between those ascriptions and the ones that the study itself necessarily makes across the transhistorical axiological network, thereby addressing one of the logical gaps in the book's argument.

Second, as suggested in the preceding chapter, the framework may provide another way to think through the thorny question of the relations of text to intertexts and other kinds of so-called contexts. These relations may all be understood as an actor's necessary mediations of the value ascriptions of other actors within the portion of the network being traced. For the typical instance of author as actor, for example, proximate other actors would include the usual array of precedent literary and non-literary texts, formal and topical conventions, actual and implied audiences, desired or real patrons, targeted or contracted publishers, and so on. What the framework would provide is an emphasis on the reciprocity of the relations among all these actors, directly or indirectly, seeing their ascriptions of value as necessarily immanent in each other and hence in the literary work.[37]

Third, keeping to the example of author as actor, the framework may help to elucidate the operative dynamics of the old chestnut that sophisticated literary works self-reflexively stage an inquiry into their own value. The framework underscores how for some authors the loose binding between textual manner and value is an especially pressing concern, since for them the stakes of whether or not their writing is 'good' may be quite high, and hence the appeal to other kinds of value may become especially salient, requiring explicit consideration in some fashion. The characteristic flexibility and mutability of connections to interlinked networks, accordingly, may be as much a threat as an asset. While interlinkages associate an author's writing with many other kinds of apparently more weighty value, they may in their very lack of firm stability also hint that those associations may not hold; so what seems worth writing one day may seem pointless the next. The props and costs of other kinds of value – whether and how much the props actually function in that way, and what sorts of costs and how much of them are expended – may consequently become urgent concerns and hence themselves key topics of the writing. As a result, the writing incorporates, in some sort of directly thematised fashion, a wide swath of its own axiological network. One subsequent critical project would then be to limn the broad and sometimes fraught axiological dynamics of the work's inquiry into own reason for existence.

To be sure, none of these three benefits would be at all new to the field. Each already characterises many projects in one fashion or another. Moreover, there are numerous projects that strike me as already exemplifying – in their own terms, of course – what a more comprehensive adaptation of an explicit axiological framework would entail. For example, outside of my research area, two of those that I have recently come across are Deidre Shauna Lynch's *Loving Literature: A Cultural History* and, in a more metacritical vein, Shai M. Dromi and Eva Illouz's 'Recovering Morality: Pragmatic Sociology and Literary Studies'.[38] My preliminary theory of literary valuing does not have the ambition to remake the field of literary studies but rather to give it some additional confidence, help it through some of its internal and external conundrums, and encourage some of the trends that it already possesses. The framework serves to underscore the nature of our accomplishments as literary researchers, clarify the relations among our various projects and highlight how, collectively, literary studies reaches ever more broadly and deeply toward values that are always in motion. If it would help to give this theory/framework/schema a name, *axiological compositionism* (to borrow a term from Latour) would be an apt one.[39] But I suspect that unhappy phrase would hamper the aforementioned aims more than further them, and thus I offer it here, at the end of my theorising, and put it aside.

Notes

1 Georg Simmel, *The Philosophy of Money*, trans. Tom Bottomore and David Frisby (London: Routledge & Kegan Paul, 1978); Barbara Herrnstein Smith, *Contingencies of Value: Alternative Perspectives for Critical Theory* (Cambridge, MA: Harvard University Press, 1988). *Philosophie des Geldes* was first published in Berlin in 1900; an enlarged edition appeared in 1907. For Simmel's account of value, see esp. pp. 59–119.
2 Elizabeth S. Goodstein, *Georg Simmel and the Disciplinary Imaginary* (Stanford: Stanford University Press, 2017), pp. 170, 155. In addition to this study, for Simmel's understanding of value I have particularly benefited from Natàlia Cantó Milà, *A Sociological Theory of Value: Georg Simmel's Sociological Relationism* (Bielefeld: Transcript Publishing, 2005); and, for or Simmel's anticipation of some elements of poststructuralism, from Deena Weinstein and Michael A. Weinstein, *Postmodern(ized) Simmel* (London: Routledge, 1993); and Bryan S. Green, *Literary Methods and Sociological Theory: Case Studies of Simmel and Weber* (Chicago: University of Chicago Press, 1988). Arjun Appadurai, 'Introduction: Commodities and the Politics of Value', in Arjun Appardurai (ed.), *The Social Life of Things: Commodities in Cultural Perspective* (Cambridge: Cambridge University Press, 1986), pp. 3–63, offers an illuminating and influential adaptation of Simmel's theory of value, one which, for example, John Frow draws upon in developing his construct of 'regimes of reading'; see Frow, *The Practice of Value: Essays on Literature in Cultural Studies* (Crawley: University of Western Australia, 2013). Ralph M. Leck, *Georg Simmel and Avant-Garde Sociology* (Amherst, NY: Humanity Books, 2000), provides a lucid account of Simmel's career and its afterlives, explaining, among other things, how Simmel's reputation in his own day as a leader among Berlin's politically and socially progressive artists and intellectuals suffered a reversal when he came out in support of the Great War. For a trenchant, Marxist-based critique of Simmel's theory of value, see Paul Kamolnick, 'Simmel's Legacy for Contemporary Value Theory: A Critical Assessment', *Sociological Theory*, 19:1 (2001), 65–85, a reference that Gabriel Meyer-Lee sent me as part of our ongoing debate about value.
3 More accurately, this is how Simmel frequently describes value. As Green points out, Simmel in fact alternates between this 'semiotic' account and one that seems more 'realist', a tendency that Green takes as evidence of Simmel's dialectical style. For my purposes, it suffices to centre Simmel's more Smith-like moments.

4 Simmel, *Philosophy of Money*, p. 86.
5 For the overlap with Saussure's ideas, see Green, *Literary Methods*, pp. 136–76. Admittedly, Simmel sometimes seems to reduce all value comparison to just one of its many modes – sacrifice – which squares neither with Saussurean semiotics nor with his own geometrical analogy. For helpful comments on the matter, see Cantó Milà, *A Sociological Theory*, pp. 158–67. Again, for my purposes I am centring Simmel's more Smith-like formulations.
6 This reformulation aligns with how Latour has described the descriptive target of ANT as 'matters of concern' in contrast with 'matters of fact'; see Bruno Latour, 'Why Has Critique Run out of Steam? From Matters of Fact to Matters of Concern', *Critical Inquiry*, 30:2 (2004), 225–48.
7 I expect readers will readily recall actual examples of such value shifts, e.g., those large-handled combs that teenagers purchased *en masse* in the 1970s, not to use as combs (at least not for many of us), but simply to display in our back pockets.
8 I adapt the metaphor of careers from Appardurai.
9 Smith, *Contingencies of Value*, p. 43.
10 From the point of view of a theory of literary value with a starting point other than Simmel, however, this statement, while uncontroversial, may simply describe a history of bad reading. See, e.g., Terry Eagleton, 'Bodies, Artworks, and Use Values', *NLH*, 44:4 (2013), 561–73, whose starting point is Marx. Although here and throughout I do not extend my claims beyond literary value, the applicability of loose binding to aesthetic value generally is obvious. Indeed, it seems applicable to what Lucien Karpik has defined more generally as the *singularity*, of which aesthetic objects are a subclass. See Karpik, *Valuing the Unique*, trans. Nora Scott (Princeton: Princeton University Press, 2010), esp. the section 'What Are Singularities' (pp. 10–13), in which the characteristics of 'multidimensional', 'structured', 'uncertain' and 'incommensurable' that Karpik describes for singularities bear relation to the concept of loose binding. That my example of bricks also illustrates loose binding, however, plainly indicates that loose binding is not restricted to singularities. Simmel provides a curious account of the origin of aesthetic value as a kind of *un*binding that occurs over time through a collective forgetting of an originally more tightly bound value, so that what we take to be, say, the aesthetic value of the beauty of cherry blossoms (or, presumably, a painting thereof) is in fact a kind of 'echo' of the originally more tightly bound value of the sustenance provided by ripe cherries. See *Philosophy of Money*, pp. 73–5. This strikes me as one of those moments of creeping realism

that, as I have mentioned, Green notices in *Philosophy of Money*, and also, perhaps, Simmel's attempt to play Marx off of Kant, or vice-versa.

11 Laura Ashe, 'How to Read Both: The Logic of True Contradictions in Chaucer's World', *SAC*, 42 (2020), 111–46 (146).

12 Azade Seyhan, 'Why Major in Literature – –What Do We Tell Our Students?', *PMLA*, 117:3 (2002): 510–12 (511–12).

13 Ashe, 'True Contradictions', 145–6.

14 This obviously means as well that differences in kinds of value, and in the relations among kinds, are not constant over time and space, as many scholars have explored from a variety of disciplinary perspectives. Diane Cady, *The Gender of Money in Middle English Literature: Value and Economy in Late Medieval England* (Cham: Palgrave Macmillan, 2019), for example, examines how the historical differentiation of economic value from such values as 'friendship, love, and poetics' has obscured the relation of the former – and, crucially, its entanglement with 'gender ideology' – to the latter (p. 51).

15 I realise that this conceptualisation of axiological constellations as at once both separate and linked, with ascriptions both 'inside' a constellation but also necessarily defined by those 'outside', broaches the sort of irresolvable false binaries that poststructuralism has famously identified. In this respect, I have found helpful Brian Massumi's discussion of the idea of 'immanent outside' and his related distinction between system and process, with the former roughly corresponding to my notion of constellation and the latter to interlinked networks. See Massumi, *99 Theses on the Revaluation of Value* (Minneapolis: University of Minnesota Press, 2018), esp. pp. 8–11.

16 Vincent B. Leitch *et al.* (eds), *The Norton Anthology of Theory and Criticism*, 3rd edn (New York: W. W. Norton, 2018). The other representatives of the Middle Ages are Moses Maimonides, Thomas Aquinas and Christine de Pizan. The *Norton* prints selections from Boccaccio's reflections on the nature and origin of poetry in his later *Genealogia deorum gentilium* ('The Genealogy of the Gentile Gods'), many of which repeat and develop ideas from the *Trattatello*. I quote the English translation of the latter from *The Life of Dante (Trattatello in Laude Di Dante)*, trans. Vincenzo Zin Bollettino (New York: Garland, 1990), and have benefited from Bollettino's introduction, as well as from David Wallace's text of and notes to an excerpt of the work in A. J. Minnis and A. B. Scott, with David Wallace (eds), *Medieval Literary Theory and Criticism c. 1100–c. 1375: The Commentary*

Tradition (Oxford: Clarendon Press, 1988), pp. 492–503. For the Italian, see Boccaccio, *Opere in Versi, Corbaccio, Trattatello in Laude Di Dante, Prose Latine, Epistole*, ed. Pier Giorgio Ricci (Milano: R. Ricciardi, 1965), pp. 565–650. My discussion here develops ideas about the *Trattatello* that I aired in *Poets and Power from Chaucer to Wyatt* (Cambridge: Cambridge University Press, 2007), which in turn were inspired by David Wallace, *Chaucerian Polity: Absolutist Lineages and Associational Forms in England and Italy* (Stanford: Stanford University Press, 1997).

17 To quote just one of many instances of the *Trattatello*'s rhetorically elaborate diatribes against commercial values, 'Your [Florence's] wealth is a transitory and unsure thing … Alas! Will you glory in your merchants and craftsmen, of whom you have plenty? You will do so foolishly. Commerce, continually goading one with avarice, is a menial trade; craftsmanship was at one time engaged in nobly by men of genius until a second mercenary nature made it corrupt and worthless' (Boccaccio, *Life of Dante*, p. 26).

18 *Ibid.*, pp. 35–6. As Wallace notes, in this passage, as well as in several others in the digression, Boccaccio closely adapts material from Petrarch's letter to his brother Gherardo in which Petrarch defends his poetic calling against his brother's religious objections. The irony that this engenders, given what we will shortly see to be some of the implications of other passages in the digression, was surely not lost on Boccaccio. For the extracts from the relevant letter (*Epistolae familiares*, x:4), see Minnis, Scott and Wallace (eds), *Medieval Literary Theory*, pp. 413–15.

19 Boccaccio, *Life of Dante*, pp. 37–9.

20 *Ibid.*, p. 38. Here, as well as at other moments, Boccaccio gestures to the Horatian linkage of the literary value of pleasure to the other-than-literary value of wisdom.

21 *Ibid.*, p. 41.

22 *Ibid.*, p. 40.

23 *Ibid.*, pp. 36, 37.

24 *Ibid.*, p. 37.

25 See, for example, the *scop*'s first-person account of Queen Ealhild in lines 99–102 of the text in *Old English Shorter Poems: Wisdom and Lyric*, ed. Robert E. Bjork (Cambridge, MA: Harvard University Press, 2014).

26 Quotation from the introduction to Walter Benjamin, *The Work of Art in the Age of Its Technological Reproducibility, and Other Writings on Media*, ed. Michael W. Jennings, Brigid Doherty and Thomas Y. Levin, trans. Edmund Jephcott, Rodney Livingstone, Howard Eiland,

and others (Cambridge, MA: Belknap Press of Harvard University Press, 2008), p. 15, and see pp. 23–4 for Benjamin's comments on aura most pertinent here. The notion has of course elicited vast commentary; a helpful entry point is C. Stephen Jaeger, 'Aura and Charisma: Two Useful Concepts in Critical Theory', *New German Critique*, 38:3 (2011), pp. 17–34.

27 With this notion of totalising present absences, readers will recognise the precedent of a number of familiar and famously knotty theoretical formulations – Althusser's of ideology, Derrida's of the transcendental signified and Lacan's of the Law, to name just three. But I believe that my point here is straightforward and limited enough not to require any lingering in these waters.

28 Michael Bérubé, *Rhetorical Occasions* (Chapel Hill: University of North Carolina Press, 2006), pp. 315–16, observes that the idea, as Shklovsky developed it, was contingent upon literary modernism.

29 Jan Mukařovský, *Aesethetic Function, Norm and Value as Social Facts*, trans. Mark E. Suino (Ann Arbor: University of Michigan, 1970), p. 75.

30 Ibid., p. 90. Cf. Derek Attridge's account of literary value quoted in the preceding chapter.

31 Mukařovský, *Aesthetic Function*, p. 88.

32 Ibid., p. 8 n. 5.

33 Carlos J. Alonso, 'Editor's Column: My Professional Advice (to Graduate Students)', *PMLA*, 117:3 (2002), 401–6 (401).

34 James F. English, *The Global Future of English Studies* (New York: John Wiley, 2012), p. 7.

35 David J. Alworth, 'Critique, Modernity, Society, Agency: Matters of Concern in Literary Studies', in Rita Felski and Stephen Muecke (eds), *Latour and the Humanities* (Baltimore: Johns Hopkins University Press, 2020), pp. 275–99 (291).

36 Rita Felski, *The Limits of Critique* (Chicago: University of Chicago Press, 2015). Although Felski does argue with forceful urgency against the mode of inquiry that she defines as critique, she nevertheless leaves room for it in the field, along with other modes. More strident calls for rethinking the field in Latour's terms include some of the contributions to Felski and Muecke (eds), *Latour and the Humanities*, e.g., Muecke, 'An Ecology of Institutions: Recomposing the Humanities', pp. 31–51; and Yves Citton, 'Fictional Attachments and Literary Weavings in the Anthropocene', pp. 200–24.

37 Cf. Smith's point that 'Every literary work ... is thus the product of a complex evaluative feedback loop that embraces not only the ever-shifting economy of the artist's own interests and resources as they

evolve during and in reaction to the process of composition, but also all the shifting economies of her assumed and imagined audiences' (*Contingencies of Value*, p. 45).

38 Deidre Shauna Lynch, *Loving Literature: A Cultural History* (University of Chicago Press, 2015); Shai M. Dromi and Eva Illouz, 'Recovering Morality: Pragmatic Sociology and Literary Studies', *NLH*, 41:2 (2010), 351–69. In my *Literary Value and Social Identity in the* Canterbury Tales (Cambridge: Cambridge University Press, 2019), I attempt an explicit application of the framework to traditional author-centred criticism, at least as far as I had developed the framework to that point. See also, among several other recent medieval literary studies, Nicholas Perkins, *The Gift of Narrative in Medieval England* (Manchester: Manchester University Press, 2021), which 'follows the actors', so to speak, by way of gift theory.

39 Bruno Latour, 'An Attempt at a Compositionist Manifesto', *NLH*, 41:3 (2010), 471–90.

4

Canonicity

> The return of 'the' canon, the high canon of Western masterpieces, represents the return of an order in which my people were subjugated, the voiceless, the invisible, the unrepresented, and the unrepresentable. Who would return us to that medieval never-never land?
>
> – Henry Louis Gates, Jr

> Indeed, the minute the word 'judgmental' became pejorative, we should have known we made a misstep. Which isn't for a moment to concede that anybody actually stopped judging. Literary evaluation merely ceased to be a professionally accredited act.
>
> – Henry Louis Gates, Jr, later in the same volume[1]

Among the several dead horses on display in this book, the canon has perhaps been beaten up the most. As it was the centrepiece of multiculturalism's critique of the traditional structure and emphases of the field of literary studies, the controversies over its status over the last half century or so have provoked an unmatched volume of scholarly angst and ire, and very few of the field's topics have elicited concern of similar scale outside the academy. Perhaps its most provoking problem over these years has been the one that Henry Louis Gates voices in the first epigraph above (putting aside, for the moment, the implications of his phrase 'medieval never-never land'). Gates uttered this *cri de coeur* over three decades ago, yet even then it was already something of a retrospective lament, as the institutional and attitudinal changes were well afoot that have at this point loosened – and in some instances broken altogether – the curricular grip, in university English departments at least, of 'the high canon of Western masterpieces'. Nonetheless, the problem that Gates's remark identifies continues to be a provoking one, suggesting some unfinished business. For example, a more generally formulated version of it serves as a point of departure for Ankhi Mukherjee's recent *What Is a Classic?: Postcolonial Rewriting and Invention of the Canon*. As Mukherjee observes near the outset of this book, 'The canon has historically been a nexus of power and knowledge that reinforces hierarchies and the vested interests of select institutions, excluding the interests and accomplishments of minorities, popular and demotic culture, or non-European civilisations.'[2] To recycle my metaphor from Chapter 1, the canon has functioned as an aesthetic Trojan Horse of ideology and domination, one that has helped to perpetuate the naturalisation of specific norms and to enforce principles of social and political exclusion. Yet recognition of this fact is, for Mukherjee and Gates, not itself a solution but a starting point, one that leads them to the more difficult question of what sort of response is called for.

With Gates, Mukherjee and many others, most of us without hesitation will lament the damage the canon has caused and condemn any continued operation in this regard. Yet, also with Gates and Mukherjee, we will discover that we have not thereby solved the problem. This problem, this chapter argues, resides in the fraught relation between the readiness with which we may affirm the sentiment of the chapter's first epigraph and the recognition, expressed in the second, that despite 'judgment' falling out of use as a description of the literary critical enterprise, we have never 'actually stopped judging'. The continued haunting of the ghost of judgement, as I called it in Chapter 1, bespeaks the persistence of the category of literary value in the enterprises of literary criticism and teaching, however much it may be acknowledged or suppressed. Indeed, with this latter remark, Gates aligns himself with those critics who, as I mentioned in this book's introduction, began in that period to voice concern about the neglect of literary value or literary distinctiveness in the scholarship being pursued under the banners of historicism and cultural studies. Mukherjee, a quarter of a century later, voices similar sentiments.[3] In my terms, both critics at some level recognise that inasmuch as the adjective *literary* remains a meaningful qualifier to the projects that they pursue, the category of value is part of those projects' most basic apprehension of the object of study. Hence, not surprisingly, while both Gates and

Mukherjee move quickly from a singular canon to plural canons (plural in both synchronic and diachronic dimensions), neither then seeks to do away with the latter. Instead (to oversimplify, massively, their complex and quite differently focused arguments) they attempt to understand the role canons may have in a more just society.[4]

How successful they are in this effort I will leave their readers to assess. Certainly, extending from before Gates through Mukherjee and beyond, there have been many literary theoretical calories burned in the effort to defend, or at least to analyse, the endurance of canons.[5] Yet the very fact that this work continues to be pursued suggests that a palpable if sometimes rather vague discomfort with the idea of canons persists within the field of literary studies. To be sure, the practicalities of syllabi, anthologies, graduate reading lists, and so on ensure that something akin to canons in effect still shape teaching and scholarship in English departments generally. But my sense is that they do so typically at a sort of arm's reach – as, say, porously delimited sets of provisionally selected texts, sets that may have a particular focus and do not present themselves as necessarily excluding the claims of others.[6] Unquestionably (to me at least), the flexibility and broadening accomplished by this pluralisation are to be celebrated. For example, assuming that one may not retain both, one may feel that the gain outweighs the loss if, for a second-year course on the bildungsroman, one makes room for Tsitsi Dangarembga's *Nervous Conditions* by dropping *Great Expectations*. Nonetheless, despite this pluralisation's apparent success, the notion of canonicity that it still necessarily involves remains, at some conscious or subconscious level, troubling to many of us, and the reason for this (or at least one of the principal reasons) is, again, the relation between the ideas underlying the two epigraphs from Gates.

Drawing on the formulations of the preceding chapter, we may, on the one hand, understand the problem of canonicity identified in the first epigraph as an affordance of the subterranean working of literary value's characteristic loose binding. As we saw illustrated with Boccaccio's meditations upon Dante's value vis-à-vis that of his pagan predecessors, ascriptions of literary value tend to seek strengthening through interlinkage with networks of other kinds of value, with literary value and those other kinds of value thereby constituting a mutually affirming circuit. Because of loose binding, that is, literary value, in practice, is almost never just literary, and as Gates's remark identifies, one of the networks of value with which the value of the canon has been traditionally interlinked has been that of white supremacy. One of the affordances of loose binding, in short, is a reciprocal linkage between the canon and white supremacy. Obviously, once we have unearthed this particular interlinkage, we may reject and seek to undo it. On the other hand, however, as the second epigraph insists, and as I have argued throughout this book, insofar as our projects are conceived as *literary* study, we cannot escape the category of literary value and the activity of value ascription – the acts of judgement – that in practice constitute that study. Because of literary value's characteristic loose binding, then, we may hardly evade some interlinkage with networks of other kinds of value, at greater or lesser levels of indirection, of which we are more-or-less conscious. And those interlinkages, in affirming some sets of values, necessarily do so in some differential relation with others sets of values. Hence, in the privileging, however provisionally and porously, of some texts over others that the activity of value ascription necessitates, we also privilege some other-than-literary values over others.

Facing this situation, we may be tempted to begin by identifying those other-than-literary values that we believe are right and good and then exercising literary judgement in explicit correlation with those values. This sort of response to the problem is a topic that I take up in the next chapter, in relation to literary interpretation. Here, we may simply note that the fact that both the Right caricaturises the Left, and the Left the Right, as performing this bully pulpit exercise should give us pause. More fundamentally, that the literary value of, say, *Othello* may easily be interlinked with any number of mutually hostile sets of other-than-literary values indicates that loose binding (as we saw with the Boccaccio example) cuts both ways. As much as it affords connection to networks of other kinds of value, its very looseness entails that those connections are never sure. In linking *Othello*'s literary brilliance to the value of a critique of white supremacy, we may thus inadvertently elevate a text that may continue to reinforce white supremacy, or something just as bad.

To translate this back into Gates's terms, any act of canon recognition, no matter how politically and socially nuanced, grants a voice to some at the expense, potentially, of rendering others voiceless, and therefore incurs the risk of committing the kind of injustice that Gates identifies in the first epigraph. Not surprisingly, therefore, many of us hesitate to provide, if not simply avoid altogether, the rationale, aim or basis (at least a fully articulated one) for the literary selection – that is, the literary valuation – that we have not ceased to perform, since such formulations seem inevitably to tend toward canon affirmation. The result is the same sort of inchoateness or lacuna in respect to literary value that I have noticed throughout this book: a gulf within the everyday practice of criticism and teaching between what we are willing to claim that we are doing (e.g., assembling reading lists) and what we actually are doing (canon-making). Despite several decades of arguing about, for and against canons, we still find ourselves bumping up against canonicity, even if – perhaps especially if – we would rather just put that category aside. It is this particular gulf between thinking and doing, as made evident in these everyday practices, that this chapter explores.

In the pages that follow, I turn first to a recent, baldly defensive moment in the history of Chaucer studies to provide an extended example of this gulf within the practical, institutional realities that govern our work and to delineate some of the gulf's characteristics. Next, to underscore how the gulf is not merely an idiosyncrasy within Chaucer studies, I consider in this respect a couple examples of similarly practical but more general defences of literary study, as they appear in departmental administrative documents and opinion pieces in professional periodicals. As we will see, in all these instances literary value – and more specifically a defence of the value of the canonical text – becomes the proverbial elephant in the room. As one might expect, then, this uneasy refusal to acknowledge the obvious has provoked in other forums a rather voluminous stream of attempts to account for canonicity and to advocate for canons in some form. Hence I next turn to an illustrative trio of such attempts, one pertaining to Chaucer studies, one to medieval literary study more broadly and one to literary study in general. Holding this trio up to the account of literary valuing that I developed in the preceding two chapters, I suggest that inasmuch as these three defences of canonicity are representative, they disclose how the very problem with which this chapter begins – the problem of canonicity marked out by its two epigraphs – in some fashion ineluctably reemerges. In this chapter's conclusion, then, I offer some suggestions for how to respond to this dilemma between wishing, for good reasons, not to acknowledge the elephant in the room, and acknowledging that elephant but then bearing out those very reasons that had prompted our avoidance. By no means claiming to have found a solution to this dilemma, I instead seek to reframe it in terms of this book's account of literary valuing and to offer ways to think about the impasse that aim to make it scholarly and pedagogically generative rather than a sort of spot on the carpet upon which we have set our feet.

Defending the MLA Chaucer Division

Medievalists will readily recognise the ironies in Gates's offhand reference to a 'medieval never-never land'. The medieval functions here as the familiar paradoxical bogeyman, simultaneously an eclipsed period of ignorance and barbarity (think Vikings in horned helmets) and a point of origin for idealised (rightly or wrongly, depending on one's point of view) social, cultural or political values (think Camelot, or, more starkly wrongly idealised, Ku Klux Klan 'knights'). The *Peter Pan* allusion plainly signals that we are to understand this instance of the trope as politically retrograde nostalgia for an era in which the 'high canon of Western masterpieces' rested untroubled (except, presumably, for border skirmishes involving this or that minor poet). One irony, of course, is that, at least for literatures in English, in the Middle Ages there were only the trace beginnings of anything like a canon, and these appeared only at the very end of the period and possessed a cultural and institutional footprint that was miniscule – that is, profoundly marginal – in comparison to the total artistic and intellectual output of the time.[7] Another irony, therefore, is that in so misprojecting a contemporary injustice onto the premodern past, Gates's othering of the medieval follows the same general logic as the racial othering that he sees performed by the 'high canon'. This irony does not, obviously, excuse that racial othering. Rather, it suggests that the medieval, and more specifically the marginal position of medieval literature within the field of English literary studies, has special purchase on the ongoing problem of canonicity.

Most of the English literary medievalists whom I know have, however grudgingly, grown to accept their marginal position in university curricula and in scholarship. (Indeed, that such a seemingly large proportion become department chairs perhaps owes something to how unthreatening they seem in their acceptance of their marginality.) Their collective outcry in 2013 was hence all the more remarkable. The triggering event was the decision by the MLA Executive Council to reconsider the division and discussion group structure into which the MLA had long parsed the many and ever-increasing literatures that fall under its umbrella (a structure last revisited in 1974). One of their proposals was to collapse the three divisions devoted to medieval British literature – Old English, Chaucer, and Middle English Language and Literature Excluding Chaucer – into one. In 'imagining a structure that works for the MLA in the twenty-first century, that reflects members' current field affiliations, and that makes space for areas that are currently underrepresented or absent', they asked the following of the members of the Chaucer Division Executive Committee:

> Given the disproportionate number of divisions in English in relation to other fields like African and East Asian, would you consider consolidating with Old English Language and Literature and with Middle English Language and Literature, Excluding Chaucer? ... Should Chaucer studies continue to be a separate division?[8]

The basic rationale for the proposal, that is, was to make room for other, formerly silenced or newly emergent voices, Gates's 'invisible ... unrepresented ... unrepresentable' – a rationale that, as a general principle, I suspect most medievalists today would affirm and even incorporate into their own practice, precisely in the fashion of my dropping Dickens in favour of Dangarembga. Nevertheless, every medievalist whom I spoke to about the proposal was outraged by it.

Unavoidably, part of what provoked this response was merely self-interest. Feeling as though our bowl of gruel was already small enough, we balked at the demand that we accept one-third of our usual portion. The then-Executive Director of the New Chaucer Society (NCS), Ruth Evans, made no attempt to disguise this motive in the email notifying society members of the proposal. I quote in full her entire second paragraph:

> The most disturbing proposal for change that they asked us to consider was that the three current medieval Divisions be consolidated

into one division. If this proposal were to go through, in place of the six sessions that are run at the MLA every year under the aegis of 'English Literature before Shakespeare' we would only have only two sessions. That is a huge reduction. It is also something of an absurdity: can one imagine representing work that covers a millennium in only two sessions? The consequences would be disastrous: fewer medieval faculty and graduate students attending MLA (less opportunity to give papers), fewer reasons to hold job interviews for medieval positions at MLA. In effect, medieval English Literature would be severely marginalized within an organization that supposedly represents the interests of all in the field of modern languages and literatures – modern, that is, in the sense of 'post-classical'. We would be giving up nearly all our places at a very important table.[9]

The threat, Evans indicates, is to our very viability as a subfield: fewer sessions at the MLA means fewer medievalists giving papers, fewer medievalists in attendance, fewer job interviews for medievalists and hence, presumably, fewer of those jobs themselves. To be sure, Evans does briefly mention a more conceptual objection – the 'absurdity' of 'representing … a millennium in only two sessions' – but she does not elaborate. Her readers in this case were not likely to pause to observe that the six division sessions have never been the only ones at the convention representing the Middle Ages, nor to weigh the relative injustice of the scarcity of sessions pertaining to a whole millennium against that of the scarcity of those pertaining to a whole continent, such as Africa. (I certainly did not so pause.) And nor would we wonder whether our smaller footprint at the MLA would in fact simply be the inevitable effect, rather than a further cause, of our smaller footprint in the field of literary studies as a whole: that is, whether the MLA would simply be accommodating itself to the real loss of medievalist tenure lines in English departments, and the cascading effects of that, rather than furthering such loss. Instead, facing the threat of losing 'our places at a very important table', we were determined not to go gently.

But of course this threat to our existence does not by itself argue against the proposal, as anyone knows who has sought to explain why the extinction of an obscure animal species matters to someone not prone to worry about such things. The question our outrage begs is why medieval English literature – and in particular Chaucer studies – continues to deserve its place at that important table. It was naturally this question, then, that the formal response sent to the MLA from Evans and then-NCS president Alastair Minnis strove to answer. Acknowledging the anomaly of 'Chaucer and Shakespeare' as 'the only two named authors with separate Divisions' (and so obliquely acknowledging the inheritance of those authors' canonical status), they locate the origin of that anomaly for Chaucer in the institutionalisation of Chaucer studies in the nineteenth century separate from the study of Middle English language and literature.[10] Quite aware, however, that the original establishment of Chaucer studies as a distinct subfield is not in itself a reason to preserve it, Evans and Minnis proceed to make their case on other bases:

> But 'Chaucer' emphatically continues to define a vitally important category within the discipline of English today. The field has its own scholarly organization, the New Chaucer Society, with a growing (and increasingly younger) membership that rivals that of the Shakespeare Association of America (1,035 and 1,250, respectively). The society has its own prestigious, peer-reviewed journal, *Studies in the Age of Chaucer* (with 7,119 downloads of its articles via Project Muse in 2012); there is also another major peer-reviewed journal in the field devoted solely to Chaucer: *The Chaucer Review*. NCS holds a biennial Congress that attracts up to 600 participants, and our members produce agenda-setting work within the field, work that has been a stimulus for scholarship done in later periods. For example, in sexuality studies and the 'new new historicism', scholars as diverse as Heather Love, David Halperin, and Valerie Traub have responded vigorously to the work of leading Chaucerians such as Carolyn Dinshaw and Aranye Fradenburg; the Chaucerians Paul Strohm and Helen Cooper are internationally known beyond the confines of medieval studies and contribute regular reviews to the *London Review of Books*; and the Chaucerian Seth Lerer teamed up with the book historian Leah Price to edit a special issue of *PMLA* on 'The History of the Book and the Idea of Literature'.

The initial move in this passage is shrewdly savvy. Placing Chaucer in scare quotes at once obliquely references the prior legitimating function of the poet's canonical status and signals acceptance, even approval, of the now post-canonical sensibility of the field. It is hence no longer Chaucer the poetic genius, but rather 'Chaucer' as the name of a sort of scholarly neighbourhood that continues to prove an attractive place to reside, that necessitates its continued privileged status. Attesting to this attractiveness is the sheer number of scholars who have taken up residence there and the corresponding volume of their scholarly activity: two journals, thousands of downloads, hundreds of conference attendees, and so on. Moreover, far from a gated community, this neighbourhood is one with frequent and mutually enriching exchanges with the cosmopolitan downtown of, for example, sexuality studies and *PMLA* itself.

I do not know how the numbers that Evans and Minnis cite compare to their parallels in, say, Milton studies. My hunch is that the Chaucer neighbourhood may not be as conspicuously distinctive in these respects as their arguments suggest, but of course achieving some quantitative threshold is not really the letter's rhetorical intent. Rather, the point that the paragraph as a whole makes is that the reason to keep the Chaucer Division is not Chaucer but the scholarship that 'Chaucer' continues to engender (even and especially among 'increasingly younger' researchers). A moment's reflection, however, may prompt the suspicion that this is rather akin to claiming that it is not pizza that one likes but the feeling of contentment that one has when one eats it. If that feeling of contentment may be had other ways, then there is no basis for privileging pizza, so the question circles back to whether there is something special about pizza itself. In other words, the question circles back to whether the 'vitally important' scholarship that resides under the heading 'Chaucer' actually depends upon something distinctive about Chaucer's works. If it does not, then the rationale for having both a Chaucer Division and an other-than-Chaucer Middle English division becomes more difficult to fathom.

Perhaps sensing this, in the next paragraph of their letter, Evans and Minnis argue,

> For such reasons, it makes no sense to get rid of the Chaucer division and to fold up the interests of a highly distinctive group of scholars into the interests of two other groups that, to be sure, share some of our interests, but also represent very different institutional and intellectual approaches, different histories (pre- and post-Conquest), different agendas, different constituencies.

That Middle English literary scholarship is 'highly distinctive' in respect to scholarship on Old English literatures is perhaps a claim that both groups of scholars would at least to some degree be willing to accept, if for the linguistic differences alone – although this is far from a settled or uncontested view (e.g., while the Conquest demarcates at least somewhat 'different histories', to what degree do the subfields' 'intellectual approaches' differ today?). But for those of us who have devoted much of our research to other-than-Chaucer Middle English texts, the claim that at present we have 'very different institutional and intellectual approaches, different histories ... different agendas, different constituencies' may seem simply nonsensical. (And for some Langlandians and Gowerians, I would guess that it may provoke no small amount of irritation.) I am quite sure that Evans and Minnis were aware of this when writing the above sentences. Both well know that the prepositional phrase 'in the age of Chaucer' in the title of the society's flagship journal performs the important work of, among other things, recognising the shared perspectives and interests of those working on post-Conquest English literatures. But their audience in this letter was not those scholars but instead those who were perceived as threatening the viability of medieval literary studies as a whole. And because their argument for the preservation of three divisions is based not on canonicity but on the distinctiveness of scholarly activity, they inevitably found themselves overstating that distinctiveness.

Nowhere in the letter do Evans and Minnis attempt to argue that Chaucer's works have any special value in themselves, as of course to do so would be to invoke the idea of canonicity, which, as they were no doubt acutely aware, no longer has suasive efficacy in the field at large. Nonetheless, as I have suggested, that idea remains stubbornly half-submerged, in the form of an aporia or inchoateness, in their defence of a Chaucer Division. Likewise, the formal letter sent by the Executive Committee of the MLA Chaucer Division (which at the time included Holly Crocker, Kathy Lavezzo, Jessica Rosenfeld, Mark Miller and Kellie Robertson), while broader in scope and more detailed, runs into much the same problem.[11] The authors of the letter eloquently defend the study of medieval British literatures generally as at once distinctive and in mutually productive conversation with the rest of the field. With regard to the Old English Division, the authors emphasise 'fundamental' linguistic differences, 'cultural and political factors' distinguishing the pre-Conquest period and the 'different methodologies and different habits of thought' of Old English scholars (no doubt aware, as we may assume for Evans and Minnis, of the eyebrows, or hackles, the latter characterisation may raise in some quarters). For the Chaucer Division, then, the letter begins by recognising 'the poet's unique place in the history of English'. Yet, lest their addressees suspect a canonical argument, the authors immediately clarify that they mean the history of English as a language and thus Chaucer's 'incorporation of French words and his sensitivity to dialectical diversity'. Notwithstanding the fact that Christopher Cannon has taught us to be sceptical of Chaucer's actual impact on the language,[12] the authors surely understood that such old philological arguments would carry little weight, and hence they quickly move on to an assertion that closely echoes the primary justification offered by Evans and Minnis:

> Chaucer still organizes a great deal of the critical conversation in medieval literary studies … By using Chaucer as a focal point for critical discussions that are emerging across the field, our division has worked hard to ensure that these panels remain vital and central to a diverse, multi-lingual, and interdisciplinary medieval studies.

The resonance here with the remarks of Ralph Hanna that we saw in Chapter 1 – that, despite his wish not to write about Chaucer, 'the canonically central medieval poet demands the attention of anyone involved with Middle English textual dissemination' – is striking.[13] Similar to how Hanna draws upon and further promulgates Chaucer's literary value, despite his explicit desire to do otherwise, the arguments of the Chaucer Division letter rest upon a literary value that they not only push aside as that division's *raison d'être* but also avoid even acknowledging. The reason to preserve the division, the letter claims, is not Chaucer but 'Chaucer as a focal point'; it is not anything special about Chaucer's works but the 'critical conversation' those works engender. The implication that remains (strategically) unstated is that, say, *Piers Plowman* does not provoke 'critical conversation' of the same scope and value, and hence combining the Chaucer and the other-than-Chaucer divisions would impoverish the subfield of late medieval literary study generally (a scenario that the authors phrase diplomatically as 'crowd[ing] out other field interests'). The implication, that is, is that Chaucer's works are special.

For both letters, therefore, the necessarily unstated reason to preserve a separate Chaucer Division remains the reason why that division was established in the first place, which is essentially the same reason for the equally anomalous separate Shakespeare Division: the author's longstanding and repeatedly reaffirmed canonical status. To be sure, as Evans and Minnis note, Chaucer is no Shakespeare in this respect. Each functions as a literary value touchstone that at once measures and legitimates the literary quality (including poorly judged quality) of the works of others that fall within its orbit. But for Chaucer the latter include primarily just late medieval English texts, while for Shakespeare they potentially include virtually all literatures – and dramatic productions – in English, not to mention in other languages. As I reviewed in Chapter 1, from the able research of David Matthews, Stephanie Trigg, Tim William Machan, Thomas Prendergast and others, we have a satisfyingly historicised and conceptualised account of Chaucer's function in this respect.[14] As these scholars have shown, it was the combination of Chaucer's self-evident, apparently timeless literary excellence, his uncanny ability to seem always current, with the manifest historical distance of his language, manuscripts and culture that enabled the birth of modern Chaucer studies in the nineteenth century. For the founder of the original Chaucer Society, Frederick J. Furnivall, Chaucer's poetry was self-evidently worth recovering, reconstructing, preserving and transmitting. And also for Furnivall, this presumed value, and the necessary scholarly activity it engendered, in turn anchored Middle English studies more generally. As the logic went, if one medieval poet was so valuable, then others might be so too, once the scholarly work of recovering their achievements has been performed; or, at the very least, these others can help us see just how valuable that one is.

This logic – of Chaucer's paradoxically simultaneous exceptionality and representativeness – has proven quite enduring. To highlight just one institutionally impactful repetition of it, I offer the editors' introduction to the 1966 inaugural issue of *ChR*:

> It would be easy to justify a journal focusing on Chaucer on the grounds that lesser writers than he, from Castelo Branco to Kipling and Schnitzler, have one or more scholarly publications devoted to them ... But the real justification is the vital and continuing interest in the study of medieval English literature, a study that has in the past decade or so been enjoying a renaissance – and experiencing a

revolution ... These and other approaches ... have resulted in a general feeling that many writings have not in the past been properly understood and appreciated ... With this renaissance has come a recognition in the colleges and schools that medieval literature is really honest-to-goodness literature that can hold its own with the writing of any age ... more and more teachers and students are finding in medieval literature an artistry and a *Weltanschauung* which make it as fascinating as the most contemporary literature – and perhaps even more worthy of study.[15]

Chaucer's canonical status is here, from the first sentence on, explicitly assumed. It needs no defence in itself, but rather in its very stable certainty it may serve as a means to recognise the literary value of 'many writings [that] have not in the past been properly understood and appreciated'. In the terminology of Chapter 2, inasmuch as recognition as 'literature' is one and the same as ascribing literary value (however much or little), the manifest value of Chaucer provides the axiological anchor point from which one may recognise 'in [other] medieval literature an artistry ... perhaps even more worthy of study' than the 'contemporary literature' that is axiologically more proximate to 'teachers and students'. Chaucer's self-evident value, amid the controversies and excitements of 1960s literary criticism (and with the canon wars still around the corner), once again led the way, thenceforth to be institutionalised in one of the still-thriving journals that bears the poet's name. (And given this rationale for Chaucer-centrism, it is all the more striking that back in 1926, as Patricia Clare Ingham reports, the forty members of the MLA 'Chaucer Group' in attendance at the association meeting voted against merging with the 'Middle English Language Group', as the thirty-seven members of the latter proposed, with the decision resting on a single vote.[16] Apparently, Chaucerian *noblesse oblige* only extends so far.)

That this self-evident literary value has in fact never ceased to function in this manner, despite the pluralisation of canons and widespread suspicion towards canonicity as a principle of privileging some texts over others, was undoubtedly recognised on some level by the authors of both letters to the MLA, as well as by other leaders within Chaucer and Middle English Studies. For example, the questions that the MLA proposal exhumed in this respect spurred the other-than-Chaucer division to devote one of its 2015 MLA convention sessions to the topic 'Rethinking the Place of the Author', a roundtable in which Evans participated, contributing a talk entitled 'What Is a Chaucer?'[17] Indeed, Evans in particular has repeatedly returned her penetrating gaze to the issue of Chaucer's institutional centrality and value, with her research and reflections in this regard culminating in her 2021 NCS Presidential Lecture. Entitled 'On Not Being Chaucer', this talk reconnoitred the rocky critical terrain to provide an explanation for why Evans 'still want[s] to read Chaucer'.[18] Yet, at the time of the earlier controversy and for the missives directed to MLA leadership, Evans and the others just as certainly recognised that – for the purpose of resisting a proposal whose rationale plainly shares the general sentiment of this chapter's first epigraph – they could scarcely mount any defence that even remotely suggested, as Gates puts it, the 'return of "the" canon'. As a consequence, the defences they did mount beg the question of whether the undoubtedly impressive scholarship that 'Chaucer' has engendered actually needed Chaucer at its centre, other than for the scholarly findings pertaining to Chaucer specifically; or, if it did, whether it continues to so need Chaucer.

Let me be clear, however, that in pointing this out, I am in no way questioning the wisdom or prudence of the authors of these letters. Quite the contrary: I am profoundly grateful to them and relieved that they achieved their aim. In their shoes, I would have attempted the same arguments but much less eloquently. My purpose here, instead, is to underscore how the category of canonicity persists in our basic practices and institutional manoeuvres, despite our laudable desire to remedy the social injustices of which it has been one instrument among many. Inevitably, the conflict between this persistence and this desire appears, within the practical occasions that these letters represent, as a degree of conceptual incoherence – one facet of the general problem of literary value.

Defending literary studies

Chaucer studies, as it is centred around a poet who is simultaneously canonical and marginal, likely exhibits this facet of the problem of literary value more baldly than other areas under the literary studies umbrella. Nonetheless, a similar incoherence is not hard to spot even in the most general defences of the field of literary studies, especially in those relatively unguarded ones with practical aims directed toward external audiences who do not already assume that the field has value. In particular, as the graduate students who absorbed the critiques of the canon in the 1980s and 1990s have grown into senior faculty in the 2000s and 2010s, the departmental self-definitions over which they preside have come to reflect their unease with canonicity as a defining justification. Recognising the conceptual tautology, ideological and socioeconomic instrumentality and historical relativity of literary value, they are no longer likely to advertise notions of literary greatness and genius in, say, their departmental promotional material. They have accepted that these notions were often vague and never subject to demonstration that (as we will witness again below) was not either logically circular or pendant on external authority, with the latter always potentially in service, at some level, to the sort of retrograde ideology targeted in this chapter's first epigraph.

For example, about eight years ago from the time of this writing, as part of the assessment plan for the English major at Indiana University South Bend (a regional branch of the Indiana University system offering BA and MA degrees in English), the department was required to develop a mission statement for the undergraduate major, 'a clear and concise description of the ultimate principles that guide the work of the program', as the university assessment experts communicated to us. This is what we agreed upon:

> Students earning a BA in English at IU South Bend engage with texts across a historical and generic spectrum of the many traditions of literatures in English, thereby developing their critical thinking, creative expression, cultural and historical knowledge, skills at and methods of textual analysis and research, and elegance, vision, and precision in writing. These abilities are central to the liberal education that the College of Liberal Arts and Sciences as a whole provides, designed to prepare students 'to meet the challenges of our ever-changing world'.[19]

Despite the not insignificant effort it took to compose and agree upon this statement, my hunch is that in this post-canon age, its tenor and even details are fairly typical of English departments' self-characterisations composed for similar purposes. In several ways, for example, it is merely a more measured, blander version of the claims that Azade Seyhan makes for the value of the English major that I quoted in the preceding chapter.[20] It foregrounds, especially, skills (more so than Seyhan in this respect), lays claim to broad, self-evidently valuable categories of knowledge ('cultural and historical'), is careful to include a nod to its creative writing constituencies ('creative expression') and even finds a way to preserve something of a rationale ('many traditions of literatures in English') for past investments in literary specialisations in periods and genres that still at that point characterised the department's organisation of faculty lines and, hence, curriculum.

In these regards, it may be usefully set alongside Paul Jay and Gerald Graff's 2012 exhortation, in an *Inside Higher Ed* piece, for humanities departments to reorganise themselves around 'critical vocationalism', giving voice to what has become a prominent trend in twenty-first-century English department self-refashioning.[21] Although the IU South Bend mission statement was drafted in ignorance of the article, it was motivated in no small part by the same anxieties about the status of the humanities and accordingly echoes many of the article's prescriptions. Jay and Graff urge humanities departments to abandon their resistance to 'our culture's increasing fixation on a practical, utilitarian education' and instead embrace the fact that 'many heads of philanthropic foundations, nonprofits, and corporate CEOs … have lately been extolling the professional value of workplace skills grounded in the humanities'. The critical vocationalism that they advocate

> is neither an uncritical surrender to the market nor a disdainful refusal to be sullied by it, but … an attitude that is receptive to taking advantage of opportunities in the private and public sectors for humanities graduates that enable those graduates to apply their training in meaningful and satisfying ways.

In particular, humanities departments should emphasise both to their internal and external constituencies 'the range of useful professional competencies with which a humanities education equips 21st-century students'. Such students learn 'to read carefully and to write concisely'; they learn to 'analyze and make arguments in imaginative ways, to confront ambiguity, and to reflect skeptically about received truths'; and, in encountering 'texts of diverse cultures', they are able 'to put themselves in the shoes of people who see and experience the world very differently from their own accustomed perspectives'. All these abilities are 'skills that are increasingly sought for in upper management positions in today's information-based economy' and 'transnational marketplace'. While Jay and Graff continue to believe 'that studying philosophy, literature, and the fine arts ... have a value in and of themselves apart from the skills they teach', for them in the end it is those skills, not that value, that justifies the continued existence of humanities departments: 'there is no defense of the humanities', they declare, 'that is not ultimately based on the useful skills it teaches'.

Faced with declining numbers of majors, no few English departments have, I would guess, adopted at least some of the language and emphases advocated by Jay and Graff (among many other such advocates), especially in self-justifying documents like the IU South Bend English major mission statement. Notably in the latter, entirely absent is any recognition of literary value, just as in Jay and Graff's article the notion of 'value in and of themselves' yields place to 'the useful skills it teaches'. Taking note of this absence, a sceptical reader of the mission statement – that is, the very reader to whom it is directed – might reasonably hesitate over its inclusion of 'the many traditions of literatures in English': why must literary texts be the vehicle – or even part of the vehicle – for the development of the listed skills? Aside from 'creative expression' – which this sceptical reader might find merely tautological with 'traditions of literatures' – what special claim do literary texts have on 'critical thinking ... cultural and historical knowledge, skills at and methods of textual analysis and research'?

Given that the anthropologist sitting next to me when first I typed the preceding sentence vigorously affirmed that all those skills are ones fostered by his field – as I suspect they are by many others – the answer would seem to be: no special claim at all. To be sure, as we have seen in the preceding chapters, no small number of attempts have been made within what I have been calling ontological accounts of literary value to substantiate this sort of special claim. I consider a very small subset of similarly oriented attempts below. At this point we may simply observe, as I did in Chapter 3 in respect to Seyhan's claims, that the inclusion of 'traditions of literatures' in the mission statement must rest on the implication that the study of literary texts facilitates the development of the listed skills in a uniquely efficacious manner (or, at least, that literary study lends the skills unique qualities); or on the unstated assumption that literature is worth engaging for its own sake, even if just as a side-effect of developing the skills; or on the banal fact that in literature departments literature is what is read. But since the first two of these justifications depend in turn on an unstated claim about literary value – literature's distinctive efficacy at fostering the listed skills, or its intrinsic value – and the third is no justification at all, the absence of any recognition of literary value produces the same sort of incoherence that we saw with the letters protesting the elimination of the MLA Chaucer Division.

Obviously, if there is little-to-no justification for the inclusion of literary texts, then there is even less justification for the inclusion of any particular literary text – that is, justification for any canonical selection of texts. Conversely, however, if we do admit one of the above justifications – say, the most modest one, that the study of literature lends unique qualities to the skills of 'critical thinking ... cultural and historical knowledge, [and] skills at and methods of textual analysis and research' – then the question arises as to whether some literary texts facilitate this better than others. Most literary scholars, even those sympathetic to the position of Jay and Graff, would, I believe, answer this question in the affirmative. For example, Robert Scholes, in his book *English after the Fall* urges English departments to put aside literature as their disciplinary centre in favour of what he terms 'textuality', arguing that 'the business of English departments is to help students improve as readers and writers, to become better producers and consumers of verbal texts ... It is a humble business, but it is the only justification for the existence of these departments.' Nevertheless, towards this 'humble' end, Scholes retains the category of literariness as a scalar quality. He just would neither limit the category to a predefined set of text types nor insist upon a hard line between literary and non-literary:

> We ['editorial groups' that have included Scholes] would not deny that certain kinds of texts, like instructions, are usually very low on the literary scale, but we all believe that there is a scale, and that there are poems, plays, stories, and expository texts all along that scale. This scale is a measure of a quality we may call 'literariness' (which

I would define as a combination of textual pleasure and power), but it is neither easy nor right to draw a line across the scale at some point and call everything on one side of the line literature.[22]

As I pointed out in Chapter 2, even a poor judgement of literary quality ('very low on the literary scale') registers the literary by means of a minimal ascription of literary value, and here for Scholes that value, offhandedly given within parentheses, is the more-or-less Horatian one of 'combination of textual pleasure and power'. Putting aside the (no small) question of what this 'pleasure and power' consist of and how they can be measured comparatively, we may therefore recognise that even in this proposal for shifting the central concern of English departments away from literature, literary value still has a place (if a less prominent one). Because certain texts have more of this value than others, they presumably ought to be privileged in some fashion, even if just within that diminished place. If for Scholes the net cast by the notion of literariness is wider than that of English departments past (and in fact Scholes's net is not much wider than the one medievalists have long used, as it includes, for example, biblical texts), there are nonetheless still better and worse fish.[23]

Hence, while the 'Sample Program in Textuality' that concludes Scholes's book may only fitfully resemble Gates's spectre of 'the high canon of Western masterpieces', the canon-making impulse – that is, canonicity – persists. Indeed, it makes an unmistakable appearance, if an indirect and brief one, even in Jay and Graff's exhortation of humanities departments to focus on skills. As evidence for the 'range of expertise' and 'concrete value' provided by a humanities education, the authors cite the example of Damon Horowitz, 'a leading figure in artificial intelligence and the head of a number of tech startups', who 'took a break from his lucrative career to enroll in Stanford's Ph.D. program in philosophy'. They report that Horowitz discovered that his sabbatical from the technology world actually increased his value in it. As Horowitz himself concludes in the *Chronicle* essay cited by Jay and Graff, 'You go into the humanities to pursue your intellectual passion; and it just so happens, as a by-product, that you emerge as a desired commodity for industry.'[24] Horowitz's initial work in artificial intelligence focused on natural language processing, and he writes about how, upon confronting limits to what he was able to have machines accomplish, he went to graduate school with questions about 'the nature of thought, the structure of language, the grounds of meaning'. He discovered to his happy surprise a long and rich history of seeking answers to those very questions, not just in 'analytic and continental philosophy', but also, among other disciplines, in 'literary theory', one of the fields in which 'thinkers explore different aspects of how we create meaning and make sense of our world'. Revealingly, after mentioning this inclusion of literary study among Horowitz's panoply of humanities pursuits, Jay and Graff conclude their summary of Horowitz's experience by reporting how he realised that his previously merely 'computational' understanding 'of cognition failed to account for whole expanses of cognitive experience (including, say, most of Shakespeare)'. Horowitz realised, that is, that without the humanities, computer science could not account for the texts of Shakespeare. To the unstated question of why it should need to account for those texts, the assumed answer is that they are a key source for 'whole expanses of cognitive experience': presumably, they are uniquely capacious representations of human consciousness – which view, albeit cryptically implied, seems at base not so different from Harold Bloom's uber-canonical view of Shakespeare.[25] In Jay and Graff's report, therefore, the value to the technology industry of Horowitz's humanities training is corroborated by the canonical literary value of Shakespeare.[26] It is hence a deepened appreciation for Shakespeare (alongside whatever higher salary Horowitz could demand) that helps to justify a humanities PhD – the very appreciation, of course, that used to justify a PhD in English, because Shakespeare, as the most canonical of 'the high canon of Western masterpieces', was self-evidently worth appreciating in ever deeper ways.

Defending canonicity

The canon-making impulse, then, or the reemergence of some principle of canonicity – the 'expanses of cognitive experience' encompassed by Shakespeare or Scholes's Horatian 'combination of textual pleasure and power' – persists even in those very forums that seem intent on providing an alternative to literary value as a disciplinary rationale. It appears there as a species of the return of the repressed, as that which the adjective 'literary' requires but which, for all the reasons summarised above, we would just as soon not dwell upon, perhaps not even acknowledge. It is precisely that which we have seen was repressed, in a much more focused manner and rather more consciously, in the letters of protest to the MLA. In other forums, however, literary scholars have not been so coy. Provoked in part by this very impetus towards repression over the last several decades, they have been increasingly interested in unearthing, accounting for and defending this repressed. They have endeavoured to return to the problem of literary value, typically in some ontological fashion, in order to provide firmer ground for a discipline that still has 'literary' as part of its name.

For this chapter's purposes, a particularly revealing instance of this effort is Mark Miller's NCS blog post entitled 'Why Do We Care about Chaucer?'[27] As mentioned earlier, Miller was one of the signatories of the Chaucer Division letter to the MLA, and since his post appeared just over a year later, it seems not unlikely that it was at least partially inspired by his recognition of that letter's axiological lacuna. Indeed, Miller seems to call attention to this very gap when at the outset he declares that 'we must have an answer' to the 'fundamental question' voiced by the blog's title, 'since we enact answers to it all the time whether we think about it or not'; and in what follows he proceeds to contrast Chaucer with two Ricardian contenders for canonicity, those stars of the other-than-Chaucer MLA division, Langland and Gower. Seemingly recognising both the continued dependence of Chaucer studies on some claim for the special value of Chaucer's texts and our reluctance to articulate that claim, Miller sets out to provide such an articulation. And with the admirable succinctness and directness encouraged by the blog form, he proposes two explanations for that value ('embarrassingly retro' ones, he worries), the first baldly ontological, the second apparently more genealogical: '1) Chaucer's a genius; 2) Chaucer's poetry, particularly the *Canterbury Tales*, is exceptionally well suited to the material and ideological conditions of higher education'.

As the latter explanation is more readily elaborated, Miller begins there. He argues, 'Unlike the equally brilliant *Piers Plowman*, the *Canterbury Tales* lends itself wonderfully to the extraction of a short stretch of text for sustained examination.' The key phrase 'equally brilliant' signals that this particular special value of extractability, while ascribed to an aspect of textual manner (to use my terminology from Chapter 2) that distinguishes *Piers* from the *Tales*, does not distinguish the two in respect to literary value more broadly considered, but rather in respect to the more utilitarian value of alignment with our typical pedagogical practices. Simply put, the *Tales* helps us appear to be better teachers, because in contrast with *Piers* its 'difficulties … often chunk themselves into bite-sized morsels'. Miller, in genealogical fashion, is well aware of the historical contingency of this value, or, in my terms, its position within the historically persistent axiological constellations that have determined and sustained these typical pedagogical practices – those constellations that, as no few scholars have discussed, from the second half of the nineteenth century led to the emergence of English as a discipline.[28] It was, Miller writes, a 'sheer historical accident that Chaucer, unlike Langland, wrote in a way that the institutional structures of 20th-century higher education ended up finding convenient'. This special value ascribed to the manner of Chaucer's text, therefore, is not an ontological value-in-itself but rather functionally serves (that is, is linked to and hence strengthened by) the value of those 'institutional structures'.

Yet, even if we put aside the question of why we should in turn care about those structures (the question that might be asked, not by employees within those structures, but by, say, the sceptical legislators funding them), we may recall, genealogically, what those structures have depended upon. In particular, in the US at least, the regimen of close reading and the accompanying pedagogical and professional privileging of short, nuanced passages of text were, of course, the results of the academic institutionalisation of New Criticism. And, as I reviewed in Chapter 1, at the heart of New Criticism lay judgement, the comparative assessment of literary value, with something like Gates's 'high canon of Western masterpieces' serving as both anchor and outcome of that assessment – a 'high canon' that had, moreover, always privileged Chaucer. Thus, as it turns out, if we should 'care about Chaucer' because his texts lend themselves to the way that we teach, then we are caring about Chaucer because he has been and remains canonical. The 'sheer historical accident' of the privileging of Chaucer is no accident at all, but rather a historical chain of contingent ascriptions of value across axiological constellations. As recalled above, an already canonical Chaucer played a key role in the institutionalisation of English as an academic subject, and so not surprisingly English pedagogy has been influenced by the characteristic features of his texts. Chaucer fits our teaching because our teaching, at least to some degree, has been fitted to Chaucer. As I have suggested in the preceding chapters, when we follow the interlinkages of the axiological constellations of current 'institutional structures' with constellations of the institutional past, genealogical analyses almost inevitably lead back to ontological claims.

Characteristically perspicacious, Miller is well aware of this relation between genealogy and ontology (although not in those terms, obviously), and hence he goes on to consider his first answer, Chaucer's 'genius', in relation to the second, Chaucer's functional suitability to the classroom. One 'sign of genius', he suggests, is that Chaucer's text 'so persistently interrogates its own grounds that it leaves its best readers in a state of suspension', but this quality, he notes, it shares with Langland's.[29] What distinguishes it, again, is its accessibility in 'bite-sized morsels', '10–20 line chunks of poetry'. But now, beyond their pedagogical utility, Miller emphasises how those morsels remain fresh: they remain present to us in ways that 'reward continual reexamination, that always seem capable of producing fresh insights, that always seem to be there ahead of us as we learn to think in new and different ways', so that 'we are tempted to say that Chaucer somehow anticipated the insights of feminism, or psychoanalysis, or whatever combination of discourses we happen to have learned from'. The feature of textual manner underlying this freshness, Miller then suggests, is the 'very condensed condensation' of Chaucer's writing, by which he means how frequently Chaucer packs complex, multifaceted signification into single lines, phrases and words. Hence, even after six hundred years of being read, Chaucer's texts still prompt new understandings of their intricate webs of meaning. This feature sets Chaucer's oeuvre apart, Miller argues, from that of Gower, which, while similarly accessible in chunks, 'has not proven nearly as receptive' to the broad sort of interpretive freshness that Chaucer's has.

Not many scholars of Middle English literature, I think, would contest Miller's characterisation of these two features of textual manner in Chaucer's works – its extractability and condensation. A few, perhaps, might query how much they truly distinguish those works, pointing to the extractability and semiotic density of, say, the first twenty-one lines of *Piers Plowman*. And these few might further wonder whether Chaucer's texts just seem to possess these features of manner more so than others because considerably more energy has been invested into the scholarly and pedagogical recognition of them. But this nitpicking would not be fair to the aphoristic spirit of the blog format in which Miller, to his credit, was willing to put forth answers to a question that indeed needs answering. Nor would it be fair to voice reservations about the predictability of the features that Miller highlights (otherwise phrased, perhaps, as resonance, textual polysemy and self-referentiality), which have featured in many prior attempts to define the nature of canonical texts. Miller himself labels his explanations 'retro', and, as his longer-format work ably attests, he would be entirely capable of providing more richly theorised versions of them.[30] And, in any event, these reservations are mere border skirmishes in comparison with the more crucial question that the identification of the features seems irresistibly to beckon, a question that Miller (again to his credit) voices explicitly in his concluding paragraph: if we grant that Chaucer matters because of the extractability and condensation of his texts – if we follow Miller and ascribe value to those features of manner, and if we assume that those features are more available in Chaucer's texts than elsewhere – then, as Miller puts it, 'why do we care about *that*'? What, in other words, is the value of this set of specific literary values?

To answer, 'we care about extractability and condensation because this is what makes texts valuable', would be, of course, to respond tautologically, to declare in effect that we value what we value. And in a tightly bound situation, this is often enough (e.g., I like to eat pizza because it's yummy, and I like to eat yummy food because, well, it's yummy). But the very voicing of the question here indicates the obvious – that, as typical with literary value, the situation is one of loose binding, in which such tautologies are usually not enough. When we granted the values of extractability and condensation to Chaucer's texts, we did so on the implied promise that some other, greater value would confirm or prop those more strictly literary ones. To move beyond the latter, we necessarily enter into the network of valuing, in which value ascriptions arise as mediations of other value ascriptions. The answer, then, to the blog's titular question, 'why do we care about Chaucer', will ultimately involve the axiological ballast that I described in the preceding chapter. We will care about Chaucer because doing so means giving attention to something that we care even more about. Understandably – but also strategically – Miller makes only vague gestures toward this something in the conclusion of his post. He points to a pair of value systems ethical in nature and conversely related to one another: on the one hand, 'a kind of Arnoldian humanism, newly revitalised, among other places, in the return to formalism, the recent critical emphasis on ethical self-cultivation, and some of the directions taken in affect theory', and, on the other, 'the cultivation of something very different: not the self, but critical habits of mind that interrupt the circuits of identification that make for Arnoldian horticulture'. Again, it would not be in the spirit of the blog format to ask for more explanation and defence of these value systems or justification for why Chaucer, or even the literary as a category, is especially well suited to them. It suffices to observe that the formulation of such an explanation, a defence and a justification would be a difficult, highly contestable task, and that the justification in particular – as suggested by Miller's invocation of Arnold and the latter's famous formula for culture as 'the best that has been thought and said in the world' – would almost certainly circle back, logically, to the fact of Chaucer's persistent canonicity.[31]

What Miller's blog thus illustrates with such admirably succinct clarity is how, when we set out to defend canonicity, we may offer it as its own defence, tautologically, as consisting of those features of manner that most appeal to us in an already canonical text, and/or we may wish it to consist of something more than that sort of academically cultured taste – and because of loose binding, the latter move is difficult to forestall. But once we move into the network of valuing in search of that something more, we encounter both the circularity and indefinite extension of that network. The circularity entails that, say, 'Arnoldian humanism' and Chaucer's canonical value become mutually defining of one another. The indefinite extension means that however counter to our intentions, an 'Arnoldian humanism' may possibly wind up underwriting something like Gates's 'high canon of Western masterpieces', that is, it may underwrite social and political values that we find anathematic.

The possibility of the latter is provocatively made evident in a blog post by Lynn Arner. Wryly entitled 'Why Do We Care More about Chaucer than Gower?', it diplomatically advertises itself as an affirmation of Miller's post but in fact constitutes a neat counterpoint, venturing into the network of valuing and settling in a rather different place.[32] Arner accepts Miller's claims for Chaucer's suitability to 'the material and ideological conditions of higher education' and for the semiotic density of his texts. She relates the former, however, to the twenty-first-century value most North American and British universities ascribe to diversity, a value to which the 'motley crew' of the *Canterbury Tales* pilgrims and the work's 'wide range of genres and poetic forms' seems well-tuned. Yet for Arner the *Tales* merely creates 'the illusion of an inclusive world'. Although it is not the aim of her post to substantiate this view, she persuasively points both to the fantasy status of the *Tales'* depicted inclusivity and to the actual social narrowness of even that fantasy. Arner then understands the higher education institutional ascription of value to diversity as 'a neoliberal rhetoric of inclusion', suggesting that this ascription itself serves in practice not social justice but a system of global capitalism. Whereas for Miller the notion of the 'ideological conditions' of higher education leads him to consider the privileging of short passages of texts, for Arner it leads to the disciplinary formation of subjects suited to the social order.

Similarly, Arner follows the ascribed value of resonant, semiotic density – the 'endless proliferation of meaning' within Chaucer's texts – to the 'ideology of individualism' that higher education seeks to promulgate. In typical Chaucer pedagogy, 'readers are encouraged to invent their own innovative readings, a multiplicity that acts as proof of each student's own unique talents and capacities'. At the same time, Chaucer's semiotic density 'thwart[s] a stabilization of politics', resulting in the ambiguous, mobile, self-contradictory politics of his texts. For Arner, this is part of Chaucer's strategy for insulating art from social instrumentality, evidence of his belief – in stark contrast with Gower – 'that authors who explicitly attempt to produce socially responsible poetry generate dull, sterile art'. For these reasons, Chaucer becomes 'an ideal figure to celebrate in humanist approaches to authorship. Chaucer seems to speak from no position in particular but seems to stand above the fray; he appears to occupy a position outside social conflict in his day, providing a neutral, enlightened vision of society'. Arner points out, however, that Chaucer actually speaks from the position of 'the proto-bourgeoisie'. Chaucer's easy irony and poetic *sprezzatura* thus make him 'a model to emulate for those who aspire to the types of bourgeois characteristics and aesthetics rewarded in our educational system'. In contrast, Gower is more honest, forthright and even visionary about the politics of literature. While Arner fully acknowledges the more unpalatable aspects of Gower's social position and politics, she nonetheless understands Chaucer's contemporary as striving for 'a more politicised version of literature with readers ultimately acting in more socially conscious ways as a result'. And this is why 'we' – by which Arner means the neoliberal institution of higher education – care more about Chaucer than Gower.

It is not my purpose here to assess the merits of Arner's response to Miller. My point, rather, is the simple one that both scholars begin with the same or similar features of manner in Chaucer's texts, and both follow the values that they ascribe to those features into the network of valuing towards other values that they perceive as most proximate, which is to say, all the way to those values that matter to them. Hence canonicity – whether Chaucer's or the competing possibility of Gower's – cannot be defended or critiqued without an appeal to values that either are ultimately not especially relevant to literature (e.g., neoliberalism) or, to the extent that they are relevant, are ultimately not wholly distinguishable from the claim for canonicity that started the venture (e.g., Arnoldian humanism). As we have seen, it is this very axiological slipperiness and circularity that in many quarters have encouraged canonicity's exile, especially in practical rhetorical situations, such as the letters to the MLA and English major mission statements. Yet, also as we have seen, exiling canonicity (as in the letters to the MLA) has not vanquished it but has rather had the effect of encouraging its return in some more-or-less reformulated, newly justified fashion (as in Miller's blog).

It would not be difficult to show that the general characteristics of Miller's defence of canonicity, just as with the general characteristics of defences of Chaucer that do not mention his canonicity, are not merely idiosyncratic of Chaucer studies but are in various permutations rather typical of other recent defences marshalled with more extensive theorisation and at a wider scope of application. The ontological approaches to literary value mentioned in earlier chapters, for example, could be recanvased in this light. Here, however, I will consider just two other such defences, which, given their authors' well-established critical accomplishments, I hope will be sufficiently illustrative: very briefly, a short essay by Thomas Prendergast directed toward Middle English scholars, and, at rather more length, a mini-monograph by Frank Kermode addressed more broadly to the field of literary studies. Both of these explicitly take as their point of departure approaches to canonicity of a genealogical nature, find those approaches lacking in some respects (albeit to rather different degrees) and offer an ontological account of literary value as a defence of canonicity.

In his chapter on 'Canon Formation' in *A Handbook of Middle English Studies*, Prendergast acknowledges the explanatory power of historicising or genealogical accounts of canon formation but argues that they are not by themselves sufficient – that 'the larger forces of history are inadequate to explain the canon'. He sets out, then, to identify 'a quality that is necessary (if not always sufficient) to make a text canonical', or, in my terms, he sets out to identify those features of textual manner that necessarily possess literary value and hence justify canonicity. Or, more precisely, he ascribes value to those features in the process of recognising them and proposes that value as the basis for canonicity. Although Prendergast devotes a large section of the essay to Chaucer, he takes as his exemplary text *Sir Gawain and the Green Knight* and focuses on the way in which it both calls attention to its own mystifications and yet remains, in the end, mysterious. It signals its repressions, but 'what truly sets the poem apart is the extent to which the poem's repressions are irrecuperable. And it is this lack of epistemological certainty that seems to underwrite the canonicity of the poem.' The traditional label for this intractable epistemological uncertainty, Prendergast tells us, is 'wonder', which the poem both evokes and 'meditates on' in a way that teaches us that 'demystification is never quite complete'.[33]

Having then, like Miller, isolated a canonical textual quality (which, as a kind of inscrutability in which meanings proliferate because they are always just out of reach, shares a family resemblance

164   *The problem of literary value*

to the semiotic density that Miller identifies in Chaucer's text), at the end of his essay Prendergast seems to acknowledge – again like Miller but more obliquely – that this identification is somehow insufficient. By itself, it amounts to the claim that canonical texts are those that possess the quality that make them canonical. Hence the pressure of loose binding is felt, impelling the nagging question of why this quality is a valuable one – why, if we are indeed to accept this as a quality attached to the manner of *Gawain*, we should care about it so much that we privilege texts that possess it. In response, Prendergast informs us that 'what recent work on wonder reveals is that wonder is that which we experience when confronted with novelty, potentially leading to revolutionary or utopian thinking', although, like Miller – and for the same reasons – he does not elaborate. Instead, he concludes by asserting that *Gawain* and other Middle English texts considered canonical (even if not always considered so) 'all share this quality'.[34] As in Miller's blog, therefore, canonicity first seeks to be its own justification but then, urged forward by loose binding, also seeks justification in other-than-literary values ('revolutionary or utopian thinking') that stretch far beyond the horizon of the traces of their mediations.

Kermode, in a pair of essays based on his 2001 Tanner Lectures at Berkeley that were published as his penultimate monograph, similarly seeks to define the qualities of the canonical text in the face of genealogical critiques that understand the canon in terms akin to those of Gates's in this chapter's first epigraph – as Kermode puts it, for example, 'a wicked myth, designed to justify the oppression of minorities – a political propaganda weapon now at last revealed as such and, as the word goes, "demystified" '. But, much more intensively than Prendergast or Miller, Kermode seeks to insulate literary value from the taint of utility that may accompany any recourse to other-than-literary values. He seeks to define the specifically literary value that ought to lie at the heart of literary criticism instead of those values associated with critical work on 'for instance, gender and colonialism'.[35] In my terms, he seeks to define a tightly bound literary value, one that is nonetheless explicable in non-tautological terms even while being autonomous, in the sense of not mediated by other ascriptions of value.

In his first essay, drawing upon Jan Mukařovský and Roland Barthes, Kermode offers a reading of Wordsworth's 'Resolution and

Independence' to illustrate his contention that '[a]gain and again we find in the best of the poetry a curious blend of delight and dismay'. It is this specifically literary value of 'juxtaposition or collision of pleasure and dismay', he claims, that marks the canonical text, not such other-than-literary values as 'collusion with the discourses of power'. In his second essay, Kermode seeks then to account for the relativity of value by addressing the manifest historical determinations of canonicity, initially by acknowledging the 'element of chance', which of course for medievalists – aware of the sheer luck that has given us, say, *Sir Gawain and the Green Knight* or the *Book of Margery Kempe* – goes without saying. More important for Kermode, though, is the way in which canons are tested and modulated according to the manner in which readers at any given historical juncture experience (or fail to experience) the requisite 'juxtaposition or collision of pleasure and dismay'. Drawing upon Gadamer, Kermode observes that the 'canonical text ... must be made to answer to our prejudices, and they are necessarily related to the prejudices of our community, even if in reaction to them'. 'So a canon changes' according to these prejudices (or, in my terms, the axiological environments of a particular time and place), and 'the changes renew the supply of both pleasure and its potent derivative, dismay'.[36] Hence, while the specific set of texts that constitute the canon is subject to historical determination through axiological network pathways, the specific literary value that canonical texts possess, the combination of pleasure and dismay, remains historically constant and, so tightly bound, may therefore serve as a transhistorical principle of canonicity. Literary value per se escapes mediation, even while any given experience of literary value, Kermode in effect acknowledges, is necessarily mediated through the axiological constellations that determine that experience. Kermode's tightly bound pleasure principle, in turn, may ground the discipline of literary criticism as an intrinsically literary endeavour, one that is distinct from, say, the more-than-literary ideology critique that exposes 'collusion with the discourses of power'.

To work through the implications of Kermode's argument, we have the benefit of the responses by Geoffrey Hartman and John Guillory, which were published in the same volume. Since Hartman, over his long, storied career, had of course himself proffered many a searching consideration of literary value, we should not be surprised to find that he expresses reservations with Kermode's attempt to provide literary value the particular tight binding that he specifies. Hartman queries Kermode's choice in a way that suggests the pressure of loose binding, posing a question that is in effect a more elaborated version of Miller's 'why do we care about *that*?': 'what general cogency, beyond being a *promesse de bonheur*, a reward for a more complex understanding of tradition or acculturation, does the criterion of "pleasure" have, revived by Kermode?' While registering the pleasure that he, like Kermode, receives from canonical texts, Hartman ultimately finds that the particular pleasure that Kermode identifies is not self-evident in a way that enables it to carry value-in-itself weight. Drawing upon Lionel Trilling, he sees Kermode's literary value as in fact anchored by a politics – 'the eudaemonic nihilism of a liberal, progressive politics' – that stands in (blind) opposition to 'an anticonsumerist force calling itself spiritual, and often in total contempt of pleasure, indeed of worldly society as such'.[37] Hartman in effect suggests that Kermode achieves tight binding simply by ignoring the other-than-literary values that actually prop up his pleasure principle.

To build his case, Hartman offers a counter-reading of 'Resolution and Independence' that understands the poem's primary dynamic not as one of pleasure but of power, claiming that the 'powerlessness' of the leech gatherer, 'who seems scarcely alive, has to become a source of power for the poet'. Recalling Wordsworth's ambivalence even toward The Terror, Hartman argues, 'Unpower/power, not the pleasure/unpleasure complex, is the [poem's] problematic subject.' Hartman concludes that Kermode's defence of canonicity, by insisting on the tight binding of the value of pleasure, therefore 'skirts the political impasse that presently makes literary criticism, not only literature, a troubled mirror of our culture'.[38] In my terms, Hartman points out that not only are the ascriptions of the literary value of pleasure/dismay to specific texts necessarily mediated through 'prejudices' – axiological constellations of political and other values – but so is the very conception of that value itself. (By the same token, Kermode's other species of change, the force of chance, emerges out of axiological constellations that determine what sorts of happenstances are possible to begin with.) As I discussed in Chapter 3, any one kind of value is only conceivable through reciprocally distinguishing relations with other kinds of value, whether those relations are supportive or hostile. We care about pleasure/dismay (or Hartman's alternative, unpower/power) because, whether we acknowledge it or not, we care, or do not care, about the other values that enable us to conceive of that very sort of pleasure, and, in a loose binding situation, those other values cannot be left unacknowledged without incurring some incoherence. Thus, despite Kermode's evasions, literary judgement (pleasure/dismay) still resides on the slippery slope of, say, Gates's 'medieval never-never land' (politics).

In contrast, Guillory – whose *Cultural Capital* remains among the most influential of genealogical examinations of literary value – is wholly willing to grant pleasure the status of a value that needs no further justification. Given a world in which literary value is, as Guillory has argued, linked in practice to the other-than-literary value of cultural capital, one may seek to resist the larger value system encompassing the latter by identifying and then refusing that linkage. In some ways mirroring, therefore, the final movement of *Cultural Capital*, Guillory embraces the idea that 'the pleasure of the literary work is ... its chief reason for being, and ... the communication of that pleasure to the readers of criticism is at least one of the purposes of criticism'.[39] But in a loose binding situation, to refuse a linkage without putting another in its place is also to refuse to answer Miller's question of why we should 'care about *that*'. With loose binding, that is, such a refusal foregrounds the arbitrariness of the choice of value. Guillory – unlike Kermode – accepts this arbitrariness, and thus what he objects to in Kermode's argument is the privileging of the specific sort of pleasure that Kermode identifies as the principle of canonicity, since without the axiological ballast of an other-than-literary value, that privileging no longer possesses any rationale. Guillory does not question, in other words, why we should care about pleasure (he is happy to answer, in effect, 'because it is pleasurable'), but instead rejects the claim that we ought to care about one particular sort of pleasure so much more than others, aesthetic or otherwise, as to require the very business of canon-making and the discipline that performs that work. To so privilege one such pleasure, Guillory suggests, is to give up the refusal of the linkage that in fact enables one to embrace pleasure as the end of the literary experience.

Since Guillory is unwilling to grant 'a higher status' to the pleasure that Kermode identifies, he also does not extend special privilege to 'the domain of culture the higher authority upon which cultural criticism was and continues to be based', as that would simply be broadening the linkages that he wishes to refuse. Rather, to sever pleasure-finding from canon-making, Guillory locates the former in a host of other value constellations: 'Our speech, our manners, our bearing, our dress, our houses, our furnishings, our public spaces and private entertainments should all be beautiful, should deliver their measure of aesthetic pleasure.' In effect, as long as 'aesthetic value' is everywhere, its inevitable linkages do not as much matter, and so in its very ubiquity it gains a kind of quasi-independent status. In contrast, to identify one species of aesthetic pleasure as more important than another necessarily involves – as we have seen with Hartman's critique – the 'prejudices' that are something more than pleasure, and so Guillory declares that we cannot 'generalize any principle from the experience of aesthetic pleasure that would ground a principle of evaluation or canonicity'. Since the 'complex pleasures' of so-called high art must then constitute just one kind of pleasure among others, no more or no less valuable than any of the rest, we must 'retreat from attempting to make the connection between the quality of pleasure and the judgement of canonicity', not the least because the latter judgement, in necessarily moving beyond pleasure per se, undoes pleasure's quasi-independent status and thus threatens the very pleasure that was so elevated.[40] In short, in a loose binding situation, to relish in good faith pleasure as of value in and for itself, as Guillory is willing to do, requires us to recognise the arbitrariness of its selection over other values and hence its inability to serve any larger axiologically anchoring function.

Since it is possible (though, I believe, inaccurate) to understand Hartman as keeping canonicity in place but arguing for a different grounding principle, Kermode, in his response to the critiques that concludes the volume, directs the most heat toward Guillory and in a manner especially revealing for present purposes. Summarising Guillory's argument, he states that the latter 'attacks the notion that some things give more pleasure than others, holding that it is unfair to claim privilege for the "higher", since what is normally thought to deserve that label can be regarded as a "very minor subculture in a vast domain of cultural production"'.[41] Yet, as we have seen, while Guillory does indeed reject the privilege granted 'the "higher"', he does not make any claims about relative amounts of pleasure, and this slippage between quality and quantity enables Kermode to sidestep Guillory's actual critique, which targets the privileging of one kind of aesthetic pleasure over another.[42] By assuming instead a single kind of aesthetic pleasure that is provided in different quantities (not unlike, interestingly, Scholes's 'literary scale'), Kermode in effect merely repeats, without offering any defence of, his privileging of 'the "higher" ', wondering aloud whether Guillory 'does not have experience of the difference between serious fiction and rubbish' and expressing regret that those who know better 'say ... that they have wholly comparable experiences from a television soap and Dante'.[43] Because of Kermode's singular tightly bound value, all cultural products are measurable by the same scale, and thus a canon necessarily follows. And in practice the measuring stick turns out to be, despite the forces of chance and change, uber-canonical texts such as Wordsworth's and Dante's. Just as with Miller's and Prendergast's defences, then, we arrive at a position in which canonicity is its own justification. For Kermode, it is a self-evidently 'higher' pleasure that bestows canonicity upon a text across the flux of historical change, and yet it is already canonical texts that define what constitutes this pleasure in respect to all other texts. The autonomy of Kermode's literary value turns out to rest upon the familiar tautology that canonical texts are so because they possess the quality of canonicity – as indeed is inevitable, because such a tautology is ultimately one and the same as a claim for tight binding.

As we have seen, both Hartman and Guillory take Kermode to task for his occulted incursion of this tautology, each in effect recognising the demands of loose binding, with Hartman accepting those demands by pointing to possibly defining other-than-literary values, and Guillory seeking to evade those demands by embracing the anticanonical implications of the tautology. Kermode, in simply reasserting the autonomous, privileged status of his chosen literary value in his more informal concluding remarks, cannot help but to betray the lacuna in his reasoning. For example, in the rather tart remarks that frame his response to his interlocutors, he states,

> If it should chance that literature as such means very little to you, having no nose you can trust, nothing you say on the subject will have a value appropriate to comment on that subject. You may say many things about other topics that some work of literature happens

to present to your mind, but their value would pertain to another subject and have little to do with a topic your activities suggest you know and care very little about. Call that topic 'poetry' and ask whether you have any in your head – any that is truly part of your mind. If not, keep on doing something else instead.[44]

The business of the critic, Kermode insists, is the discerning and communicating of specifically literary value (the sort of pleasure that he has identified), not 'other topics that some work of literature happens to present', whose 'value would pertain to another subject'. Inasmuch as a critic focuses on those 'other topics', Kermode avers, she is simply not doing her job. But in respect to keeping those other topics at bay, and hence literary value autonomous, the phrase 'no nose you can trust' is (to mix his metaphor with my own) the card falling from Kermode's sleeve. Although in its specific context this phrase refers back to Kermode's invocation of William Empson's remarks on the use of theory in criticism, in the larger context of what has preceded and what will follow, it also cannot help but to invoke, through an irresistible synaesthesia, the category of taste (and, indeed, when initially referring to Empson's remarks, Kermode acknowledges an 'enological analogy'). Kermode, not surprisingly, does not elaborate on what having a 'nose you can trust' entails nor addresses whether or how one may obtain such a nose. Tellingly, when expressing disbelief at Guillory's supposed flattening of 'the difference between serious fiction and rubbish', he simply remarks that the experience of this difference 'is a fact of life, however difficult it may be to philosophize it'.[45]

Although I cannot here embark upon any adequate discussion of the category of taste, we may simply observe that by invoking that category, Kermode inadvertently discloses how firmly he has backed himself into a corner. On the one hand, Kermode invokes the category precisely so that he does not need to explain 'the difference between serious fiction and rubbish', since taste, as Lucien Karpik (drawing on Hannah Arendt) notes, 'is idiosyncratic, and therefore no argument can prove any overall superiority'. But on the other hand, by implying that true literary critics would share his taste (and that those who do not ought to find other employment), he suggests that taste is emphatically not idiosyncratic but rather a shared judgement that definitively separates, for anyone actually paying attention, the 'serious' from 'rubbish'. Yet as Karpik further notes, in contrast to taste, judgement 'is totally in the world. Because it embodies a norm, it is inseparable from all other judgments'.[46] In my terms, judgement is a value ascription performed by an actor as a mediation of the value ascriptions of other actors, within an infinitely receding axiological network. Judgement expressed as taste, then, is a species of value ascription that presents the mediation of other value ascriptions as not such mediation, and thereby gains authority through that stratagem. In Pierre Bourdieu's famous formulation, taste is 'a class culture turned into nature, that is, *embodied*'.[47] It is an immensely powerful mechanism by which aesthetic value may command all sorts of other values (or vice-versa).

Kermode's terse acknowledgement of how difficult it is to 'philosophize' the distinction between 'serious' and 'rubbish' hence serves as an abrupt erasure of the axiological constellations within which any such distinction must necessarily be made. Indeed, in naming this distinction a 'fact of life', he renames as *fact* what are quite plainly *values* (the judgements of 'serious' and 'rubbish') – and facts, of course, are the one thing that values are not. (Or, more precisely, they are always already saturated with values from the moment that they are experienced as facts.) Kermode's attempt to secure his literary value of pleasure/dismay from any sort of axiological mediation thus eventually bumps into a sort of conceptual incoherence kindred to what we have seen in other defences of canonicity, only Kermode seems wistfully to imagine judgement-as-taste as also becoming the ground of and gatekeeper to the profession. By refusing to acknowledge the other values that would prop up his insistence that the 'collision of pleasure and dismay' is present in canonical texts in the fashion he has described and worth caring about so much as to serve as the basis for an entire profession, he can only say, in effect, either you get it or you don't, and if you don't, you should stop talking about literature.[48] Faced with the prospect in which literary value is only experienced as such within an infinitely receding axiological network, he would like to transform the portion of the network comprising the institution of literary criticism so that all its actors ascribed value in the same way – the way that he does (if not necessarily to the same text). Unfortunately, for Kermode, there will always be those who favour the cheap wine.

Canonicity is dead: long live canonicity

In the wake of this perhaps ungenerous reading of Kermode's defence of canonicity, let me reiterate that I am not arguing that his or any of the other defences that I have considered is inadequate – in the sense that categorically better defences might be marshalled – or that this general endeavour is not a worthwhile one. Rather, as I mentioned in the preceding chapters, defences of canonicity, as ontological defences of literary value, are among the crucial tasks of the field of literary studies. Complementary with rather than antagonists to genealogical analyses of literary value, they help to chart the expanse of the network of literary valuing. A further consideration of why this is so, what its implications are for how we go about teaching and studying literature, and how we might then navigate the problem of canonicity, is the task of this final section.

What the prior sections of this chapter have sought to trace is the double-bind of canonicity, the basic idea of which I introduced with the chapter's pair of epigraphs. If we avoid defending canonicity, being aware of its ideological and conceptual pitfalls, but retain the category of the literary (in however limited a fashion), canonicity inevitably reemerges in some unformulated but logically mandated way whether we acknowledge it or not. But if we do acknowledge this reemergence and accordingly seek to provide some formulation for canonicity, we find it always slipping from our grasp into the endless relays of interlinked networks of value. To refuse to recognise that slipping is to chase our own tails, arguing some untenable form of the tautological claim that canonicity is the quality of canonical texts. Yet to recognise those networks, even vaguely, is to discover that the values that would finally give canonicity axiological ballast both keep circling us back to where we started and are always just around the corner (of the next mediation), never quite in reach, and that we cannot prevent those cascading mediations from potentially involving values that we may find anathema.

One seemingly ready solution to this double-bind is that which Guillory proposes in his response to Kermode: why not just discard canonicity but keep literary value? Once we have recognised that there is no single scale upon which the value of all texts may be weighed, should not our canonical burden be lifted – should not we be free to enjoy literature, and the study of literature, without needing literature also to serve some larger purpose that is ultimately not literary and perhaps ideologically problematic? The ethically and politically charged nature of critical discourse at present suggests that we cannot so easily be let off the hook, and the formulations of the preceding chapters help explain why. If ascriptions of value to features of textual manner occur differentially by way of mediations of other ascriptions of value across the axiological network, then in most if not all cases, among the most proximate mediating ascriptions will be ones involving like features of perceived manner in other texts. Hence, our ascriptions of value to textual manner emerge differentially not just in kind but also in degree. In short, within the network of literary valuing, judgements of literary value inevitably include judgements of relative literary value.

I am of course just stating the obvious, in a rather abstract, convoluted fashion, which the simplest example illustrates. If I find, say, the stress pattern of two lines of text musical, I am able to do so in part because 'musical' is an established literary value that other pairs of lines have in greater or lesser amounts, as made available to me through mediated value ascriptions, whether mine or other actors'. Thus, while we may readily follow Guillory in refusing to enthrone a single quality as the principle of canonicity, we may not so easily follow his assumption that we may have literary value without hierarchy. Although there is not a single scale of literary value as Kermode seems to wish there were, as long as texts seem to possess similar features of manner, the value ascribed to them, because it is differential, is in practice unavoidably scalar. Indeed, as the sheer ubiquity of 'top ten' lists for this or that attest, one the greatest pleasures that we seem to get from literature, or any aesthetic experience, is that of relative judgement and the construction of hierarchies of value.

Such hierarchies of value are necessarily idealising within the vector of the scale that they delineate, and they therefore entail a version of the present absence dynamic that we saw with extensions to totalising values in Chapter 3. Once value becomes scalar, every judgement involving that value – however provisional, spontaneous or minute – is haunted by the shadow of that value imaginable as fully realised, perfectly achieved, available in the greatest plenitude possible. Integral to each act of scalar judgement is an invocation of the phantasmagorical perfection required for that judgement to occur – an invocation that may be more-or-less conscious, more-or-less conceptually definite and more-or-less temporally stable. In an axiological network constellation of any persistence, these invocations may crystallise into a palpable principle of hierarchy, which is to say more simply that what may emerge out of any top ten list is a principle of top-ness, however implicit or inchoate that principle may be.

Canonicity is this principle of top-ness writ large. It is the notional ideal that any act of scalar judgement, which is to say virtually any recognition of the literary, necessarily invokes. It is the simulacrum of the ideal literary work, according to whatever specific ascription of value is being performed, that that ascription requires and invents.[49] It is, for example, the imagined perfect realisation of Scholes's 'combination of textual pleasure and power', Miller's 'very condensed condensation', Prendergast's 'wonder' and Kermode's 'collision of pleasure and dismay'. But it is also the more inchoate or even wholly unacknowledged principle at work when we select texts for syllabi, choose an anthology or decide which conference sessions to attend. It is that which any defence of the value of literature or of literary study – on the basis of, say, literature's facilitation of critical thinking, empathy, negotiation of ethical complexity and cross-cultural understanding – necessarily invokes, as the imagined vessel conveying the maximum possible amount of all those virtues. In short, we cannot study something that we call literary without positing the category of canonicity, whether or not that category explicitly enters into our research or classrooms. Nor can we avoid canonicity within a cultural studies framework that features literary texts merely as one cultural artefact among others. For, as I argued in Chapter 1, insofar as we recognise that someone has registered those texts as literary, someone else's canonicity – through a series of transmutations through the network of literary valuing – becomes also our canonicity.

While canons themselves are wholly mutable, therefore, we cannot eliminate canonicity without also eliminating the category of the literary. And this returns us, one final time, to the dilemma that has been this chapter's overarching purpose to describe. On the one hand, many of us hesitate to formulate principles of canonicity because of what we have come to learn about canonicity's conceptual pitfalls and ideological liabilities. And then, with the resulting aporia in the centre of our object of study, we find that in some important respects we have nothing to counter scepticism towards the value of our subfield or discipline as a whole, since these institutional formations cannot escape resting upon the value of that object. On the other hand, those of us who do venture to formulate principles of canonicity produce accounts that cannot withstand the very conceptual pitfalls and ideological liabilities that keep the rest of us at bay. When we attempt to fill the aporia left by our reluctance to judge, we cannot help but reproduce the problems that led to that very reluctance. The question, then, is where do we go from here?

Although any answer must necessarily be provisional, if we approach the problem in the simple terms of bad faith (relying on canonicity even while not believing in it) versus blind faith (committing to canonicity, regardless of the consequences), one possible response readily emerges: to have faith in the necessity of having faith. That is, we may explicitly embrace the central role of canonicity and simultaneously make reflection on the intractable challenges of formulating canonicity's principles itself one of the field's defining tasks, both in scholarship and in the classroom. As I suggested in the preceding chapter, some degree of an explicit adoption of an axiological framework may be beneficial in this regard. By simply acknowledging something like that framework as the field's big tent, we would bring to the surface the axiological negotiations that we are already performing, and the field as a whole might thereby be better oriented towards understanding the intractable challenges of canonicity as one of its ongoing tasks. If we were then to draw on this framework as way to delineate our own positionality within the axiological network, as I also suggested, we might better recognise the everyday work that we do – say, putting together a syllabus, writing an annotated bibliography, producing a critique of a scholarly tradition – as scalar ascriptions of value that are mediating others' scalar ascriptions of value and, in this way, invoking canonicity by creating hierarchies of value. We could then turn some of our attention to those invocations, investigating in some form or another the manner and extent of the traversal of the axiological network that our work necessarily involves. In other words, in performing the work that we are already doing, we would also be putting our axiological cards on the table, so to speak, so that both we and our scholarly and pedagogical interlocutors may consider what it means to have a winning or losing hand. This disclosure, moreover, would have the benefit of possessing a ready answer to the question of 'why should we care about *that*', for it is precisely an explanation of why we care.

As a pedagogical example of this sort of response to the problem of canonicity, I offer an instance of my own recent experience – or, less arrogantly and more accurately, an example of an awkward pedagogical collision with the problem of canonicity that baldly exhibits the very inchoateness that I have described for others, in response to which I sought to cobble together a more coherent approach. Not long after I arrived at Agnes Scott College in 2015, I recognised that my new institutional home afforded an opportunity to rework the *Canterbury Tales* course that I referred to at the beginning of Chapter 1, to transform the course formally in ways that for years it had been informally tending. As its mission statement reads, 'Agnes Scott College educates women to think deeply, live honorably and engage the intellectual and social challenges of their times', and students embrace this mission passionately. Exceptionally diverse racially, socioeconomically and in sexual orientation, the students as a group are nonetheless generally united in their progressive attitudes toward gender and LGTBQ+ issues.[50] Given this institutional context, the fact that over the years gender and sexuality had increasingly been taking centre stage in my pedagogical approach to the *Canterbury Tales* and the lack of any specific mandate for teaching Chaucer at all, I decided to refashion the course to make it one of the rotating topics for the 'Studies in Gender and Sexuality' course that is cross-listed with the Women's, Gender and Sexuality Studies department, rechristening it 'Gender, Sexuality and Chaucer'.

The first time that I taught the course, I naturally focused on the importance of the cross-listing. In the terminology of this book, I presented as the course's axiological network anchor point progressive values regarding gender and sexuality, assuming that what we would care most about would be feminist theory and criticism, gender and sexuality theory, and the injustices that these focuses would bring into view. Chaucer and his works were, in this respect, one or more mediations away in the network, nudged from the centre in favour of an initial set of values that I believed I shared with the students. Hence the aim of the course was to discover what light the study of a premodern literary text such as the *Canterbury Tales* could cast on our more central concerns, most often by way of comparisons and contrasts between medieval and modern.

As the semester progressed, however, I increasingly felt the pressure that this approach put on the rationale for focusing on Chaucer rather than any other premodern author or just any text whatsoever. When students inquired into what the study of Chaucer could tell them about modern feminist theory, for example, Chaucer's massive shortcomings as a feminist quickly and often became the most imposing topic in the room. We continually bumped into the question of why, in order to study gender and sexuality, we were studying texts by a relatively prosperous white fourteenth-century Englishman, one whose literary representations of gender and sexuality – no matter how ironic, ambiguous and self-reflexive – plainly reproduce elements of Western misogyny.[51] We bumped into the very question, that is, that has recently been cogently and urgently reiterated by a number of feminist medieval literary scholars – the question of whether, in respect to progressive values of gender and sexuality, Chaucer's works are not just beside the point but in fact detrimental. As Suzanne Edwards puts it in one of the two recent special issues of *ChR* that, broadly speaking, consider this topic,

> [F]eminist scholarship [by continuing to centre Chaucer's works] has risked upholding the heteronormative, misogynist, and white supremacist presumptions that have made Chaucer a privileged object of academic study. The question of whether Chaucer is the proper object of feminist medieval studies remains an open one.[52]

Or, as Sarah Baechle and Carissa Harris query in their introduction to the other special issue, 'How can we, as scholars committed to ethics and social justice, write about or teach Chaucer's work without upholding the patriarchal and white supremacist institutions the poet and his oeuvre have advanced?'[53]

To be sure, I began the semester equipped with what I believed was a set of student-friendly prompts for considering this question, but I soon had to admit (to myself) that none of them was wholly adequate. The axiological orientation of the course asked students to find ways to link Chaucer to the more urgent concerns of gender and sexuality, and most students achieved this by taking the ready path of focusing their contributions to discussion and especially their papers on Chaucer's shortcomings or just plain toxicity in those respects. Such a focus as a scholarly project has performed and continues to perform the salutary work of disenchantment, of inspecting the House of Chaucer and discovering the holes in the roof and the skeletons in the basement that overeager prospective purchasers wilfully overlook. Inasmuch as other scholarly projects (my own not excepted) continue to perpetuate Chaucer's enchantment, the former project bears repetition and elaboration.[54] In the context of my course, however – in which most students had at best only a very vague sense of a House of Chaucer to begin with – I found myself in the awkward position of needing to build that house for a sceptical audience just so that we had a reason to tear it down.

One solution to this awkwardness would have been simply to walk away from the falling-down house altogether, as Edwards in particular seems to recommend. But in the middle of the semester that remedy obviously would have incurred an even more disorienting awkwardness, and so I stuck with the basic plan, tweaking it as best I knew how. Over and over, the students expressed informed, perceptive views about Chaucer's shortcomings as a feminist, but the sheer repetition of this line of argument, applied to this text and that, began to feel like shooting fish in a barrel. While on the whole the students did gain a more historically detailed, nuanced understanding of the longevity and intricacy of Western misogyny and patriarchy, this served mostly to fill in the gaps of the picture of the past that they had already largely drawn. Pedagogically, I felt that I had let them down, as they deserved an educational experience that went beyond such a repetitive confirmation of expectations.

Very likely, a more skilled, knowledgeable and creative teacher would have had greater success with the same course framework. And there is no doubt, too, that my identities as a white-passing Asian straight cis man, occupying the authoritative position of professor, affected classroom dynamics in respect to the course's thematic focus. Nonetheless, I am vain enough – and had close enough relationships with some of the students – to believe that no small portion of the awkwardness lay in the course's framework and not just in its delivery. Working on this present book during this time, I was prompted to realise that I had incurred a blind spot very similar to the one that I have described for, say, the letters to the MLA Executive Committee, only in my case it scarcely achieved those letters' strategic success. There was a yawning conceptual gap between the values ascribed to issues of gender and sexuality and the pedagogical requirement to consider these issues in relation to Chaucer. I had sought to provide a rationale for what was manifestly still a practical centring of Chaucer (despite his relegation to the third term in the course title) that did not rely on the proposition that there was something special about Chaucer's works – the very same sort of gap, or inchoateness, that we have seen in the attempts to defend literature without recourse to canonicity.

The actual most basic rationale for the continued centring of Chaucer was, obviously, my own investment in Chaucer's literary value, the inheritance of Chaucer's longstanding canonical status that pervades my experiences of his writing. By leaving that rationale to the side, I founded the course's framework, in effect, on a non sequitur. In response, taking cues from my work on this book, the next time that I taught the course I reversed the axiological polarity of my approach. Laying my axiological cards on the table, in place of the basic question of what we can learn about gender and sexuality by studying Chaucer, I framed the course as an inquiry into what we can learn about Chaucer by way of feminist, gender and sexuality theory. The value of Chaucer's texts, that is, I established as one of the course's premises, just as it had been positioned for countless other courses back in the era before the so-called culture wars – Gates's 'medieval never-never land'. But, in contrast to what I suppose to have been the case in that never-never land, I made this premise explicit and described it as what it is: contingent. Chaucer's literary value would not be an unquestionable, mysterious aura of greatness, but an institutionally established and perpetuated privileging of one author over others, a privileging that has without question been sometimes complicit with other kinds of privileging through the various networks of other-than-literary values with which his literary value has been interlinked.

Within this framework, the course evolved into an exploration of why anyone might value Chaucer's writing enough to find rewarding the discovery of the complex ways that it represents and meditates upon gender and sexuality, no few of which ways, notwithstanding their complexity, we might find discomforting or simply reprehensible. While students once again readily perceived that Chaucer was no feminist, they more often took that perception as point of departure rather than a conclusion. That point of departure led them to see how, among other things, Chaucer's artistry so often depends upon the contradictions and repressions of a patriarchal social order that shaped him and in which he was complicit. As a result, we gained more insight into both Chaucer's artistry and those contradictions and repressions and their long histories. In effect, we more successfully traced the complex relays among value ascriptions – my own, but more importantly those of the students, those within Chaucer's texts and intertexts and those within Chaucer scholarship – following them from literary values (Chaucer's and others') to the values of various other kinds that attend diverse understandings of gender and sexuality. In presenting canonicity explicitly as an institutional fact and also a problem to be explored, I found that even anticanonical impulses led to rich critical discussions. The problem of canonicity proved to be generative rather than limiting.

I do not wish to generalise this experience beyond what its circumstances may bear. Agnes Scott's distinctive student population, my identities and teaching style, the particular classroom dynamic, the agency I had in respect to the curriculum, and so on, were all inextricable contributors to the outcome. Under different conditions – say, with a classroom including many cis white men, under an institutional mandate to teach Chaucer every year – something more in line with my first approach could be a better fit. I do not mean, therefore, to suggest how Chaucer ought to be taught or even to insist that he be taught at all. Additionally, I do not mean to claim that my revised approach represents any special innovation. Rather, I suspect that wiser teachers than I have long taught Chaucer in a similar fashion.[55] In fact, this suspicion significantly motivated my choice of this example, as it suggests that my recommendation of having faith in the necessity of having faith does not necessarily require major adjustments to current practice. In my case, the adjustments consisted of just foregrounding a previously occluded belief in Chaucer's literary value and simultaneously encouraging an inquiry into the conditions that sustain that belief.

In a rudimentary way, the example of my pedagogical having faith in the necessity of having faith points to a more general, far-reaching affordance of an explicit, reflexive inquiry into the problem of canonicity, namely, a route to the effect that I described in the previous chapter's discussion of defamiliarisation. Canonicity, as the idealised simulacrum of literary value that any scalar act of literary valuing invokes, lends itself rather directly to extension from features of textual manner to totalising kinds of other-than-literary value – as we saw exhibited in Boccaccio's extension of features of textual manner to the duelling totalising values of God and power, by way of the canonical value of Dante's literary achievement. Canonicity, as itself a present absence that may be manifested in any specific act of literary valuing, easily draws into itself more totalising present absences, functioning in this way rather like an axiological black hole. Because canonicity is quite catholic in the range of these totalising kinds of value that it attracts, the more energy that we put into a reflexive negotiation of the problem of canonicity in any particular situation, the more that negotiation may disclose of our axiological environment. The more thoroughly, precisely and reflexively that we explore why, say, Chaucer's works deserve canonisation, the more profoundly and exhaustively we may plumb our own axiologies. By this I do not only mean that we confront our own value ascriptions in an unusually broad and deep manner. I mean also that we recognise both the contingency of those value ascriptions and, simultaneously, the necessity that they function in any given moment as if they were not merely contingent. In respect to this chapter's epigraphs, we recognise that in judging, we risk aligning ourselves at some level with values we find anathema, but we also recognise that we nonetheless may not cease judging: once again, we have faith in the necessity of having faith. And so at the very least we are on guard, and we empower others to hold us to account for the judgements that we cannot cease making but which we can alter.

This kind of converse, dynamic and indeterminate pair of axiological recognitions, I argue, is one that literary study in both its scholarly and pedagogical forms is particularly well suited to foster. Although these recognitions are potentially available in virtually any field, within literary studies, because of the very problem with its object of study – the problem of literary value, the problem of canonicity – they may powerfully facilitate a richly varied and extensive engagement with the category of value per se. They may shine a spotlight on our being as actors in an axiological universe, on how value ascriptions are begotten by and beget other value ascriptions, and on the relations between values and the actors ascribing those values, which include the so-called objects to which values are ascribed. Whether in a monograph, syllabus or class discussion, if we bring to the surface the relays from 'I like this book' to 'you ought to read this book' to 'this book is good for you' – even while still seeking, in good faith, to construct those relays – literary studies can illuminate the mediations that link 'like' to 'good' across a wide range axiological domains.[56] In short, that we cannot avoid canonicity, even if we would like to, may itself be worth making one of our central concerns – as it is something that we all share within the experience of literary study. And we may then use to our advantage the fact that canonicity also happens to be that which much of the extra-academic world has already long understood to be our area of expertise.

Notes

1 Henry Louis Gates Jr., *Loose Canons: Notes on the Culture Wars* (Oxford: Oxford University Press, 1992), pp. 35, 178.
2 Ankhi Mukherjee, *What Is a Classic? Postcolonial Rewriting and Invention of the Canon* (Stanford: Stanford University Press, 2014), p. 9. Even more recently, Sarah Baechle and Carissa M. Harris, 'The Ethical Challenge of Chaucerian Scholarship in the Twenty-First Century', *ChR*, 56:4 (2021), 311–21, have trenchantly voiced this sentiment in respect to Chaucer's canonicity specifically. For a personal reflection on the ideological complicity of Chaucer's canonicity and that of the white male canon more generally, see Sierra Lomuto, 'A White Canon in a World of Color', *Medievalists of Color*, http://medievalistsofcolor.com/race-in-the-profession/a-white-canon-in-a-world-of-color/ (2019; accessed 4 January 2020); and for Lomuto's thoughts on the complicity of the wider field of medieval studies, 'Becoming Postmedieval: The Stakes of the Global Middle Ages', *postmedieval*, 11:4 (2020), 503–12, as well as other contributions to this special issue devoted to 'Race, Revulsion, and Revolution', guest edited by Mary Rambaran-Olm, M. Breann Leake and Micah James Goodrich. For just one example of literary critical work in this

regard, see Nahir I. Otaño Gracia, 'Borders and the Global North Atlantic: Chaucer, Pilgrimage, and Crusade', *English Language Notes*, 58:2 (2020), 35–49. For an extension of this critique to the humanities more generally, as well as a set of recommended responses, see Waqas Khwaja, 'Reimagining the Humanities in a Transcultural, Post-Truth World', in Waseem Anwar and Nosheen Yousaf, *Transcultural Humanities in South Asia: Critical Essays on Literature and Culture* (New York: Routledge, 2022), pp. 28–40. For an opinion piece that argues, somewhat contrastingly, that 'those from non-privileged and black and ethnic minority backgrounds' should not be 'robbed of the chance to read texts foundational to the history of English literature', especially Chaucer (written in response to the University of Leicester's proposal to eliminate courses in medieval literature), see Shazia Jagot, 'Students from All Backgrounds Need Access to the Literature of Every Age', *Times Higher Education*, www.timeshighereducation. com/blog/students-all-backgrounds-need-access-literature-every-age (2021; accessed 14 September 2021).
3 E.g., in her consideration of the heated exchange between Rita Dove and Helen Vendler regarding Vendler's 2011 review of Dove's *Penguin Anthology of Twentieth-Century Poetry*, Mukherjee – although mostly sympathetic to Dove – declares as 'justified' Vendler's 'valorization of difficult art over lazy demands for instant gratification' (p. 12).
4 In respect to late medieval English study, such is also more-or-less the nature of the project that Laura Saetveit Miles and Diane Watt, 'Introduction: Women's Literary Culture and the Medieval English Canon: Gender and Genre', *SAC*, 42 (2020), 285–93, have recently outlined.
5 These studies include many of those that I termed ontological in orientation in Chapter 2. In addition to those that I consider below, for just few other, relatively recent ones, see William Franke, *The Revelation of Imagination: From Homer and the Bible through Virgil and Augustine to Dante* (Evanston: Northwestern University Press, 2015); Robert Alter, *Canon and Creativity: Modern Writing and the Authority of Scripture* (New Haven: Yale University Press, 2000); and David Fishelov, *Dialogues with/and Great Books: The Dynamics of Canon Formation* (Brighton: Sussex Academic Press, 2010). Of course, genealogical analyses of canon formation have continued to appear over the same period, which together with the latter collectively reproduce the field's ever-swinging pendulum between belief and scepticism. See, for example, Günter Leypoldt, 'Singularity and the Literary Market', *NLH*, 45:1 (2014), 71–88.
6 This impression gains some confirmation in the findings of James F. English, *The Global Future of English Studies* (New York: John

Wiley, 2012), which suggest that when information about actual curricular practice is broadly considered, the canon – in the form of a variable, evolving selection of exemplary literary works – has scarcely receded from its central role, although its historical centre of gravity has, predictably, shifted forward.

7 For incipient fifteenth-century vernacular canon-making activities, see, *inter alia*, Trevor Ross, *The Making of the English Literary Canon: From the Middle Ages to the Late Eighteenth Century* (Montreal: McGill-Queen's University Press, 1998); Seth Lerer, *Chaucer and His Readers: Imagining the Author in Late-Medieval England* (Princeton: Princeton University Press, 1993); and my *Poets and Power from Chaucer to Wyatt* (Cambridge: Cambridge University Press, 2007).

8 Marianne Hirsch, 'D023 – Possible MLA Division Changes: Your Advice Needed', email to Kellie Robertson *et al.* (28 March 2013).

9 Ruth Evans, 'Update on MLA Proposals and Chaucerians' Responses', email to New Chaucer Society membership (20 April 2013). Let me emphasise here, as I will again below, that I intend no criticism of Evans – or any of the other leaders within Chaucer studies – for their responses to this proposal. They rather have my admiration for their success. I owe thanks in particular to Professor Evans, who has been unfailingly supportive of my work on this topic.

10 Alastair Minnis and Ruth Evans, letter from NCS President and Executive Director to Marianne Hirsch and Margaret Ferguson, email attachment (17 April 2013).

11 Holly A. Crocker *et al.*, letter from MLA Chaucer Division to Marianne Hirsch and Margaret Ferguson, email attachment (19 April 2013).

12 Christopher Cannon, *The Making of Chaucer's English: A Study of Words* (Cambridge: Cambridge University Press, 1998).

13 Ralph Hanna, *Pursuing History: Middle English Manuscripts and Their Texts* (Stanford: Stanford University Press, 1996), pp. 14–15.

14 David Matthews, *The Making of Middle English, 1765–1910* (Minneapolis: University of Minnesota Press, 1999); Stephanie Trigg, *Congenial Souls: Reading Chaucer from Medieval to Postmodern* (Minneapolis: University of Minnesota Press, 2002); Tim William Machan, *Textual Criticism and Middle English Texts* (Charlottesville: University Press of Virginia, 1994); and Thomas A. Prendergast, *Chaucer's Dead Body: From Corpse to Corpus* (London: Routledge, 2004).

15 Robert W. Frank and Edmund Reiss, 'Bringing Comfort and Mirthe', *ChR*, 1:1 (1966), 1–3 (1–2).

16 Patricia Clare Ingham, 'Why Chaucer Now?', *The Chaucer Blog*, https://chaucerblog.net/2015/05/why-chaucer-now/ (2015; accessed 4 January 2020). Ingham concludes this piece by defending the continued division between the two groups on the basis of the scholarly productivity that has been in part spurred by their separation. As with the letters to the MLA, she does not attempt to defend Chaucer's value but instead the scholarship that Chaucer inspires.
17 The presider of the session, Eve Salisbury, has posted on *Humanities Commons* an overview of the session's topic and rationale, as well as Evans's 'What Is a Chaucer' and the papers of three of the other four panellists. See Eve Salisbury, 'Rethinking the Place of the Author', *MLA Commons*, https://mla.hcommons.org/groups/middle-english/forum/topic/rethinking-the-place-of-the-author/ (2015; accessed 13 October 2021).
18 Ruth Evans, 'On Not Being Chaucer', *SAC*, 44 (2022), 3–26 (10). See also, in addition to the aforementioned 'What Is a Chaucer', Evans's 'The Chaucer Society, Victorian Medievalism, and the Nation-State: Englishness and Empire', *The Chaucer Blog*, https://chaucerblog.net/2018/03/the-chaucer-society-victorian-medievalism-and-the-nation-state-englishness-and-empire/ (2018; accessed 4 January 2020).
19 My familiarity with this text (and my decision to pick it apart here as an exemplar of incoherence) derives from the fact that I produced the first draft of it in my role as Associate Chair of Curriculum in the IU South Bend English department.
20 Azade Seyhan, 'Why Major in Literature – What Do We Tell Our Students?', *PMLA*, 117:3 (May 2002), 510–12.
21 Paul Jay and Gerald Graff, 'Fear of Being Useful', *Inside Higher Ed*, www.insidehighered.com/views/2012/01/05/essay-new-approach-defend-value-humanities (2012; accessed 4 January 2020). For just one example of a recent editorial that similarly emphasises the skills fostered by humanities majors (in this instance specifically literature majors), see Paula M. Krebs, 'Our Majors Can Fix Things', *MLA Newsletter*, 53:1 (2021), 1, 5, although here Krebs focuses more on activist skills than professional ones.
22 Robert Scholes, *English after the Fall: From Literature to Textuality* (Iowa City: University of Iowa Press, 2011), pp. 34, 24–25.
23 In 'The English Curriculum after the Fall', *Pedagogy*, 10:1 (2010), 229–40, an earlier formulation of some of the arguments of *English after the Fall*, Scholes offers English faculty strategies for how to retain 'great books in English' in their courses despite the fact that

such books 'have lost much of their appeal and interest' and that what 'people want from us' are 'those things we consider most trivial and annoying: instruction in the basic functions of language' (p. 233).

24 Damon Horowitz, 'From Technologist to Philosopher: Why You Should Quit Your Technology Job and Get a Ph.D. in the Humanities', *The Chronicle of Higher Education*, www.chronicle.com/article/from-technologist-to-philosopher (2011; accessed 4 January 2020).

25 As in Harold Bloom, *Shakespeare: The Invention of the Human* (New York: Riverhead Books, 1998).

26 In Horowitz's piece the Shakespeare reference is given as just one realisation among many others.

27 Mark Miller, 'Why Do We Care About Chaucer?', *The Chaucer Blog*, https://chaucerblog.net/2014/05/what-do-we-care-about-chaucer/ (2014; accessed 4 January 2020).

28 See, e.g., Gerald Graff, *Professing Literature: An Institutional History* (Chicago: University of Chicago Press, 1987); Ian Hunter, *Culture and Government: The Emergence of Literary Education* (Basingstoke: Macmillan Press, 1988); and Gauri Viswanathan, *Masks of Conquest: Literary Study and British Rule in India* (New York: Columbia University Press, 1989).

29 Cf. my discussion near the end of Chapter 3 of the applicability of an axiological framework to critical descriptions of the dynamics of these sorts of self-interrogating texts.

30 See, e.g., Mark Miller, *Philosophical Chaucer: Love, Sex, and Agency in the Canterbury Tales* (Cambridge: Cambridge University Press, 2004).

31 Matthew Arnold, *Culture and Anarchy* (Cambridge: Cambridge University Press, 1993), p. 190. As John Willinsky, 'Matthew Arnold's Legacy: The Powers of Literature', *Research in the Teaching of English*, 24:4 (1990), 343–61, has observed, Arnold's 'entire poetic project was decidedly interested in elevating a literary canon that assisted a nation in finding what he believed to be its best self, whether insensibly in schools or openly through criticism' (p. 358).

32 Lynn Arner, 'Why Do We Care More About Chaucer Than Gower?', *The Gower Project*, https://thegowerproject.wordpress.com/2015/01/03/why-do-we-care-more-about-chaucer-than-gower/ (2017; accessed 21 July 2017). For the much more expansive arguments about Chaucer and Gower that this blog post transmits in capsule form, see Arner, *Chaucer, Gower, and the Vernacular Rising: Poetry and the Problem of the Populace after 1381* (University Park: Pennsylvania State University Press, 2013).

33 Thomas A. Prendergast, 'Canon Formation', in Marion Turner (ed.), *A Handbook of Middle English Studies* (Hoboken: John Wiley, 2013), pp. 239–51 (243, 244, 247).

34 *Ibid.*, pp. 247, 248.
35 Frank Kermode, *Pleasure and Change: The Aesthetics of Canon*, ed. Robert Alter (Oxford: Oxford University Press, 2004), pp. 15, 16.
36 *Ibid.*, pp. 28, 29, 30, 34, 38, 50.
37 Geoffrey Hartman, 'The Passing of the Canon', in *Pleasure*, ed. Alter, pp. 53–64 (57, 61, 62).
38 *Ibid.*, pp. 63–4, 64.
39 John Guillory, 'It Must Be Abstract', in *Pleasure,* ed. Alter, pp. 65–75 (65).
40 *Ibid.*, pp. 68, 70, 74.
41 Kermode, *Pleasure*, p. 87.
42 Guillory: 'I believe that the greatest art gives us very complex pleasures indeed, but I don't think that such pleasure must come at the expense of other kinds of pleasure, or require their derogation as merely simple' ('Abstract', p. 75).
43 Kermode, *Pleasure*, p. 88.
44 *Ibid.*, pp. 85–6.
45 *Ibid.*, pp. 85, 88.
46 Lucien Karpik, *Valuing the Unique*, trans. Nora Scott (Princeton: Princeton University Press, 2010), pp. 38, 39.
47 Pierre Bourdieu, *Distinction: A Social Critique of the Judgement of Taste*, trans. Richard Nice (Cambridge, MA: Harvard University Press, 1984), p. 190, emphasis in original.
48 'Not everybody has a nose in this sense', Kermode observes, and 'if you don't have one, you should seek some other form of employment.' He then adds, 'Of course a great many people do that, and it is no disgrace' (*Pleasure*, p. 85).
49 Cf. the formulation for the 'classic' of Pascale Casanova, *The World Republic of Letters*, trans. Malcolm DeBevoise (Cambridge, MA: Harvard University Press, 2004): 'The classic embodies the very notion of literary legitimacy, which is to say what is recognized as *Literature:* the unit of measurement for everything that is or will be recognized as literary' (p. 15).
50 According to its 2020–2021 Fact Book, in that year 34.8 per cent of the college's undergraduates were 'Black or African-American', 31.0 per cent were 'White', 14.6 per cent were 'Hispanic' and 6.2 per cent were 'Asian', with smaller percentages for other racial/ethnic categories or 'Two or more races'. Unusually for a selective small private liberal arts college, therefore, it has no racial majority. The proportion of Pell-eligible students was 41.3 per cent. According to data made available by *The New York Times*, in 2017 the median family income of an Agnes Scott undergraduate was $63,600, whereas that of Mount Holyoke College, similar in many other respects to Agnes Scott, was $110,400 (and that of my alma mater, Williams College, was

$185,800). There is, in other words, solid basis for the college's typically strong showing in *US News & World Report*'s 'social mobility' category. For the Fact Book, see www.agnesscott.edu/institutionalresearch/fact-book.html; for the median family income data, www.nytimes.com/interactive/2017/01/18/upshot/some-colleges-have-more-students-from-the-top-1-percent-than-the-bottom-60.html; for the social mobility rankings, as of this writing, www.usnews.com/best-colleges/rankings/national-liberal-arts-colleges/social-mobility.

51 Although perhaps not also an author whose personal history includes a rape charge, as long believed. See Euan Roger and Sebastian Sobecki, 'Geoffrey Chaucer, Cecily Chaumpaigne, and the Statute of Laborers: New Records and Old Evidence Reconsidered', *ChR*, 57:4 (2022), 407–37, as well as the several appendices and response essays in the same issue.

52 Suzanne M. Edwards, '"Burn All He Has, but Keep His Books": Gloria Naylor and the Proper Objects of Feminist Chaucer studies', *ChR*, 54:3 (2019), 230–52 (231). This number on 'New Feminist Approaches to Chaucer' was guest edited by Samantha Katz Seal and Nichole Sidhu.

53 Baechle and Harris, 'Ethical Challenge', p. 314. For a particularly searching reflection on this question, see Emma Margaret Solberg, 'Response to '#MeToo, Medieval Literature, and Trauma-Informed Pedagogy',' *New Chaucer Studies: Pedagogy and Profession*, 2.2 (2021), 134–53. An important predecessor to this line of inquiry is Elaine Tuttle Hansen, *Chaucer and the Fictions of Gender* (Berkeley: University of California Press, 1992). For the charge that views such as these (specifically citing Seal and Sidhu) are contributing to the waning of Chaucer in the postsecondary curriculum, see A. S. G. Edwards, 'Gladly Wolde He Lerne? Why Chaucer Is Disappearing from the University Curriculum', *Times Literary Supplement* (1 July 2021), pp. 7–8.

54 As Baechle and Harris observe, 'At the same time that Chaucerians are breaking new ground in interrogating Chaucer's formative role in enduring discourses of misogyny, racism, rape culture, and antisemitism, many are still reluctant to acknowledge the magnitude of this role' ('Ethical Challenge', p. 316).

55 See, for example, Mary C. Flannery, 'Good Fun: Cecily Chaumpaigne and the Ethics of Chaucerian Obscenity', *ChR*, 56:4 (2021), 360–77, who offers really helpful reflection on how to approach one of Chaucer's most famous – and increasingly recognisably problematic – canonical qualities.

56 I am riffing here on Catharine R. Stimpson, 'Introduction: Where Is Value Now?', *Profession* (1991), 5.

5

Interpretation

Even more so than the preceding chapter's ambition to treat in the limited space of its pages the ponderously debated topic of canonicity, an attempt to consider the topic of interpretation in the confines of a single chapter would seem at best presumptuous if not merely foolhardy. As with Chapter 4, however, I have sought to calibrate my aim and method to the modest scope of this book's overall project. My objective is simply to explore some of the implications of the ideas so far presented in this book for this particular basic activity of literary scholarship and teaching, in the hope that the very ubiquity of that activity may make the book of some use. My method, as in Chapter 4, is to work dialogically between particular instances of practice and the conceptual knots that they manifest. In no way do I attempt anything resembling a survey of the concept and practice of interpretation. Rather, I follow narrow pathways into the topic, identifying thereby a problem within concrete interpretive practice, considering the problem in light of this book's preliminary theory of literary valuing and, finally, proposing a response.

In the section that follows, I clarify more precisely the chapter's topic and provide an illustrative pair of snapshots of actual literary interpretation in action, so to speak. These examples then serve as touchstones for the next section's identification of a particular problem endemic to the practical activity of interpretation, which takes as its point of departure Stanley Fish's early 1970s critique of the approach to literary study known as stylistics. After suggesting how Fish's critique still applies – and applies generally – to interpretive practice up to the present, at the end of this section I reintroduce my preliminary theory of literary valuing, redescribing in its terms the problem thus far elaborated. In the third section, I trace within the framework of that preliminary theory some of the implications of the problem and provide another illustrative snapshot of interpretation in action. With the basic contours of the problem then established, the fourth section considers the sustained efforts of one celebrated Chaucer scholar, Lee Patterson, to come to grips with it. Serving as a kind of case study, this consideration brings to the fore several of the specific challenges involved in formulating a response to the problem for the purpose of establishing a firm grounding for academic literary study. Using those challenges as cues, the chapter's final section then proposes an alternative response that, while certainly no solution, may nonetheless be generative. The chapter concludes with a description of a pair of recent medievalist literary interpretations that, although in no sense conceived in this book's terms, exemplify the sort of response that its framework may help to facilitate.

Definitions and examples

Given what Rita Felski has called the 'method wars' within literary criticism over the last fifteen years or so, and heeding her observation that 'the fate of a particular phenomenon turns on how narrowly or broadly one defines one's terms', I should clarify here at the outset how I am using the label *interpretation*.[1] In line with my pragmatic definitions elsewhere in this book, I mean to include under that label all the everyday activities that the field of literary studies has for many decades now more commonly designated as *reading*, as in the ordinary locution of so-and-so's 'reading of Chaucer's *Squire's Tale*'. But with the proliferation of qualifiers that critics today may wish to place before the term *reading* – as a recent handbook lists, 'deep, descriptive, denotative, distant, hyper, just, mere, paranoid, reparative, slow, surface, symptomatic, uncritical, even large' – my umbrella use of *interpretation* must necessarily be very basic.[2] For this book's purposes, I will define the activity of interpretation, I hope uncontroversially, as the registration of some semantic effect of a set of signifiers, for example, the registration of the letters, colours, shape and roadside placement of a stop sign as the command to stop one's vehicle. In the simplest terms, we may call the set of signifiers a *pattern* and that semantic effect *meaning*, and thus interpretation is ascribing meaning to a pattern. All the aforementioned sorts of reading, I contend, may readily be described in these simple terms, although, that said, I do not mean to suggest their identity. Plainly, significant differences remain, which in my simpler terms are matters of the number of relays between meaning and pattern, and of the frameworks in which one conceives of their relation. (Later in the chapter I briefly consider a couple examples of these differences.)

As Felski has observed, the tendency of literary scholarship to avoid the term *interpretation*, along with its philosophical elaboration as hermeneutics, derives from the perception in some quarters that it refers to 'the dogged pursuit of an ultimate, hidden, all-determining truth'.[3] Long before the method wars, the term *reading* was therefore adopted to signal an activity that is in contradistinction more provisional, contingent and plural, in short one that recognises, among other things, the indeterminacy that twentieth-century poststructuralism has taught us to be the condition of all engagements with texts. As Felski elsewhere points out, however, the latter recognition has scarcely impeded the field's actual interpretive activity, when that activity is more generally understood as 'trying to figure out what something means and why it matters'. To the contrary, the poststructuralist axiom of the unreliability of signs has proliferated suspicious approaches to texts, goading 'the impulse to decipher and decode', so that 'more suspicion means ever more interpretation'.[4]

Felski perceives these suspicious approaches to be ubiquitous within literary studies, a perception with which a number of other combatants in the method wars would agree, such as Stephen Best and Sharon Marcus, who have famously named the approaches 'symptomatic reading' and contrasted them with 'surface reading'.[5] Nonetheless, while I do not doubt that suspicious or symptomatic reading corresponds to a longstanding scholarly habitus, I would add as a complementary observation that – at least within the subfields with which I am most familiar – a great deal of considerably less paranoid interpretation remains prevalent. And much of that sort of interpretation (as well as, in fact, much of the symptomatic variety) proceeds more-or-less as if the lessons of poststructuralism regarding the indeterminacy of the act of reading and the intractable uncertainty of establishing meaning had never been aired.[6] Indeed, at least within these subfields, I would judge that the majority of scholarship over the last several decades, while most likely fully aware of the lessons of poststructuralism, has simply shrugged its shoulders and proceeded to construct interpretations – whether large-scale literary arguments about entire works or just local construal of individual passages toward some other end – as if those lessons do not apply. Most of today's most prominent Chaucer scholars, for example, generally operate in this fashion. I will supply brief instances from just two recent studies, chosen on the basis of how celebrated they have been, how exceptionally perspicacious I have found them and my certain knowledge that both authors are conversant with poststructuralism.

With his monograph *Voice in Later Medieval English Literature: Public Interiorities*, David Lawton has revitalised how the category of person or subject is conceived in relation to a text's speaker. At one point in Chapter 7's account of the *Squire's* and *Franklin's Tales*, Lawton argues that the frequent use of narratorial *occupatio* in the *Squire's Tale* serves as a device that radically revises the attitude towards cultural otherness found in the narratives 'of friar travellers to Tartary in the thirteenth and fourteenth centuries'. In those narratives, the first-person narrators are 'puzzled and repelled by the [Tartar] religious beliefs and social practices ... distrusting the people and their culture, diplomatic, angry, and overawed'. In contrast, with the device of *occupatio*, Chaucer's Squire 'takes all these considerations – beliefs, practices, food, manners, even gender and sexuality – and ascribes inability to describe or internalise them not to the interplay of cultures but to that of genre and style, assimilating what is unknown and unknowable to an Arthurian golden age'. Chaucer's resulting 'great achievement is not to exoticize – or to orientalize – but to naturalize what in the earlier accounts was profoundly and forbiddingly alien'.[7] There is plainly no trace in this snippet of interpretation of concern over, say, the indeterminacy of language or how a rhetorical device such as *occupatio* might destabilise propositional inference (nor of a suspicious prying into what Chaucer represses). To the contrary, as is readily evident in the larger context of his argument, in this instance Lawton seeks to replace one definite meaning that other critics have assigned to the frequency of *occupatio* in this tale – namely, that it serves as a characterisation of the narrator, conveying in particular the dramatic irony of the *Squire's* narratorial inadequacy – with a quite different definite meaning, that of a revisionary response to cultural otherness.[8]

Similar moments abound in the otherwise very differently oriented *Chaucer: A European Life* by Marion Turner, a remarkable biography that weaves together a densely textured set of contexts with penetrating readings of Chaucer's oeuvre, developing thereby a capacious account of the meaning and significance of Chaucer's life and works in tandem. In Chapter 19, Turner tackles the end of the *Canterbury Tales* and specifically how readers are to understand the relation of the *Parson's Tale* to the near entirety of the work that precedes it. She acknowledges Lee Patterson's influential account of this relation that 'sees the tale as offering meaning relevant to all human experience, voicing an authority that shifts the text away from the play of the tale-telling contest', so that 'this final tale has a greater authority than the tales that precede it', which suggests in turn 'that Chaucer now capitulates to a religious vision of life, crossing a boundary and closing the text'.[9] Rejecting this account, Turner argues that the tale 'is presented to us as the partial perspective of an individual, like all the other tales', and this perspective 'has a limited vision', one that in particular 'codifies the self in relentlessly simplifying ways'. For Turner, the Parson assumes a 'natural order of social hierarchy' that emphasises 'the inferiority of churls and women' in a way that 'contrasts starkly with the ethical and compassionate emphasis on gentilesse as a quality not determined by gender, class, or age in other tales'. She concludes, 'We have not passed through the liminal zone of the playful tale-telling contest and ended up in the transcendent world of the spiritual Jerusalem', and so the work remains, at the end, 'radically egalitarian'.[10] The underlying interpretive challenge in this case is what to make of the sprawling prose penitential treatise that terminates the *Canterbury Tales* – whether to take it, to put the question in Chaucer's terms, as in earnest or game. Patterson chooses the former, Turner the latter. Neither entertains the poststructuralist possibility of, say, simultaneously both and neither, that is, of undecidability.

My point with these examples is most certainly not to suggest that Turner or Lawton (or Patterson) ought to have recalled poststructuralism or any of its consequences but rather just to illustrate that they plainly felt no need to do so, even though each elsewhere shows familiarity with poststructuralist ideas. Moreover, not only do I believe that these critics are much more typical than unusual in this respect (and certainly my own scholarship is filled with similar moments), but I also suspect that many if not most of us approach our pedagogical activities in this way – teaching, say, Derrida in the morning and encouraging a student to formulate a clear, firm interpretative thesis about the *Wife of Bath* in the afternoon. For many of us, therefore, the everyday activity of interpretation harbours an inchoateness similar to that which in prior chapters I have observed within the everyday activity of literary valuing: namely, a gap between theory and practice that characterises our work in its several dimensions. In the rest of this chapter, I will build the case that these two gaps are not just parallel but mutually implicated – that the problem of literary value necessarily reproduces itself within the sphere of interpretation.

The problem, according to Stanley Fish

My simple definition of interpretation – ascribing meaning to a pattern – directs us to one of twentieth-century literary critical history's starkest articulations of problems endemic to interpretation, as that articulation was formulated more-or-less in those terms. This is Stanley Fish's blistering early 1970s critique of the approach to literary study pursued under the label *stylistics*, a critique which, in the heavy lines with which it was drawn, will quickly lead us to the basic crux with which this chapter is most concerned. Stylistics today, perhaps because of Fish's critique, is not as immediately familiar as many other approaches to literary study, especially in the US, although it remains relatively popular – and indeed practicing stylisticians may greet the recent efforts toward a 'descriptive turn' in literary study with a sense of déjà vu.[11] One of the lines of development out of Russian formalism, stylistics is at once more broadly conversant with the field of linguistics and more humanist in orientation than its cousin, structuralism.[12] As a pair of recent handbooks attest, its range of linguistic concepts and analytical methods is wide and diverse, having branched out from structural linguistics to incorporate ideas from functional, cognitive and pragmatic linguistics, among many others. But all flavours of stylistics share an emphasis, as the editor of one of the handbooks puts it, on establishing 'physical evidence in the text that can either support or falsify' what the editor a bit earlier describes as 'critical statements from the world of literary studies of interpretation and evaluation'.[13] More so than most other approaches to literary study, therefore, stylistics is quite explicit about its identification of pattern as a discrete step in the interpretive process, using linguistic analysis to generate 'physical evidence' that seemingly possesses more-or-less independent status. In this way, the meaning ascribed to pattern, if not free from indeterminacy, in principle obtains a ground firm enough to be verifiable, even falsifiable.

In his 1973 essay 'What Is Stylistics and Why Are They Saying Such Terrible Things About It?', Fish surveys a representative sampling of then-recent stylistic studies of literary texts. What he decisively demonstrates – as even the committed stylistician Michael Toolan admits – is that in each case the stylistician's ascription of determinate meaning to pattern is ultimately either unwarranted or simply a restatement of the pattern as meaning.[14] In the most straightforward instance of this, Fish considers an essay by Louis Milic that focuses on Jonathan Swift's 'habit of piling up words in series and [on] Swift's preference for certain kinds of connectives'. When Milic turns to the meaning of these patterns, he declares that Swift 'is a writer who likes transitions and made much of connectives' and that Swift's 'use of series argues a fertile and well stocked mind'. The first claim, as Fish points out, just restates the pattern (transitions and connectives) as meaning, and the second is merely 'asserted rather than proven because there is nothing in the machinery Milic cranks up to authorize the leap (from the data to a specification of their value) he makes'.[15] The same 'data' or pattern might just as easily be attached to a different, even opposite 'value' or meaning, for example that Swift's mind is overgrown and cluttered. The rest of the instances of stylistic analysis that Fish considers are rather more involved, but nonetheless he easily and persuasively arrives at the same conclusion for each.

Far from providing falsifiable evidence for an interpretation, stylistics therefore underscores one of the basic problems of interpretation that it sets out to solve – the problem, most simply stated, of the hermeneutic circle.[16] Stylistics's inevitable restatement of pattern or unwarranted ascription of meaning really amount to the same sleight of circularity, which is, as Fish remarks in respect to a critique of a stylistic analysis in a later (even more polemical) essay, that 'the pattern emerges under the pressure of an interpretation and does not exist as independent evidence of it'.[17] Either the decision to undertake a particular form of stylistic analysis (e.g., counting connectives) serves the function of an interpretation that is ultimately just restated as the results of that analysis, or an interpretation of another sort directs the stylistician to a pattern that may perhaps plausibly, but in no way necessarily, confirm it. In both cases, like Saussure's signifier, the pattern only materialises through its attachment to meaning.

In the years following Fish's critique, stylisticians have often taken more nuanced or guarded approaches to their work. Toolan, for example, concedes that stylistics cannot serve as 'a discovery procedure for finding interpretations or a means of validating an interpretation', but rather, much more modestly, it establishes 'public' or common evidentiary reference points among readers who might otherwise disagree about a text's meaning.[18] This seems a sound, admirably pragmatic position, but set next to the above examples of Chaucer criticism, it also reveals how much of the ambition of stylistics that it gives up. For plainly those examples of criticism also involve common evidentiary reference points about which readers have disagreed, just ones that have been established in a less systematic, linguistically dense fashion. Yet the fact that the more widespread kind of interpretation that Lawton and Turner practice coincides with stylistics in this respect does not so much further impugn stylistics as it suggests the general applicability of Fish's critique. Just as stylisticians do, Lawton and Turner sight their respective patterns – the *Squire's* use of apostrophe; the tenor, form, position and size of the *Parson's Tale* – well within the horizon of their developing interpretations. As the hermeneutic circle predicts, literary evidence, whether systematically elaborated as in stylistics or more informally established as in the examples of Lawton and Turner, 'emerges under the pressure of an interpretation and does not exist as independent evidence of it'.

Fish's own recognition of the general applicability of his critique, as is well known (and as he charts in *Is There a Text in This Class?*), led him away from the text – as well as from his initial alternative, the reader – to locate determinations of meaning in the 'interpretive communities' in which they occur. Those communities, rather than the text or reader, determine any particular instance of literary meaning by establishing 'the structure of meanings that is obvious and inescapable from the perspective of whatever interpretive assumptions happen to be in force'.[19] This notion, at once intuitive and vague, has provoked no small amount of sometimes heated discussion.[20] For this chapter's purposes, we can put aside Fish's more categorical claims about it and just accept the relatively straightforward premises that shared 'interpretive strategies exist prior to the act of reading', that 'the thoughts an individual can think and the mental operations he can perform have their source in some or other interpretive community' and that any interpretive community involves 'a bundle of interests, of particular purposes and goals'.[21] These premises are generally in line with, say, accounts of the social construction of knowledge, such as the one long ago developed by Thomas Berger and Peter Luckmann, or as extended to practice somewhat less long ago with Pierre Bourdieu's concepts of field and habitus.[22] The three premises may be folded together into the single formulation that interpretations involve mediations of prior interpretive activity that has been institutionalised in some persistent fashion and that carries discernible values.

Put this way, the premises clearly hold for the examples of Chaucer criticism that I have cited and for countless other acts of interpretation in the record of literary scholarship more generally, so much so that the formulation may seem merely a periphrastic amplification of the term *literary criticism*. But I have obviously offered this formulation to emphasise its affinity with the preliminary theory of literary valuing that I developed in Chapters 2 and 3. For whatever in practice actually constitutes an interpretive community (and this remains a sticking point of Fish's theory), such a community, as it carries 'a bundle of interests, of particular purposes and goals', must be coextensive with some portion of the axiological network. Specifically, what must help to hold an interpretive community together as such, functioning in a sense as its skeleton, are what I have termed *axiological constellations* – diffuse, dynamic sets of actors' mediations of the value ascriptions of other actors, organised in proximity to some vector of difference, and extending across time and space.

In this light, *contra* Fish, we may then restore the text to the class, as the text, as well as other nonhuman actors, certainly serves as one of these mediating actors, as I have discussed in earlier chapters and will consider again below. Furthermore, what I have referred to in this chapter as *pattern* is clearly equivalent to – or perhaps a subclass of – what I have in those earlier chapters named textual *manner*, and so the ascription of meaning to pattern would seem wholly parallel with the ascription of value to manner. In fact, the activities are not just parallel but two sides of the same coin. According to Chapter 2's schema for the activity of literary valuing – 'we register a text as literary when we ascribe value to some aspect of its perceived manner' – the perception of aspects of textual manner is reciprocally enabled by the ascriptions of value to them: to perceive aspects of manner as such is already to ascribe value to them. Hence, since pattern is assimilable to manner, the ascription of value to manner must necessarily accompany the ascription of meaning to pattern, for it is the former ascription that makes that pattern recognisable as such. Moreover, as I discussed in Chapter 3, ascribed value obtains definition only in relation to other ascribed values, and in relation to other kinds of value. Thus, since ascriptions of value involve the mediation of prior ascriptions of value, and ascriptions of value necessarily accompany ascriptions of meaning, the activity of interpretation – defined as involving mediations of prior interpretive activity that carries discernible values – is coextensive with, if not identical to, the activity of literary valuing. To consolidate the points in this and the preceding paragraph into a single formulation: meaning emerges in and through the axiological network, and hence *interpretation, at some level and in some fashion, consists of articulation of mediations of value ascriptions transposed as the content of signification*. Or, more simply, meaning is made through mediation of value ascriptions.

To return to the question of why interpretations may proceed untroublingly despite however much interpreters recognise their intractable uncertainty, we may see that the journey from pattern to meaning may occur unhesitatingly because meaning, as it at some level and in some fashion rests upon value ascription mediations, is what makes the pattern visible in the first place. Hence, if today's literary critics seem so often to push aside the lessons of poststructuralism and offer unqualified meanings for a literary work, they do so in part because the alternative would be to pretend that they have not already laid the ground for such meanings when recognising that work as literary in the first place. To consider again my examples of Chaucer interpretation, not only do we see that Lawton's recognition of the Squire's use of *occupatio* as a textual pattern is inseparable from prior interpretations of the meaning of that pattern, but we also see that Lawton's own interpretation involves an ascription of value to the device as a means to represent an alternative to cultural chauvinism and intolerance. His specific reading of the device – as an 'inability to describe' that assimilates 'what is unknown and unknowable to an Arthurian golden age' – transposes as the content of signification ethical values pertaining to the encounter with cultural others. Similarly, Turner's recognition of the pattern of the distinctive disposition of the *Parson's Tale* plainly mediates Patterson's interpretation thereof, among those of others. And her reading of that disposition as in fact not so distinctive but rather as presenting the 'limited vision' of its teller 'like all other tales' – in this instance a vision that 'codifies the self in relentlessly simplifying ways' – transposes as the content of signification the value of egalitarianism, 'the ethical and compassionate emphasis on gentilesse as a quality not determined by gender, class, or age in other tales'.

To be sure, in neither case do I mean to suggest that the interpretive process reduces to the critic's ascribing his or her own values to Chaucer. Although in these instances I find it likely that the critics do hold the values identified, elsewhere both critics have not hesitated to ascribe values to Chaucer that they certainly do not hold. Rather, as I will further elucidate in the next section, my point is that the end product of interpretation, while in no way necessarily predetermined by any set of values, cannot be neatly divided between meaning and value, since when interpretation is carried out under the sign of the literary, value permeates meaning from start to finish.

Value permeation

Admittedly, even with the above qualifications, despite all their abstractions my arguments to this point may still seem to reduce to the commonplace that interpreters' own values, at some level and in some fashion, shape their interpretations – an impression perhaps encouraged by the passages from Lawton and Turner that I selected, which illustrate the general relation between meaning and value unusually straightforwardly. Obviously, countless other instances of interpretation, in their studies and elsewhere, possess more complexity in this regard, and so would require more elaborate unfolding. But in fact my aim here has been not so much to transcend this commonplace as to complicate it, to brush from it the accumulated dust of banality and uncover in the terms of this book's preliminary theory of literary valuing various dimensions of the still vexatious problem underneath. In particular, that the problem of the hermeneutic circle is fed by the spring of the problem of literary value has several implications, a couple of which are readily evident in the Lawton and Turner examples.

First, while I have identified the relation between ascriptions of value and meaning as transpositional, let me reiterate that this does not necessarily – probably not even usually – entail a simple imposition of the interpreter's values upon the text, with 'values' here more narrowly denoting, say, political, ethical, or religious commitments. While such impositions do of course occur, they constitute only a small fraction of possible outcomes. As I described in Chapters 2 and 3, the activity of literary valuing is a reciprocally dynamic one performed in concert with other actors, nonhuman as well as human, and involving a broad and fluid range of kinds of value. Hence, while, say, a particular ethical value may feature prominently in a critic's initial approach to a text, that value's necessary mediations of other actors' ascriptions of that value and others are far from determinate. To see this, we need only to grant (I believe fairly) that Turner and Patterson share the value of egalitarianism. For both of them, in other words, that value was somewhere active in the axiological environment in which they produced their interpretations. What differs, then, are their respective particular sets of mediations of other actors' ascriptions of value that for them in some way connect the disposition of the *Parson's Tale* to the value of egalitarianism – the differences in their respective *pathways* through the network constellations that those mediations trace. Clearly, for example, especially significant are the different ways that each critic mediates Chaucer's relative – even conflicting – ascriptions of literary and spiritual value to the *Parson's Tale*, which along with other mediations lead them to establish opposing meanings for the tale.

In general, especially given the account of the characteristic loose binding of literary value in Chapter 3, we can expect such pathways to be as numerous as there are interpreters, involving mediations of this and that actor's value ascription in this or that fashion. Importantly, sometimes mediations occur as affirmative relations, as with Turner's association of egalitarianism with Chaucer, and sometimes as disavowing ones, as with Patterson's understanding of Chaucer as turning towards a more authoritarian position. Obviously, though, in practice there is typically a great deal of overlap among pathways, especially when one of the actors is the same physical object (e.g., the *Riverside Chaucer*) and others are those that constitute the same general critical approach (e.g., historicism).

Hence, while it is a commonplace that our values, at some level and in some fashion, shape our interpretations, how they do so in any particular interpretive act does not follow merely from just those values. Moreover, let me reemphasise that the shaping does not occur in a single direction. In the activity of ascribing value to particular aspects of textual manner, those aspects in their material instantiations become themselves actors, relay points of mediation in the pathways through axiological constellations that a specific interpretive act traverses. Aspects of textual manner may therefore have discernible if not necessarily predictable effects on the ascriber/interpreter, which is to say, on the determination of the pathways. Put more simply, the values – and hence also the meanings – that we bring to a text are not necessarily those that we leave with, as our encounter with a text involves a hazy set of value mediations, of encounters with other actors' ascriptions of value, whose outcome is not predetermined. Precisely how this reader-text dynamic works is difficult question that for this book's purposes I can at best dance around.[23] Here I will simply reaffirm another commonplace widely held in the field, which is that, while readers' values shape their interpretations, those values in turn may be shaped by those interpretations. I cannot of course speak for Lawton and Turner on this point, but I am certainly aware of moments in my own activities of interpretation – as I am sure my readers are in theirs – in which my understanding of a value that I hold has been altered in the course of that activity. Moreover, as elaborated above, these reciprocal relations may have affirmative or disavowing characters, or some ambivalent combination thereof.

The second and related implication evident in the above examples is that the perceived aspects of textual manner involved in interpretive pathways occur at an enormous range of possible scales and quantities, in these examples from instances of a single rhetorical device in a single tale to all the instances of teller/tale relations across the entirety of the *Canterbury Tales*. It is easy to see, in fact, that no theoretical limits may be placed on these scales or quantities, inasmuch as the aspects of manner that may potentially emerge in relation to ascriptions of value are limited only by the perceptual acumen, energy, opportunity and interpretive creativity of the ascriber. Most typically, instances of interpretive activity will move up and down the scale, and both zero in on and accumulate examples, however their pathways through axiological constellations lead them. But it is plainly methodologically possible to focus on one end or the other, as in, say, the contrasting formalisms of William Wimsatt and Vladimir Propp. Or, to return to the method wars, we may consider descriptive and distant readings as representing two poles in this regard (although, given that Best and Marcus cite both of these methods as versions of surface reading, and advocates of each understand their practice in contradistinction with interpretation, these methods are by no means opposed in principle). For example, we may sight at one end Heather Love's 'close but not deep' descriptive practice as she illustrates it in her focus on the lexis of point of view in a single passage of *Beloved* – a feature of manner that ultimately (despite her disavowal of interpretation) mediates the value of the disclosure of 'the facts of dehumanization' and 'what is irrecuperable in the historical record'.[24] And, at the other end, we may sight a quantitative study by Ted Underwood and Jordan Sellers that aims to establish correlations between diction and literary prestige by applying a statistical model to a large corpus of literature. By taking as their units of analysis such lexical qualities as 'darker' and 'more concrete', they build value ascriptions directly into the identification of their data, only – in this way akin to the manuscript studies scholarship discussed in Chapter 1 – they represent those value ascriptions as someone else's, leaving obscure the mediations that necessary extend to their own activity.[25] Value ascriptions, in short, wholly permeate the activity of interpretation in all its varieties. They are active in ascriptions of meaning from the minutest to the widest levels of pattern, and in the smallest and largest aggregations of examples.

This total permeation by value leads us to another of literary interpretation's familiar conundrums, which is that there is no systematic method or even conventionally agreed upon heuristic for assessing the relative merits of one interpretation in comparison with another. To be sure, such criteria as logical coherence or sound construal of sense are widely shared means for evaluating relative strengths and weaknesses, but by themselves those will not determine the choice between equally accomplished interpretations, such as (in my view) between Turner's and Patterson's of the *Parson's Tale*. Rather – to take myself as an example judge of interpretations – insofar as I might want Chaucer, near the end of his life, to have affirmed an egalitarianism that demotes the *Parson's* dismal view of human life to just one view among others, I might discover that I favour Turner's interpretation. Alternatively, insofar as I might want to mark the distance between Chaucer's situation and that of modernity in order to underscore the values of, say, the latter's secularism and pluralism, or insofar as I might want to recognise the conditions in which an otherwise open-minded individual abandons egalitarianism, I might find myself giving the nod to Patterson's interpretation. I might in fact lean toward Turner's interpretation one day in one context and Patterson's the next in another context. Or I might decide that both hold: that Chaucer, in proto-postmodern fashion, simultaneously embraced and rejected the *Parson's* view. In all instances, inextricably intermixed within my assessment of the critics' argumentation and evidence, though not straightforwardly determinative of it, would be my own ascriptions of literary value to Chaucer in mediation with ascriptions of other values, such as social and ethical ones. To conclude that judgements between interpretations at some level incur value judgements, then, by no means entails a simplistic 'my side or your side' procedure of alignment. It is rather just to say that judgements between interpretations are necessarily made within the axiological network and so are suffused with value at each step. And it is to acknowledge that as a value-permeated activity, responsibly constructed interpretations are not subject to final verification any more than value commitments are, notwithstanding what some stylisticians, the line of hermeneutical thought leading up to and extending from E. D. Hirsch, and other objectively inclined scholars might argue.[26]

Let me provide an additional, slightly more detailed example of Chaucer interpretation – this time an artificially constructed one – to illustrate this conundrum of verifiability, as well as several of the other points above. If there is any passage of Middle English poetry that may be said to be widely familiar, it is this:

> Whan that Aprill with his shoures soote
> The droghte of March hath perced to the roote,
> And bathed every veyne in swich licour
> Of which vertu engendred is the flour;
> Whan Zephirus eek with his sweete breeth
> Inspired hath in every holt and heeth
> The tendre croppes, and the yonge sonne
> Hath in the Ram his half cours yronne,
> And smale foweles maken melodye,
> That slepen al the nyght with open eye
> (So Priketh hem Nature in hir corages),
> Thanne longen folk to goon on pilgrimages,
> And palmeres for to seken straunge strondes,
> To ferne halwes, couthe in sondry londes;
> And specially from every shires ende
> Of Engelond to Caunterbury they wende,
> The hooly blisful martir for to seke,
> That hem hath holpen whan that they were seeke.[27]

One very frequently noticed pattern in this first sentence of the *Canterbury Tales* is its division into two parts, with its initial eleven lines emphasising renewal of the physical world and the following seven emphasising renewal of the spirit. This division, as Roman Jakobson might have described it, is enacted both within the axis of selection (the lexis of spring and penance, respectively) and within the axis of combination (the syntactical organisation in which the first eleven lines serve as an adverbial clause for the next seven).[28] Also usually noticed is how the *rime riche* of the concluding couplet suggests then a blending of the physical and spiritual, in which the spiritual potency of the 'hooly blisful martir' carried by the first homophone serves as remedy for the physical malaise of the second.

I would guess that the vast majority of readers would readily agree that the passage contains this pattern, and yet there would also likely be (and obviously there has been) wide disagreement about what it means. Some might extend the pattern to the trajectory of the entire work and argue, for example, that it synecdochically signals the project – the blending of physical and spiritual – that the rest of the work seeks to realise across myriad dimensions of human life. Others might argue precisely the opposite: that the passage's blending of physical and spiritual signals the problem that besets fallen humanity, which the work illustrates in countless ways and which is finally, with the *Parson's Tale*, transcended, at least in theory. Still others – say, those taking a new materialist approach – might question the nature of the pattern as described, and specifically whether the supposed turn to the spiritual in the twelfth line is instead a false turn and really an extension of the physical, since the ensuing seven lines emphasise what was for Chaucer an actual physical journey undertaken by flesh-and-blood human beings seeking relief from their real corporeal ailments. And of course other ascriptions of meaning to the pattern are not just possible but have been compellingly argued in the long recorded history of the commentary on this sentence.

Since some of these ascriptions of meaning are mutually exclusive, they cannot all be 'correct' in the ordinary way that we understand that judgement. But by now we recognise that the question of correctness, assuming more-or-less equivalent critical competence, ultimately involves values and that it finds its basis in the particular pathways through the axiological constellations of any given interpretation and those of our critical responses to it. The decision about whether the first sentence of the *Canterbury Tales* advocates or condemns a blend of spiritual and physical (and about what sort of blend it might be) depends upon a complex set of reciprocal mediations of others' value ascriptions, including, among many possible actors, mediations of the perceived ascriptions of value to that blend by Chaucer, other medieval actors (e.g., Augustine, Aristotle as transmitted by Arabic writers, etc.) and select modern ones (e.g., global warming, the reader's church, etc.) – mediations that may be affirmative, disavowing or somewhere in between. Furthermore, while the majority of readers will recognise this pattern, that recognition in fact depends upon particular axiological pathways.

Namely, to perceive the pattern as interpretively significant is already to ascribe some sort of value to the very distinction between spiritual and physical, since only within such a metaphysically binary axiological system (and, say, its accompanying masculinist ideology, as Emma Margaret Solberg has trenchantly identified) would the pattern be visible as such.[29] The sentence's syntax, lexis, *rime riche*, and so on, so observed, all become interpretively visible only within that axiology. In sum, as in the snapshots of Lawton's, Turner's and Patterson's interpretations, our construal of the sentence's meaning, whatever it happens to be at the moment, will be wholly permeated by ascriptions of value.

This general condition of permeation, and the consequent inability to develop broadly accepted principles of correctness among competing readings, scarcely entails, however, that the choice among interpretations is arbitrary or that all responsibly constructed interpretations are equivalent. For in few if any pragmatic situations are value commitments experienced as arbitrary, or competing values (such as, for example, justice and mercy) experienced as interchangeable. Nonetheless, inasmuch as the academic field of literary studies is largely constituted by this value-permeated activity of interpretation, the field does face the practical (and sometimes embarrassing) challenge of defining its work in a way persuasively reconcilable with the discourse of rational inquiry that governs the academy. For indeed the annoyingly familiar charge – from sceptical students, colleagues in other disciplines and interlocutors outside the academy – that *our* interpretations are merely just that cannot finally be wholly disavowed. As a result, our endeavours can generate some friction with the usual demand of the discourse of rational inquiry to issue judgements about our objects of study that lend themselves to some sort of shared criteria of evaluation. And this friction in turn takes us back to the gap between theory and practice that I mentioned earlier in this chapter.

I suspect that most of us within the field of literary studies pursue our everyday activities as if this reconciliation with the discourse of rational inquiry has been successfully achieved, even though we are probably aware that at some level it remains a challenge. In our research, we diligently work out carefully constructed rational arguments for textual meaning (*mutatis mutandis*, depending on one's approach and methods), explaining why our readings of the text deserve attention alongside or at the expense of others' readings. And in our teaching we likewise ask students to back up their claims with logic and evidence in order to learn how to intervene responsibly in critical conversations so that they, too, can aspire to producing readings deserving of attention. Most likely, we perform these activities at some level aware of, but probably not very anxious about, the fact that these judgements of critical merit, while we make them all the time, have no firm ultimate ground. Only in situations in which we find ourselves uncomfortably confronted by the value-permeated nature of our work are we likely to find this underlying challenge actually challenging in practice. When, for example, we must determine a grade for a student essay that offers a reading informed by values that we find reprehensible, but which is otherwise logical and well supported, we may find ourselves torn between our commitment to our own values and our commitment to the strictures of the rational discourse of the university.[30] Or when we are asked as part of programme assessment to provide language that substantiates a numerical scale for measuring the learning outcome of, say, 'insight of reading', we may find ourselves struggling to complete that task in a way that will satisfy the university's assessment experts.

To sum up my argument to this point, the particular problem of interpretation that I have so far adumbrated is ultimately inseparable from the problem of literary value that this book has explored in the preceding chapters, and our various inchoate responses to the former problem are essentially a repetition in a different register of our inchoate responses to the latter. As I elaborated in Chapter 4, the problem of literary value, in that case as manifested in canonicity, underlies our regular inability or reluctance to articulate why this or that author or text is more valuable than another, despite those estimations continuing to organise our praxis. What I have argued so far in this chapter is that insofar as we do not then have ready frameworks for accounting for literary value, we also lack frameworks for accounting for the activity of interpretation in those situations in which the value-permeated nature of that activity comes to the fore.

Obviously, however, as this book's several glances back at the history of literary studies attest, those inchoate responses belie the field's virtually continuous attempts to supply precisely those frameworks for value, interpretation and their relation. In Chapter 1, for example, I considered (albeit in a different context) a few of the many ways in which the field has sought to reconcile itself with the discourse of rational inquiry, and indeed it would be accurate, if only part of the story, to say that the field's history consists of these attempts. As reviewed in that chapter, one especially powerful proffered solution has been formalism, since it insists (to collapse together its many varieties and massively oversimplify their nuances) that the field's object of study is in fact a particular class of object, one that possesses something akin to objective properties. Of course, among formalism's difficulties has been (again to oversimplify) how to account for the historical contingency of this class of object, which was the very condition that its predecessor, philology, had taken as its object. If the supposedly objective properties of the formalist text actually vary according to time and place, then, in accordance with the discourse of rational inquiry, the task of the scholar must be one of the objective reconstruction of those times and places, whether that be in the form of philology in its narrow sense of recovery of linguistic usage or its broader one of describing a whole way of life of another time and place. As we know, though, one of the principal reasons why formalism so overtook philology in prominence was that in the latter approach the literary object as such often seemed to disappear (at least according to the formalists). And so the pendulum of literary scholarship swings.[31]

Nonetheless, in both cases the basic conundrum remains the same: the academy's discourse of rational inquiry wants to draw some sort of line between interpreting subject and interpreted object, but the axiologically reciprocal, value-permeated nature of literary study makes this line impossible to draw with any certainty or finality.[32] As a kind of case study, then, it will be instructive to take sustained look at one of the field's more-or-less programmatic attempts to solve this conundrum: the proposed marriage, of sorts, between formalism and philology represented by late twentieth-century historicism, in particular as described and practiced by Lee Patterson. Through this case study, we may identify *in situ*, in more detail and more precisely the conundrum's knotty perplexities. Then, cued by this attempt's relative successes and failures, we may begin to sight a way forward.

The case of Lee Patterson

Among the several prompts behind the development of late twentieth-century historicism, the particular problem of interpretation elucidated above was no small one. In this approach to literary study, the challenge of the entanglement of interpreting subject and interpreted object could be fruitfully engaged in the form of the entanglement of the present and the past. Feeding off of the literary theoretical innovations of the decades that preceded, and in contrast with the philological tradition, this approach embraced those entanglements, seeing them not as an obstacle to be overcome but as the fertile soil for a more expansive form of literary scholarship, as in (to cite just the most famous example) Stephen Greenblatt's 'cultural poetics'.[33] Within Chaucer studies, no historicist devoted more of his career to thinking through these entanglements and their implications than Patterson.[34] Indeed, it is no overstatement to observe that interpretation, and specifically interpretation's permeation by values, was one of Patterson's primary concerns across the span of his career. In the preface to his first book, 1987's *Negotiating the Past: The Historical Understanding of Medieval Literature*, after noting the ineluctable conditioning of the historian's view of the past by the historian's present situation, Patterson asserts that 'the various forms of resolution at which historicist negotiations arrive are governed neither by empirical necessity, nor (least of all) by theoretical correctness, but by values and commitments that are in the last analysis political'.[35] Similarly, if rather more simply, in the brief preface to his final book (a 2010 collection of mostly previously published essays), Patterson remarks, '[T]hose of us who seek to understand the past ... are simultaneously trying to understand the present – and, even more pertinently, our own lives, both professional and personal.'[36] And in a series of dense, bracing metacritical excursions spanning these years, Patterson repeatedly grapples with the tangled relations within and between these dyads of understanding and value and past and present, seeking to forge a coherent organisation of them as the basis for literary critical practice.

The second chapter of *Negotiating the Past* represents Patterson's first sustained attempt at this project. At the chapter's outset, Patterson rejects 'the ostensibly value-free procedures and materials of objectivist scholarship' that he perceives much of medieval studies as endorsing, and he instead insists 'that the objects with which the human sciences deal can never be wholly other from the interpreting self over against which they stand; on the contrary, they are themselves constituted by means of the very subjectivity that characterizes the interpreter', and so 'political values operate even at the microlevel of historicist methodology'. This leads him to conclude that 'however much we may be committed to the idea of original meaning, we must finally acknowledge that, in every way it counts, "original meaning" is indistinguishable from "meaning to us" '.[37] The problem of interpretation these points establish is clearly of the same genus as the one that I have aired above; the value-permeated nature of interpretation, for example, indeed makes 'original meaning' inextricable from 'meaning to us'. But Patterson's aim is as much prescriptive as critical. In response to the problem, he advocates a scholarly method that makes explicit the 'values and commitments' that, as he notes in his preface, necessarily underlie one's research, arguing that stating one's 'political commitment' does not entail, as 'traditional historicism' has disparaged, 'constraining dogmatisms' but instead may serve as 'enabling assumptions'. He exhorts the literary researcher 'to locate one's scholarly work ... in a way consistent with what one takes one's political values to be', as such an alignment 'endows the critic's activity with historical consequence: the past we reconstruct will shape the future we must live'.[38] Or, as he reiterates this point a few years later, 'The question is not whether we are going to engage in politically charged critical activity or not. It is, rather, to recognize that since all forms of criticism are evidently and by definition political, which form we choose to practice is an act with consequences.'[39]

So far, then, the way forward that Patterson proposes is (in my terms) to embrace the value-permeated activity of interpretation as such – to use one's value commitments as springboards into interpretation rather than to see them as barriers in the way of the object. As a result, our scholarship may become a mode of activism, one that helps to 'shape the future' in a consequential manner. To put this proposal into practice, the necessary first step would seem to be to articulate one's political values, and, while Patterson does not devote abundant pages to this topic, neither is he reticent. Revealingly, *Negotiating the Past* is dedicated to the memory of Jim Renwick, a leader in Ontario's New Democratic Party with whom Patterson worked. Near the end of the book's second chapter, Patterson indicates an abiding interest in 'adopting an antagonistic stance to the depersonalized, depoliticized, and tranquilized homogenization accomplished by American [individualistic] culture', yet a stance that nonetheless does not 'dispense with the category of individualism altogether', as that would 'deprive the human agent of any purchase upon the social world' and so 'signal the end of a politics we desperately need'.[40] Subsequently, in his 1991 magnum opus, *Chaucer and the Subject of History*, Patterson addresses the topic more expansively, beginning the book not with Chaucer but with the sentence, 'In late-twentieth-century America ... human life is conceived in terms of a basic unit, the autonomous, free, self-determining individual.'[41] In what follows in the book's introduction, Patterson – sympathetically drawing on, among other prompts, the 1985 sociological study *Habits of the Heart* – seeks to chart a path through the Scylla of the politically enfeebling ideology of individualism and the Charybdis of the antihumanist implications of Marxist, psychoanalytic and structuralist accounts of the individual, which he characterises as totalisations that deprive the human subject of any self-determination.[42] Patterson does not offer a label for this political position, but for convenience *social humanism* is perhaps one that we can imagine him as accepting.

With his political commitments on the table, then, the next step in the forging of a coherent literary critical praxis is to clarify the relation between those commitments and the procedures of interpretation in a way that will satisfy the strictures of academic rational inquiry. Building upon his formulations in *Negotiating the Past*, in *The Subject of History*, Patterson develops an intricate, dovetailing two-part strategy for accomplishing this task that will in turn serve as the framework for the chapters on Chaucer that follow. On the one hand, he claims that one of the key manifestations of the ills of individualism is disconnection with the past: 'If the category of the social has faded from view, so too has the category of the historical. Instead of understanding themselves as products of determinative historical processes, modern individuals tend to see themselves as autonomous and self-made.'[43] On the other hand, he argues (and here I am especially oversimplifying) that Chaucer is a particularly worthy object of study not only because he stands on the cusp between medieval and modern conceptions of the subject but also because in his literary works he meditates on the nature of both conceptions and on tensions between them. For these reasons, Chaucer models a path between Scylla and Charybdis from which we may learn. Because Chaucer's 'poetry everywhere records the attraction of modernity but is finally unwilling to annul its own historicity', it is 'worth' studying 'Chaucerian subjectivity', since 'it can perhaps contribute to understanding the issues involved in the dialectical process of self-construction per se'.[44] Put together, these two claims neatly both distinguish and conflate Chaucer's 'original meaning' and his 'meaning to us', as it is precisely by way of the former, which in *The Subject of History* consists of Chaucer's historically specific situation and his distinctive response to it, that the latter – Patterson's commitment to social humanism – may be furthered. In effect, a line emerges between interpreting subject and interpreted object because the value ascriptions that, in general, deny a categorical distinction between subject and object are, in the case of Patterson's brand of historicism, ascribing value to that very line as part of the recognition of that very denial.

There are obviously paradoxes if not simply contradictions in this strategy, which I will consider shortly. But first, to see how Patterson puts this strategy into practice, we may review one of the interpretive episodes in *The Subject of History*. For the book's readings of the *Canterbury Tales*, Patterson shrewdly refurbishes one of the predominant interpretive lenses through which the *Tales* had been read for nearly the entire twentieth century: the so-called dramatic approach, in which the primary literary function of each tale is understood to be the drawing of a portrait of its teller.[45] Patterson, in place of seeing each tale as an elucidation its teller's character, sees them as a series of competing, developing meditations upon character per se, that is, on the nature of subjectivity in relation to history. But the dramatic approach's underlying assumption, that Chaucer closely calibrated each tale to its teller, remains Patterson's enabling one. What Patterson adds is the assumption that Chaucer did so as part of seeking the aforementioned path between Scylla and Charybdis.

For example, Patterson reads the *Merchant's Tale* as a depiction of a proto-modern instance of the autonomous bourgeois subject, one that emerges as such because the mercantile subject, having no class-specific ideology of its own, experiences itself as socially undetermined. Patterson sees this experience of subjectivity exhibited in the tale in the way that its capacious and diverse array of topics all reduce to the limning of the Merchant's interiority:

> it is the *absence* of representability – of, that is, a social identity derived from a confidently articulated class ideology – that renders the Merchant vulnerable to merely personal feelings. Denied a secure prospect upon the world, the Merchant's gaze instead focuses with obsessive attention upon the inner landscape of unsatisfied desire that is staged in his own failed marriage. Lacking an ideology that would legitimize his commercial life and secure his participation in the political world of events, the bourgeois turns instead to the inner world of the self as the space of self-definition ... The *Tale* is pervaded with the contradictions of the Merchant's own feelings about himself: his shame and self-hatred for humiliating himself, his self-pity and anger at having been victimized.[46]

I have quoted this passage at length in order to highlight the proximity of Patterson's reading to the standard dramatic one. In the latter, the *Merchant's Tale* is understood as contributing to the so-called marriage group of tales because the Merchant, prompted by his feelings of 'shame and self-hatred' about 'his own failed marriage', responds to the Clerk's preceding story about an obedient wife with a sardonic story about an adulterous one. What Patterson adds is that it is the Merchant's proto-bourgeois social condition that produces his wholesale fixation on his inner bitterness, as expressed through the tale that he tells: 'Lacking a secure social identity, the Merchant is overwhelmed by an inner selfhood, what he calls at the outset the "soory herte" (1244) that his *Tale* seeks to silence but everywhere expresses.'[47]

For those who have doubted either the applicability of the dramatic approach in general or just its bearing in this fashion on the *Merchant's Tale* in particular, the sleight of hand here will be evident. For the dramatic approach to reading the *Tales*, no matter what one may believe to be its critical value, itself quite plainly issues from the ideology of bourgeois subjectivity. This approach, invented in the twentieth century as an outgrowth of the nineteenth century's increasingly novelistic understanding of the *Tales*, is wholly infused with the ascription of value to the individual that eventually develops into the late twentieth-century individualism that Patterson wishes to resist. In his introduction, Patterson briefly entertains the possibility that the dramatic approach may not in fact correspond to Chaucer's design for the *Tales* and may even be a gross distortion of it. In support of the approach, he cites the Ellesmere manuscript's portraits of the pilgrims and then quickly dismisses doubts by stating that 'it is not by definition anachronistic'.[48] Although this is not the place to contest that dismissal, those familiar with the history of Chaucer criticism will recognise that it is assuredly quite contestable. In short (and to mix metaphors), in his refurbishment of the dramatic approach, Patterson has stacked the deck: he arrives at his conclusion about the proto-bourgeois significance of the Merchant's 'soory herte' because, in mediating the preceding dramatic interpretation, he has infused the text with that significance to begin with. Insofar as Patterson's reading of the Merchant is representative of his method, it is thus on this rather unstable platform that his metacritical arguments about interpretation rest.

In the terms of those arguments, the instability of the platform derives from the possibility that the line between interpreting subject (Patterson) and interpreted object (the *Merchant's Tale*) is not so much paradoxically simultaneously present and absent but rather just absent. The value that Patterson ascribes, as an enactment of his political commitments, to Chaucer's historical distinctiveness may instead just be an ascription of value to a projection of those commitments onto Chaucer. His interpretive method, rather than enacting the reconnection with the past that he sees as essential to resisting the ideology of individualism, may be instancing that very ideology by recasting the past in its likeness.

In fact, in *Negotiating the Past* Patterson foresees this very difficulty. There, alongside his advocating for the political importance of reconnecting with the past, he characterises the identification of past and present as methodological error, a form of 'historicism that would reduce difference and opposition to sameness by collapsing together subject and object'. Instead, 'our work should seek to preserve and understand threatened categories of difference', and '[n]ot the least of these categories … is that between the present-as-subject and the past-as-object'. But lest we think that he has merely reversed here what we have seen to be his earlier denial of that very difference (e.g., 'they [the objects of the human sciences]

Interpretation 215

are themselves constituted by means of the very subjectivity that characterizes the interpreter'), he quickly qualifies the point. First, recalling 'the failure of objectivism' that he previously established, he states, 'This is not, it must be insisted, a difference that can be theorized.' He then characterises the attempt 'to understand the past' as consisting of 'elaborate and endless negotiations, struggles between desire and knowledge that can never be granted closure'. And these negotiations, he adds, 'can take place only between two equal and independent parties, and this fiction – a fiction because the past can never exist independently of our memory of it – must be consciously and painfully maintained'.[49] There is much to query about this reasoning (e.g., if the difference cannot be theorised, then how can it be recognised?), but to take it in the pragmatic spirit in which it was likely intended, we may focus on the way that Patterson finally reconciles hermeneutic sophistication with the demand for historical difference. By declaring the latter difference a *fiction*, he in effect puts the question of historical authenticity on the shelf as ultimately not applicable; to adapt Sir Philip Sidney's aphorism, fiction 'nothing affirms, and therefore never lieth'.[50] The identification of historical difference thus becomes at base a hermeneutic strategy linked to the hermeneut's political values, and its success will finally depend less on correspondence to historical actuality than on the rhetorical potency of the conscious and painful efforts to maintain the fiction of that correspondence.

We should hence not be surprised, then, when in the afterword to *The Subject of History* Patterson circles back to how the book 'witnesses to its author's political values', which he here encapsulates in the exhortation to 'think socially'. He states that in the preceding chapters he has sought to enact this practice by locating Chaucer's texts 'in relation to a discourse ... that can make explicit the social meaning of his poetry', such as the discourses of late medieval 'history, class, gender, family, and religion'. The ultimate aim, he flatly states, is not thereby to produce 'correct' interpretations, since (here recalling formulations from *Negotiating the Past*) 'historical description can never provide a norm of interpretive rectitude'. Such description, he says, rather serves to generate interpretations that emphasise Chaucer's value for the present-day political project of thinking socially, as it 'can make visible social meanings and so show how Chaucer, both in his championing of a sovereign selfhood and in his critique of it, participated and continues to participate in the making of our world. And perhaps', he adds, 'it can help us to think socially about other, more urgent matters as well'.[51] Thus, at the end of *The Subject of History*, Chaucer's literary value and Patterson's political values wholly coincide, which is of course the axiological condition that has been in place from the start. Patterson, in short, has made good on his call for literary critics to foreground the connections between their value commitments and their interpretive practice.

Nevertheless, I expect that most readers of *The Subject of History* will agree that the deep erudition and dazzling argumentation of its several hundred pages of Chaucer interpretation seem rather disproportionate to the aim of exhorting us to think socially about Chaucer and 'other, more urgent matters as well'. Manifestly, the book presents its capacious and detailed readings of Chaucer as attempts to understand Chaucer's writings better than before, thereby maintaining a commitment to the discourse of rational inquiry in this particular respect that the book belatedly disavows. Once more a lacuna emerges between theory and practice, which in this case arises because, if the difference between Patterson's values and his historical description is, as he says in *Negotiating the Past*, a fiction, Patterson may not actually be thinking socially according to how he has defined that activity. As a consequence, even though he recognises the value-permeated nature of interpretation, his very values demand that in practice he act sometimes as if that were not the case, which entails his acting as if his interpretations were more historically authentic than others. In fact, I would credit him with, more often than not, *believing* his interpretations are more historically authentic, thereby avoiding bad faith in one direction while incurring it in another.

In the aftermath of *The Subject History*, I suspect that Patterson in some fashion recognised this double-bind. Not coincidentally, also in the years between then and his work on *Negotiating the Past*, the perception of the relative dearth of explicit political commitments in medievalist scholarship that he bemoaned in the latter was replaced by a perception of relative ubiquity, and this more recent scholarship sometimes took the form of interpretations (and commitments) that he found inferior, most notoriously, those which were informed by psychoanalysis.[52] Strikingly, then, in the

1996 essay 'The Disenchanted Classroom', which at times comes across as a *de facto* methodological palinode, Patterson turns his attention, not to how align one's scholarship and teaching with one's values, but to how to insulate the former from the latter. (Written as a contribution to a symposium on 'Teaching Chaucer in the Nineties', the essay, as its title indicates, foregrounds the question of value in pedagogy. But in his consideration of the question Patterson seamlessly blends the activities of teaching and scholarship, since, in the elucidation of his methods in contrast with those of others, he must necessarily refer, as he admits, 'to the critical arguments of other Chaucerians'.)[53]

Early on in the essay, Patterson reiterates his recognition 'that the practical choices one makes derive from value commitments', but just a few sentences later presents the 'two components' of 'the debate about course content' in a way that appears to defer, if not just to disavow, this derivation:

> First, if for the purposes of analysis we think of our teaching in terms of knowledge and values, where should our emphasis fall? Second, should we teach medieval literature primarily in terms of its relevance to or difference from contemporary life?[54]

In the light of Patterson's own formulations in *Negotiating the Past*, it is not difficult to see that here, simply by articulating these questions as choices *between* 'knowledge' and 'values' and 'relevance to' and 'difference from contemporary life', he has already solved the problem (in my terms, the permeation of interpretation by values) that he sets out to address. For if knowledge and value, and past and present, are separable in the practical, instrumental way implied, then that permeation has evaporated.

In what follows, Patterson turns to Max Weber's 'Science as a Vocation' in order to articulate as a matter of scholarly/pedagogical method these binary distinctions that he has already put into place.[55] He follows Weber's insistence 'that values remain incapable of scientific – that is, empirical – demonstration', but, rather than concluding, as he did in *Negotiating the Past*, that the value-permeated activity of interpretation is therefore not ultimately a matter of empirical demonstration, he seeks instead to position his method of historical description as a version of the latter. Accordingly, following Weber he characterises the foregrounding of values in scholarship and teaching as the practice of an 'ethic of commitment', which is an ill-advised choice 'because the teacher should not promote values that are by definition beyond empirical demonstration'. The better, contrasting choice is an 'ethic of responsibility', in which 'the teacher must distinguish, as best he or she can, between the meaning of the cultural objects under scrutiny and their value', maintain 'a reticence about questions of value', provide 'knowledge not about what ought to be but about what is', and 'to explain ... historical causes and meanings ... rather than their *significance*, in the sense of their value to us'. Although again acknowledging, this time via Weber, 'that all knowledge is developed within a value-laden sociohistorical context that determines not merely the object of inquiry but the methodology and, to an important degree, the results', he nonetheless insists that a measure of *Wertfreiheit*, or 'value-freedom', is achievable by means of a 'rigorous application of empirical methods within the context of a project that is necessarily defined by the investigator's values'.[56]

Weber's arguments, of course, were directed towards sociologists. Hence, regardless of whether or how much 'the rigorous application of empirical methods' may achieve value-freedom in that sort of work, for Patterson the question must be how the interpretive methods of literary studies can be conceived as somehow empirical. Suddenly, that is, Patterson is in a boat that oddly resembles the one of the pre-Fish-critique stylisticians, only with historical rather than linguistic description serving as the proposed empirical basis of practice. Revealingly, the manner in which Patterson seeks to substantiate his position is by yoking together the rather mismatched pair of Paul de Man and E. D. Hirsch. He turns to the former to argue that while political values inevitably eventually enter into the literary critical enterprise, that entry can and should be deferred by means of 'careful textual reading', quoting de Man's emphasis on 'attention to the philological or rhetorical devices of language'.[57] He then explains the nature of this 'attention' within the Hirschian framework that he earlier imported with the distinction, as quoted above, between *meaning* and *significance* (an importation that he acknowledges in an endnote).[58] He defines 'careful textual reading' as the establishment of a text's *meaning*, which now corresponds to Weber's emphasis on empirical methods, and contrasts this activity with an articulation of a text's *significance*, which corresponds to an ascription of values that may not, as Weber says, be empirically demonstrated. On this basis, Patterson asserts that 'the central ambition' of his historical method 'is to discover original meaning'. And in a virtually complete reversal of the formulation in *Negotiating the Past* that states that 'in every way it counts, "original meaning" is indistinguishable from "meaning to us"', he declares, 'The last question it [Patterson's historicism] asks of a text is not "What does this mean to us?" but "What might it have meant to them?"' Consequently, Patterson's interpretive method, instead of serving, as he insists in *The Subject of History*, as a means to enact one's value commitments, now 'erects systemic barriers that can help to protect us from our own enthusiasms'.[59] And so, by the end of the essay, the political commitments that he so stirringly solders to academic work in his earlier writings now appear wholly severed. Whereas in 1990 he affirms the aspiration to make our 'choices ... as literary historians ... consistent with the choices we make as citizens', in 1996 he avers, 'But civic duty is a different part of life; and while all of us want to understand our lives as wholes, the way we achieve that understanding is a personal matter that is strictly irrelevant to our professional practice.'[60]

In the next and final section of this chapter, Patterson's decades-long grappling with the problem of the value permeation of interpretation will provide a point of departure for how we might reconcile ourselves to that problem in a generative fashion. For that purpose, then, we need not pick apart Patterson's sometimes eyebrow-raising reasoning in 'The Disenchanted Classroom'. It perhaps suffices to point out that de Man would likely have laughed out loud at seeing his arguments, which of course emphasise the sheer undecidability of literary meaning, being used to bolster a case for interpretive empiricism. Indeed, Patterson himself was likely aware of the sheer audacity of this ungainly move, as he quotes de Man's declaration that 'it is not ... certain that literature is a reliable source of information about anything'.[61] (Equally audacious is his using de Man's arguments to advocate for a deferral of political values in scholarship and teaching, given that by the mid-1990s Patterson was obviously aware of de Man's notorious wartime writings.) To be fair, Patterson does, as I have noted, consistently qualify his claims in ways that recall his positions in *Negotiating the Past*. Nonetheless, as is evident in his final sustained metacritical reflections in the introduction to a 2006 collection of his essays, through the rest of his career Patterson retains both those earlier positions and the quasi-empiricist ones that he voices in 'The Disenchanted Classroom'.[62] Taken altogether, this spectrum of positions rather poignantly illustrates the personal remark that Patterson offers early in the 2006 introduction, when looking back on his political work for the New Democratic Party: 'One of the challenges that most perplexed me was how to link my political life with my scholarship.'[63]

Where we might go from here

For this book's purposes, one helpful cue in Patterson's struggle with the value permeation of interpretation is that on a few occasions in 'The Disenchanted Classroom' he indicates that Weber's motivation for the advocacy of value-free scholarship was actually itself political. Specifically, Weber was wary of 'the growth of nationalist pan-Germanism', and 'much of Weber's methodological pronouncements were delivered in response to the growing pressure of the right-wing nationalism that would, after his death in 1920, develop into Nazism'. By arguing against an 'ethic of commitment', therefore, Weber was resisting 'the deep complicity of the German universities with the state that financed them'.[64] Just like Patterson, then, Weber disavows value commitments in the name of a value commitment, exemplifying the same double-bind that leads Patterson down the path of apparent contradiction. As we have seen, Patterson exhibits an unwillingness wholly to accept what he nonetheless frequently does acknowledge – the permeation of literary study by value – because he perceives that one of his deeply held value commitments, his abiding concern to resist the ideology of individualism, prohibits that full acceptance. The basic problem, as he sees it – as the contrasting epigraphs from Johan Huizinga and Søren Kierkegaard in the preface to *Negotiating the Past* signal – is that value commitments are rooted in individual subjectivity, whereas 'to think socially' demands that one seek to transcend the confines of one's subjectivity and to reach out toward, if not quite touch, subject positions that are authentically – even empirically – other. To reduce literary study to values, then, is to capitulate to the ideology of individualism, the resistance to which was Patterson's motivation for his approach to literary study in the first place.

At first glance it may seem easy enough to extract oneself from this double-bind simply by adopting a different centrally motivating value commitment, say, resistance to white supremacy. But by itself this move would just reinstall the same problem in a different guise. As long as value commitments are understood as rooted in individual subjectivity, the relation between those commitments and the object of academic literary study is at best arbitrary if not always, as in Patterson's case, paradoxical. Why study literature in order to resist white supremacy? To be sure, many literary texts would seem to have much to teach us about this resistance. But that by itself does not justify the study of literature as an academic field or lay the ground for a methodology that would distinguish that field from others, as the widespread consideration of literary texts in other disciplines readily attests. Rather, the logic of the discipline-justifying claim must go the other direction, asserting, say, that an already established distinctive methodology of literary study contributes something to the resistance of white supremacy that cannot otherwise be achieved. But this in effect puts us back with Patterson. On the one hand, in the same way that he installs an *a priori* subjective value of resistance to individualism within the historicist method that he recommends for literary study, we will have installed an *a priori* subjective value of resistance to white supremacy into whatever literary methodology we choose. On the other hand, to satisfy the strictures of the discourse of rational inquiry, like Patterson we will then be left with the task of explaining how our respective methodology does not ultimately reduce to that *a priori* subjective value commitment – how the methodology remains something more than that commitment precisely in order to serve as a discipline-justifying means of furthering it (or other commitments). We must explain, in short, how value and method are at once independent of and bear a necessary relation to each other.

This is where this book's preliminary theory of literary valuing may be of some help. For in that theory value commitments are not rooted in individual subjectivity. Rather, such 'commitments' emerge only in the activity of ascribing value, an activity that consists of the mediation of the value ascriptions of other actors, human and non-human, across a network extending indefinitely, temporally and spatially. Although each actor, as the label denotes, possesses mediating agency, any one actor's value ascriptions cannot be isolated from those of the other actors that they mediate. Any given value commitment is hence in no way distinct from the pathways through the axiological constellations in which it is enacted. Accordingly, such a commitment is certainly not housed within an individual's subjectivity but is always already social, and in fact, inasmuch as *social* is understood to refer only to human actors, it is more precisely always already *environmental*. In short, our values are never simply just ours. In my preliminary theory of literary valuing (and reflecting its derivations from ANT), the dichotomy between subject and object does not hold, and so the demand to delineate the latter from the former simply does not apply.

That this points to a way forward rather than just compounding the problem becomes evident if we consider the question of what might constitute literary study if we put aside the dichotomy between subject and object. What remains is the study of the pathways through the axiological constellations that constitute our experience of the literary. In being neither subjective nor objective, these pathways are simultaneously both us and not us, both self and other. They are, moreover, as 'real' (which is to say, as historically authentic) as anything else, as they involve flesh-and-blood people, physical books, course syllabi, and so on, as well as the ideas, information and interpretations necessarily carried by material things. What literary study can be – or, as I argued in Chapter 3, what it in fact already is – is a generative and reflexive account of these pathways, which are no more or no less objective than anything else in the humanities, if not across the academy more generally.

There is no need to repeat here Chapter 3's explanation of how various activities currently pursued under the banner of literary studies may be understood in these terms.[65] Rather, the point to reemphasise at this juncture is that pathways through axiological constellations always necessarily include, at some level of mediation, the literary scholar as one of the actors. Thus we may reaffirm Patterson's exhortation to be explicit about the value commitments that motivate our work, as that constitutes a key part of a reflexive account of that work's pathways. And we may also reaffirm his method of locating Chaucer's texts 'in relation to a discourse ... that can make explicit the social meaning of his poetry' as one pathway-generative practice, among many other possibilities, wholly reconcilable with the academy's strictures of rational inquiry. But we must recognise, too, that in literary study, 'discourse' and 'social meaning' are themselves transpositions of mediations of value ascriptions within axiological constellations that include the interpreter and hence are no more or no less 'empirical' than other mediations. Yet neither are they, as Patterson seems to fear, therefore merely subjective. Rather, insofar as they necessarily include actors other than the interpreter, they are subject to inquiry in a way that has the potential for interpreters to gain knowledge and insight beyond that which they bring to the task. As I mentioned above, interpretation, as it involves mediations of value ascriptions, is reciprocal; it may shape the interpreter as much as the interpreter shapes that which is under consideration. One form of this shaping of the interpreter is what we may call, with all the necessary caveats, the positive knowledge of literary inquiry. So, for example, quite plainly Patterson's grasp of the ideology of individualism was shaped by his placing Chaucer's poetry alongside fourteenth-century social discourses. That knowledge is real, but in the final analysis it is not so because of whatever historical authenticity those discourses may possess but rather because the axiological constellations that join Patterson to an array of other value-ascribing actors, extending from the 1990s to the late fourteenth century and beyond, are real.

The formalists' famous notion of defamiliarisation can, as I suggested in Chapter 3, be understood as a name for this kind of knowledge. Not in fact a property of the literary object, it names the experience of becoming aware of the other as such that scrutiny of one's mediation of the value ascriptions of other actors makes possible. It names the conscious recognition that our knowledge of our values always involves some mediation of the values of others. As in Chapter 3, therefore, what I am recommending is not necessarily any practical changes to the robust variety of approaches to literary study currently being pursued. Rather, in the first instance I am simply proposing that we more fully acknowledge what we are actually doing in those approaches, with the aim of thereby closing the gap between theory and practice in a way compelling both to ourselves within the field and to those outside who may have interest in or be sceptical of our work. I believe that this response to the particular problem of interpretation under consideration here, while it makes it no less problematic, may well be among the most distinctive assets that the field has to offer.

Rather than retreading this ground any further, however, in conclusion let me briefly turn to a couple of recent examples of medievalist literary scholarship, ones that have struck me as not merely redescribable in my framework but as illustrations of its potential usefulness (unbeknownst to their authors, of course). In particular, I have found these studies methodologically innovative in ways that exemplify the reflexive tracing of their own generated pathways through axiological constellations. In contrast with Patterson, who produces interpretations that may not finally be fully accounted for by his claims about his methods, these scholars adopt an interpretive practice that regularly and explicitly foregrounds the mediations of value ascriptions that constitute those pathways. In regard to the future of the field, I find this work promising in its scholarly nimbleness and reflexive rigour, although, to be sure, I am by no means suggesting that other kinds of work are necessarily any less so. Moreover, this pair of studies represents just two among many others that possess similar qualities.[66]

In *Obscene Pedagogies: Transgressive Talk and Sexual Education in Late Medieval Britain*, Carissa Harris's overall project is to investigate the 'capacity of obscenity to educate and change minds ... in order to understand its meanings in the later Middle Ages and to uncover its present-day implications'. She accordingly from the start foregrounds the mediations of value ascriptions (especially social, political and ethical ones) that inextricably connect 'the later Middle Ages' and 'present-day implications', which include relations between her own experiences of the book's topics and the presence of those topics in the texts that she interprets. As she describes,

> I link my discussion of medieval texts with my own experience, bringing personal histories into conversation with literary and cultural ones ... I cannot help but see the larger issues I write about – power, inequality, oppression, misogyny – at work in my everyday experiences, just as I cannot help but notice how the quotidian violations of inhabiting this body have structural causes and political import.

At the same time, she recognises that these linkages are simultaneously distinctions – that it is as much the differences as it is the continuity between her experiences and those represented in the texts that demand attention. While she avers that 'we need to trace the deep roots of violence and misogyny stretching back to the Middle Ages', she also remains alert to 'the differences between then and now', arguing 'for linkages without collapsing differences'.[67] In these ways her project, in my terms, takes as its object neither precisely her experiences nor medieval texts but rather the pathways of mediations through axiological constellations that include both and that are generated by the study itself.

Throughout the book, Harris pursues a methodology that juxtaposes present-day experiences, sometimes her own, with readings of late medieval texts (readings that often involve historicist collocations of the sort that Patterson recommends). For example, Chapter 1 begins with the woman raped by Ched Evans, considers the ensuing legal case that resulted in both a 2012 conviction and a 2016 acquittal, and then uses this as a springboard to examine the culture that fostered both the crime and the acquittal as that culture is reflected in, and even in part produced by, the Miller-Cook sequence in the *Canterbury Tales*. In particular, Harris identifies in that tale sequence a ' "felawe masculinity" ... centered on men teaching their peers to perpetuate rape culture'. With this juxtaposition between present and past, she produces a reading that highlights a key aspect of the tale sequence's artistic design that has gone underappreciated: its unification not just by an exhibition of toxic masculinity but as the representation of a linked series of instructional narratives – 'overtly pedagogical' tales – from men to other men about the normative modes of performance of that masculinity in relation to violence and particularly sexual assault.[68] She compellingly delineates a distinctive late medieval genre of toxic pedagogy, while keeping in view its continuities with the present. The close attention that she gives to Chaucer's text manifestly ascribes literary value to it, but she follows this value through a complex set of mediations that are as disavowing as affirming, if not more so the former. As in Patterson's reading of the *Merchant's Tale*, the interpretive framework that she brings to the *Canterbury Tales* plainly originates with her present-day value commitments, but, in contrast to Patterson's reading, the distinctions and continuities between present and past, and the mediations that necessarily create them, are much more prominently part of Harris's explicit method. In tracing in this fashion axiological pathways among actors that include herself, Chaucer, Ched Evans's rape victim, Evans and a range of others, Harris provides us with a generous helping of what I tentatively called above the positive knowledge of literary study, in this case knowledge of both the *Canterbury Tales* and rape culture.

The work of Seeta Chaganti, as most capaciously on display in her book *Strange Footing: Poetic Form and Dance in the Late Middle Ages*, offers a similarly innovative methodology, one that foregrounds, particularly with the latter study's technique of narrative reenactment, both the continuities and distinctions between past and present.[69] But for this chapter's purposes the most germane example of Chaganti's work is her plenary address for the 2021 Sewanee Medieval Colloquium, 'Boethian Privilege and the Abolitionist Position'.[70] In this talk, Chaganti's method involves a strikingly bold juxtaposition between present and past that is motivated by an exceptionally focused value commitment, a juxtaposition that at first may seem a non-sequitur. Specifically, Chaganti asks us to bring the meditations of Boethius's *Consolation of Philosophy* on Providence and temporality into conversation with twenty-first-century arguments for abolition. She sets out, as she puts it, 'to read Boethius through the abolitionist position and read the abolitionist position through Boethius'.

Chaganti begins with Derek Chauvin's trial for the murder of George Floyd, but her point of contact between this event and Boethius is not so much, as she notes, the dubious workings of the justice system then and now, as respectively instanced by the modern carceral system and Boethius's imprisonment. Rather, the considerably more complex juxtaposition that she presents is between the experience and perception then and now of inevitability – specifically, the experience and perception, on the one hand, of the inevitable necessity of the modern carceral system, and the consequent fate of its victims such as Floyd, and, on the other hand, that of human fate categorically within a system of divine Providence. What motivates this inquiry, she makes clear, is her commitment to countering the modern liberal reformist position that seeks not to abolish the carceral system but just to rid it of its problems, a position that she characterises as believing that the need for such a system, in some form, is inevitable. In a dazzling series of mediations that I cannot hope to summarise adequately, she identifies the scholarly tradition of focusing on Boethius's concern with free will as a product of the same liberalism that sees the carceral system as inevitable and, for that very reason, as providing a springboard for understanding Boethius's more crucial concern with futurity and collectivity. She suggests that bringing the lens of the apparently anachronistic abolitionist position to bear on the *Consolation of Philosophy* helps to clear away some of the smoke of liberal individualism that intervenes between our twenty-first-century present and the sixth-century *Consolation*. Reciprocally, the reading of the *Consolation* that results may speak to possibilities that twenty-first-century liberalism cannot imagine. Hence, she claims, the scholarly habitus of medievalist scholarship, once adjusted in this fashion, may help make more legible the abolitionist position. As she proposes, our 'familiarity with Boethius' may allow us

> to inhabit perhaps a somewhat rarer position as an academic, one from which [we] are focused on the fact that the structure has some outer limits whether [we] can access those or not, and thus [we] understand that what [we] can discern of the structure is bad, and thus [we] can set [our] sights and energy on breaking it down.

Importantly, however, Chaganti makes clear that she does not mean to reclaim Boethius as a kind of abolitionist *avant la lettre*. She fully acknowledges not just the immense historical span in this mediation but also the equally profound ideological differences between Boethius's work – and the tradition of scholarship on it – and the abolitionist position. 'I have every reason to believe', she remarks, 'that [Boethius] would have had no problem enacting the kinds of oppressions that his own philosophical system may have helped pave the way for'. Neither is Chaganti interested in recuperating 'the European Middle Ages' generally by attempting 'to make the argument that it existed in a time prior to white supremacy and is thus innocent'. Rather, the reciprocal power of her juxtapositional interpretation of Boethius and the abolitionist position arises as much out of their historical and ideological discontinuity as their continuity. Indeed, inasmuch as the philosophical tradition of liberalism runs through the eighteenth century on back to its mediation of figures such as Boethius, Chaganti's ideological antagonism in this regard serves also as reflexive scrutiny of the historiographical tradition in which her reading of Boethius necessarily occurs.

As I hope is evident from this summary, explicit identifications of value ascriptions and of those that they mediate, in both affirmative and disavowing fashions, pervade Chaganti's talk in a way that makes them inextricable from her interpretive arguments. The value commitment with which she begins is also the one with which she ends: the positive literary knowledge that her talk offers regarding Boethius's practical recommendations for living within a Providential system is in no way detachable from the exhortation that she makes to her auditors to involve themselves in abolition – for it is the practical imperative to engage in the latter activity that enables her to discern the nature of Boethius's advice.[71] Methodologically, Chaganti's talk illustrates that in literary study, value ascription mediation need not necessarily involve the sort of manifest topical overlap that we saw with Harris's delineation of 'felwae masculinity' in both the *Canterbury Tales* and the present. Since our axiological environments have no definitive temporal or spatial boundaries, and since our ceaseless value ascription mediations branch out in myriad directions, there is no methodological throttle limiting the germane set of mediations in any given act of interpretation, as long as the interpreter is, like Chaganti, careful to trace her pathways through axiological constellations. Literary study, precisely because it is literary in the way that I have described in this book, may for these reasons cast into relief relations among our and others' values, even very different values of very distant others, in manners that we had not before so fully appreciated.

Nonetheless – to end this chapter on a cautionary note – such a self-congratulatory account of literary studies must be tempered by recognition of the necessarily uncertain bearing of the results of an interpretive project upon the value commitments that always (if not always explicitly) inaugurate it. Some degree of this uncertainty must always remain because, while the positive literary knowledge gained by tracing one's pathways through axiological constellations cannot be separated from the value commitments that prompt the journey, there can be no assurance that that knowledge will further that commitment. Not only may the experience of interpretation, with its reciprocal dynamic, potentially affect the interpreter in a way that hinders her commitment, but more obviously the efficacy of the interpretation in respect to this commitment depends to some degree upon the unpredetermined value ascriptions of the interpretation's subsequent mediators (e.g., its human auditors, its institutional reception, etc.). Chaganti, acutely aware of this provisionality, accordingly concludes her talk by having her audience consider, for example, 'whether it is possible to take an abolitionist position as connected to a disciplinary identity, or whether that position itself is inherently contradictory because of the power dynamics that disciplinary protocol inevitably reproduces'. She wonders aloud, 'Would committing to abolition for all of us mean getting out *there*, not in *here*?' With Patterson, then, she is clearly still contemplating the nature of the linkages between her value commitments and her scholarship. And for all its abstruse axiological terminology, that sort of contemplation is primarily what this present book has sought to encourage in its readers.

Notes

1 Rita Felski, Introduction to a special issue on 'Interpretation and Its Rivals', *NLH*, 45:2 (2014), v–xi (v, vi).
2 Matthew Rubery and Leah Price, 'Introduction', in Matthew Rubery and Leah Price, *Further Reading* (Oxford: Oxford University Press, 2020), pp. 1–11 (1).
3 Felski, Introduction, p. vi.
4 Rita Felski, *The Limits of Critique* (Chicago: University of Chicago Press, 2015), pp. 10, 33.
5 Stephen Best and Sharon Marcus, 'Surface Reading: An Introduction', *Representations*, 108:1 (2009), 1–21, the formulations of which continue to be debated.
6 I assume these lessons require no elaboration. For a paradigmatic instance, see J. Hillis Miller, 'Stevens' Rock and Criticism as Cure, II', *The Georgia Review*, 30:2 (1976), 330–48.
7 David Lawton, *Voice in Later Medieval English Literature: Public Interiorities* (Oxford: Oxford University Press, 2017), pp. 166–7.
8 The debate about irony in the *Squire's Tale* is longstanding. Lawton's position here builds upon his earlier intervention in *Chaucer's Narrators* (Cambridge: D. S. Brewer, 1985). I take a position in Chapter 3 of *Literary Value and Social Identity in the* Canterbury Tales (Cambridge: Cambridge University Press, 2019).
9 Marion Turner, *Chaucer: A European Life* (Princeton: Princeton University Press, 2019), pp. 477–8. Turner is summarising the argument of Lee Patterson, 'The Parson's Tale and the Quitting of the

Canterbury Tales', *Traditio*, 34 (1978), 331–80, whose findings about the Parson Tale's more localised responses to earlier tales she cites approvingly in her preceding paragraph.

10 Turner, *Chaucer*, pp. 478–9, 364. Turner develops this general line of argument about the *Tales* in many other places across the biography, from one of which I have taken the final two-word quotation. In that discussion, she states that with the *Tales*, Chaucer 'embraced the idea of equivalence', and '[t]his ability to equalize without homogenizing is central to Chaucer's ethical stance and to his poetic art' (pp. 366–7).

11 For the descriptive turn, see, e.g., Heather Love, 'Close but Not Deep: Literary Ethics and the Descriptive Turn', *NLH*, 41:2 (2010), 371–91; Sharon Marcus, Heather Love and Stephen Best, 'Building a Better Description', *Representations*, 135:1 (2016), 1–21; Heather Love, 'Care, Concern, and the Ethics of Description', in Rita Felski and Stephen Muecke (eds), *Latour and the Humanities* (Baltimore: Johns Hopkins University Press, 2020), pp. 107–31. In the latter essay, Love remarks, 'Most critics point to close reading as the core method of the field, without necessarily being willing to commit to a definition, let alone a step-by-step protocol or directives for training students' (p. 127). It is precisely such protocols that characterise stylistics.

12 For the relation of present-day stylistics to Russian formalism, see especially the introduction to Violeta Sotirova, ed., *The Bloomsbury Companion to Stylistics* (London: Bloomsbury Academic, 2016).

13 Michael Burke, ed., *The Routledge Handbook of Stylistics* (London: Routledge, 2014), p. 2. Burke here is drawing on Mick Short, *Exploring the Language of Poems, Plays and Prose* (London: Longman, 1996).

14 See the first chapter in Michael Toolan, *The Stylistics of Fiction: A Literary-Linguistics Approach* (London: Routledge, 1990), pp. 1–27. As Toolan avers, 'Fish's book has been an invaluable corrective to the objectivist mentalist tendencies that stylistics had long nurtured' (p. 19). Toolan, however, does not see Fish's critique as making stylistics any less valid than any other sort of literary study, once stylisticians recognise what they are actually doing.

15 I quote Fish's essay from Stanley Fish, *Is There a Text in This Class?: The Authority of Interpretive Communities* (Cambridge, MA: Harvard University Press, 1980), pp. 71, 72, 77. The original publication is Fish, 'What Is Stylistics and Why Are They Saying Such Terrible Things About It?', in Seymour Benjamin Chatman (ed.), *Approaches to Poetics: Selected Papers from the English Institute* (New York: Columbia University Press, 1973), pp. 109–52. For the quotations of Milic, see Louis T. Milac, 'Unconscious Ordering in the Prose of Swift', in Jacob Leed (ed.), *The Computer and Literary*

Style: Introductory Essays and Studies (Kent: Kent State University Press, 1966), pp. 79–106 (104).
16 For an account (largely Gadamerian) of the hermeneutic circle as it applies to literary interpretation, see David Couzens Hoy, *The Critical Circle: Literature, History, and Philosophical Hermeneutics* (Berkeley: University of California Press, 1982).
17 Fish, *Is There a Text*, p. 253. The original publication is Fish, 'What Is Stylistics and Why Are They Saying Such Terrible Things about It?-- Part II', *Boundary 2*, 8:1 (1979), 129–46.
18 Toolan, *Stylistics of Fiction*, p. 21. Toolan here is following the argument of George L. Dillon, 'Whorfian Stylistics', *Journal of Literary Semantics*, 11:2 (1982), 73–7, and approvingly quotes Dillon's point that the best response one can hope for from a sceptical interlocutor of stylistic analysis is 'I see' rather than 'You've proved your point' (Toolan, p. 21; Dillon, p. 75). Other stylisticians, however, have not given up so easily. Burke's remarks about falsifiability suggest as much, and indeed Burke goes on to figure the stylistician as a 'Sherlock Holmes character' who uncovers 'the linguistic data' that thereby undergirds a 'relatively objective interpretation' (*Routledge Handbook*, pp. 2–3).
19 Fish, *Is There a Text*, p. vii.
20 For just one response, see Toolan, *Stylistics of Fiction*, pp. 12–20, who points out some clear deficiencies.
21 Fish, *Is There a Text*, p. 14.
22 Peter L. Berger and Thomas Luckmann, *The Social Construction of Reality: A Treatise in the Sociology of Knowledge* (New York: Anchor Books, 1966); Pierre Bourdieu, *The Logic of Practice*, trans. Richard Nice (Stanford: Stanford University Press, 1990).
23 One notable if ultimately only partially successful attempt to address this question was the Konstanz school of reader-response criticism and especially that of Wolfgang Iser. See, e.g., Iser, *The Act of Reading: A Theory of Aesthetic Response* (Baltimore: Johns Hopkins University Press, 1978). Fish, whose early work held many affinities with this approach, infamously took it to task in 'Why No One's Afraid of Wolfgang Iser', *Diacritics*, 11:1 (1981), 2–13. For a reflection on the impact of this moment on the history of literary criticism, and its implications for interpretation, see Michael Bérubé, *Rhetorical Occasions* (Chapel Hill: University of North Carolina Press, 2006), pp. 97–110. A more recent attempt to address this question is one of the projects of the approach to literary study known as cognitive poetics. For a recent handbook, see Peter Stockwell, *Cognitive Poetics: An Introduction*, 2nd edn (London: Routledge, 2019).
24 Love, 'Close but not Deep', p. 387.

25 Ted Underwood and Jordan Sellers, 'The Longue Durée of Literary Prestige', *MLQ*, 77:3 (2016), 321–44 (335). John Frow, 'On Midlevel Concepts', *NLH*, 41:2 (2010), 237–52, recognises a similar dependency on value ascription at the level of data identification in the work of Franco Moretti – as in *Graphs, Maps, Trees: Abstract Models for Literary History* (London: Verso, 2007).
26 I refer, of course, to E. D. Hirsch, *Validity in Interpretation* (New Haven: Yale University Press, 1967).
27 Cited from *The Riverside Chaucer*, gen. ed. Larry D. Benson, 3rd edn (Boston: Houghton Mifflin, 1987).
28 For the famous formulation upon which I am riffing, see Roman Jakobson, 'Closing Statement: Linguistics and Poetics', in Thomas Albert Sebeok (ed.), *Style in Language* (Cambridge: Technology Press of Massachusetts Institute of Technology, 1960), pp. 350–77.
29 Emma Margaret Solberg, 'Response to "#MeToo, Medieval Literature, and Trauma-Informed Pedagogy"', *New Chaucer Studies: Pedagogy and Profession*, 2:2 (2021), 134–53 (138).
30 I expect that this is not an uncommon experience. My most difficult case was with a student who wrote a tightly argued, reasonably well-informed paper about the *Physician's Tale* in which she claimed that Virginius makes the correct choice to decapitate his daughter.
31 Among the many sources informing this paragraph's admittedly crayon-level depiction of the relation of formalism and philology, the most proximate are Lee Patterson's introduction to his *Temporal Circumstances: Form and History in the* Canterbury Tales (Basingstoke: Palgrave Macmillan, 2006); and his 'The Return to Philology', in John H. Van Engen (ed.), *The Past and Future of Medieval Studies* (Notre Dame: University of Notre Dame Press, 1994), pp. 231–44. For the deep history of the emergence of literary study from within philology, see the sixth and tenth chapters of James Turner, *Philology: The Forgotten Origins of the Modern Humanities* (Princeton: Princeton University Press, 2014), which, among other things, explain how the perceived antagonism between philology and evaluative criticism on the basis of form emerges only in the decades after 1910.
32 I recognise that when put this way, the conundrum appears as just one species of the vastly more general observer effect and thus this point is by no means limited to literary study. But for the reasons that I have elaborated in Chapters 2 and 3, literary study is among the fields for which this effect is most palpable and fraught.
33 As articulated in, e.g., Stephen Greenblatt, *Shakespearean Negotiations: The Circulation of Social Energy in Renaissance England* (Berkeley: University of California Press, 1988).

Interpretation 233

34 Patterson's work has attracted no small amount of commentary of its own, as well as its share of controversy, with which I cannot hope adequately to engage without turning this entire chapter into a study of his legacy. If one were to pursue such a project, the place to begin is Kathy Cawsey, *Twentieth-Century Chaucer Criticism: Reading Audiences* (Farnham: Routledge, 2011), 131–53. See also, *inter alia*, Elizabeth Scala, 'Historicists and Their Discontents: Reading Psychoanalytically in Medieval Studies', *Texas Studies in Literature and Language*, 44:1 (2002), 108–31; John T. Sebastian, 'Chaucer and the Theory Wars: Attack of the Historicists? The Psychoanalysts Strike Back? Or a New Hope?', *Literature Compass*, 3:4 (2006), 767–77; Scala's response to Sebastian (among others) in 'The Gender of Historicism', in Elizabeth Scala and Sylvia Federico (eds), *The Post-Historical Middle Ages* (New York: Palgrave Macmillan, 2009), pp. 191–214; and, in that same volume, George Edmondson, 'Naked Chaucer', pp. 139–60.
35 Lee Patterson, *Negotiating the Past: The Historical Understanding of Medieval Literature* (Madison: University of Wisconsin Press, 1987), p. x.
36 Lee Patterson, *Acts of Recognition: Essays on Medieval Culture* (Notre Dame: University of Notre Dame Press, 2010), p. viii.
37 Patterson, *Negotiating the Past*, pp. 42–4. Patterson doubles down on these points in 'Introduction: Critical Historicism and Medieval Studies', in Lee Patterson (ed.), *Literary Practice and Social Change in Britain, 1380–1530* (Berkeley: University of California Press, 1990), pp. 1–14., asserting that, e.g., 'textual interpretation confronts the critic with acts of judgment that require continual recourse to his or her own values' (p. 3).
38 Patterson, *Negotiating the Past*, pp. 57, 69, 45.
39 Patterson, 'Critical Historicism', p. 14.
40 Patterson, *Negotiating the Past*, p. 72.
41 Lee Patterson, *Chaucer and the Subject of History* (Madison: University of Wisconsin Press, 1991), p. 3.
42 *Habits of the Heart* is now in its third edition: Robert N. Bellah *et al.*, *Habits of the Heart: Individualism and Commitment in American Life*, 3rd edn (Berkeley: University of California Press, 2007).
43 Patterson, *Subject of History*, p. 4. See also the related formulations in Lee Patterson, 'On the Margin: Postmodernism, Ironic History, and Medieval Studies', *Speculum*, 65:1 (1990), 87–108. Important to this claim of Patterson's, here and elsewhere, is Paul de Man's conception of modernity as consisting of the impossible desire to effect a definitive rupture with the past, for the present to be its own point

of origin. See de Man, *Blindness and Insight: Essays in the Rhetoric of Contemporary Criticism*, 2nd edn (Minneapolis: University of Minnesota Press, 1983), pp. 142–65.
44 Patterson, *Subject of History*, pp. 21, 12.
45 Greatly prompted by George Lyman Kittredge, *Chaucer and His Poetry* (Cambridge, MA: Harvard University Press, 1915), this approach reached a kind of apotheosis with R. M. Lumiansky, *Of Sondry Folk: The Dramatic Principle in the Canterbury Tales* (Austin: University of Texas Press, 1955), which includes actual visual portraits of the pilgrims.
46 Patterson, *Subject of History*, p. 338, emphasis in original.
47 *Ibid.*, pp. 337–8. For just one of the many instances of dramatic, marriage-group readings of the *Merchant's Tale*, see Clair C. Olson, 'The Interludes of the Marriage Group in the *Canterbury Tales*', in Beryl Rowland (ed.), *Chaucer and Middle English Studies in Honour of Rossell Hope Robbins* (Kent: Kent State University Press, 1974), pp. 164–72.
48 Patterson, *Subject of History*, p. 45. Patterson mentions the critiques of Lawton, *Chaucer's Narrators*; and C. David Benson, *Chaucer's Drama of Style: Poetic Variety and Contrast in the* Canterbury Tales (Chapel Hill: University of North Carolina Press, 1986). To those we may add, *inter alia*, two studies by A. C. Spearing: *Textual Subjectivity: The Encoding of Subjectivity in Medieval Narratives and Lyrics* (Oxford: Oxford University Press, 2005); and *Medieval Autographies: The 'I' of the Text* (Notre Dame: University of Notre Dame Press, 2012), in the latter of which Spearing notes Patterson's dependence on the approach. In the second chapter of *Literary Value and Social Identity*, I review the critical history of reading the *Merchant's Tale* as expressing its teller's bitterness and find those arguments, for a variety of reasons, wanting.
49 Patterson, *Negotiating the Past*, pp. 72–3.
50 Quoted from Vincent B. Leitch *et al.* (eds.), *The Norton Anthology of Theory and Criticism*, 3rd edn (New York: W. W. Norton, 2018), p. 279.
51 Patterson, *Subject of History*, pp. 423–4.
52 Patterson articulates this view most trenchantly in 'Chaucer's Pardoner on the Couch: Psyche and Clio in Medieval Literary Studies', *Speculum*, 76:3 (2001), 638–80.
53 Lee Patterson, 'The Disenchanted Classroom', *Exemplaria*, 8:2 (1996), 513–45, although I quote from the essay's republication in *Acts of Recognition*, here at p. 36.
54 Patterson, *Acts of Recognition*, p. 36.

55 For a translation of Weber's famous essay, see *The Vocation Lectures*, ed. David Owen and Tracy B. Strong, trans. Rodney Livingstone (Indianapolis: Hackett Publishing, 2004).
56 Patterson, *Acts of Recognition*, pp. 39, 41, 42, 43, 44; emphasis in original.
57 *Ibid.*, 45; Paul de Man, *The Resistance to Theory* (Minneapolis: University of Minnesota Press, 1986), p. 24.
58 Patterson, *Acts of Recognition*, p. 269 n. 27. In contrast, in *Negotiating the Past*, Patterson identifies Hirsch's hermeneutics as the 'lingua franca' (p. 44) of the objectivist historical scholarship that he finds so conceptually dubious.
59 Patterson, *Acts of Recognition*, pp. 46, 48.
60 Patterson, 'Critical Historicism', p. 10; *Acts of Recognition*, p. 53.
61 Patterson, *Acts of Recognition*, p. 45. Patterson drops the conclusion of de Man's sentence: 'anything but its own language' (*Resistance to Theory*, p. 11). Patterson develops his odd use of de Man to underwrite old-school philology in more detail, if not with more persuasiveness, in 'The Return to Philology', which obviously takes its title from de Man's famous essay. In fact, that relatively brief 1994 essay anticipates several of the positions that Patterson takes in 'The Disenchanted Classroom', including the introduction of Weber and the idea of disenchantment into the debate about literary critical method. Patterson airs the possibility, for example, that the 'whole enterprise [of literary studies] *cannot* be justified in terms of social effectiveness' (p. 239, emphasis in original).
62 One gets that sense that with these final metacritical reflections, Patterson is not so much seeking to reconcile his conflicting positions on interpretation as he is just gathering them together in one place (as the sometimes verbatim incorporation of material from those earlier forays would seem to confirm). Interestingly, in a personal communication, Seeta Chaganti has reported to me a conversation with Patterson in 2000 in which he reflected on how his teaching was increasingly gravitating toward an emphasis on moral purpose, and so perhaps at least in practice he had abandoned some of the more categorical positions he takes in 'The Disenchanted Classroom'.
63 Patterson, *Temporal Circumstances*, p. 2.
64 Patterson, *Acts of Recognition*, pp. 38, 41.
65 Although it is perhaps useful to reiterate that at this level of accounting for literary studies, the otherwise different methods of surface and symptomatic reading look very much the same. They both trace pathways through axiological constellations; what differs are the actors involved and the nature of mediations among them.

66 For example, less recent but clearly a precedent for these studies are Carolyn Dinshaw's *Getting Medieval: Sexualities and Communities, Pre- and Postmodern* (Durham: Duke University Press Books, 1999); and *How Soon Is Now?: Medieval Texts, Amateur Readers, and the Queerness of Time* (Durham: Duke University Press, 2012).

67 Carissa M. Harris, *Obscene Pedagogies: Transgressive Talk and Sexual Education in Late Medieval Britain* (Ithaca: Cornell University Press, 2018), pp. 3, 7, 9. Harris's Biennial Lecturer plenary at the 2022 New Chaucer Society Congress, entitled 'Chaucer's Wenches', extended this approach further into Chaucer's writings. The article version of this talk should appear in the 2023 volume of *SAC*.

68 Ibid., 29, 30.

69 Seeta Chaganti, *Strange Footing: Poetic Form and Dance in the Late Middle Ages* (Chicago: University of Chicago Press, 2018).

70 Seeta Chaganti, 'Boethian Privilege and the Abolitionist Position' (lecture given at the Sewanee Medieval Colloquium, University of the South, 9 April 2021). A somewhat different version of this paper oriented toward a wider audience for a cluster on 'rethinking exceptionalism' appears as Seeta Chaganti, 'Boethian Abolition', *PMLA*, 137:1 (2021), 144–54. I thank Professor Chaganti for providing me access to a recording of the talk and an advanced copy of the article. For more informal reflections that make use of a similar methodology, but aimed at an even wider audience, see Chaganti's 'B-Sides: Chaucer's "The House of Fame"', *Public Books*, www.publicbooks.org/b-sides-chaucers-the-house-of-fame/ (2019; accessed 14 September 2021); and 'B-Sides: "Sir Gawain and the Green Knight"', *Public Books*, www.publicbooks.org/b-sides-sir-gawain-green-knight/ (2017; accessed 14 September 2021).

71 In this respect, Walter Benjamin's famous notion of synchronicity – the idea, as his recent editors put it, 'that certain historical moments and forms become legible only at a later moment' – might be usefully set alongside of Chaganti's approach. See *The Work of Art in the Age of Its Technological Reproducibility, and Other Writings on Media*, ed. Michael W. Jennings, Brigid Doherty and Thomas Y. Levin, trans. Edmund Jephcott, Rodney Livingstone, Howard Eiland, and others (Cambridge: Belknap Press of Harvard University Press, 2008), pp. 5–6.

Postscript: losing my religion

While I have sought to be consistent in my theorising of literary value in this book, that theorising has not really been accompanied by an overarching thesis. Rather, in addition to presenting my preliminary theory of literary valuing, my basic aim has been to describe some practical dimensions of the problem of literary value within a few of the arenas of the everyday activities of scholars and teachers of literature. Those descriptions have been regularly, if relatively briefly, accompanied by suggestions for how to navigate the problem, most of which are variations on the recommendation to recognise in some explicit way the value ascriptions that pervade literary study – variations of the exhortation, 'Always be reflexive'. In lieu of a tedious recapitulation of the major points of the preceding chapters, therefore, in these few concluding pages I will heed my own advice and convey more personally and directly than elsewhere a sense of some of the axiological conditions that have prompted and shaped this book. I have organised these reflections under the headings of a pair of queries (as the Quaker tradition uses that term), each of which comprised for me one of this book's prompting provocations – doubts that, while personal, I expect that I share in some fashion with others.

Query 1: What if literature is not as valuable as the dedication of one's career to it would seem to presume?

From the moment when I sounded out the first words that I was actually reading ('Hop on Pop', if I remember correctly), books have been among my closest friends, and they were especially so during some elementary school years in which the day that the Scholastic order arrived was the very best, by far, of the term. At college, with its exhilarating opening of intellectual horizons, this already deep emotional connection with literature engendered transformative reading experiences that belied my chosen major of computer science, experiences that affected much of what may be said to constitute 'me'. (To name just three of the books involved: Harold Frederic's *The Damnation of Theron Ware*, Charlotte Brontë's *Villette* and Thomas Pynchon's *The Crying of Lot 49*.) In the emotionally turbulent years immediately following, attempts to create my own fiction, however feeble, were powerfully therapeutic. And while my eventual career as a professor of literature obviously bespeaks my devotion to it, more private reading (most recently as of this writing, Yaa Gyasi's *Homegoing*) continues to play an important role in shaping my understandings of self and world. In short, for almost as far back as I have memory at all, literature has been a large and diverse source of value in my life – a value that once, in a splendidly axiological fashion, baldly materialised as the definite price tag of the bonus that I declined when my boss in the software industry sought to waylay my pursuit of a PhD in English.

A similar testimony to literary value, substituting one set of idiosyncrasies with another, could, I expect, be easily enough composed by most readers of this book. And yet, I also expect that we all know, and likely have close relationships with, people who would not attest to literary value in this fashion but who are nonetheless, in every way that it counts (ethically, politically, socially, professionally, dispositionally, etc.), better people than we are – people who, that is, embody our own most cherished values more fully than we perceive ourselves to do. I certainly am acutely aware of some such individuals, for whom literature is simply not very important, at least relative to its importance to me, but who do not seem thereby any worse off. The conclusion must be, then, that the benefits of greatest import that I have received from literature have been available to others from different sources, and thus literature is no more valuable, at least in those respects, than those other sources – and, for all that I am aware, it may be less valuable. To claim otherwise, I have come to believe, is to suggest that those for whom literature is not as important lead lives that are in some foundational ways impoverished. Especially as voiced by someone who is paid to study literature, this claim, even in its most sophisticated varieties, strikes me now as a rather arrogant, condescending, self-congratulating species of self-justification.

In the preceding pages, I have had the occasion to point to some other possible justifications for the study of literature. Rather than reiterate those here, I will cite a more obvious, much simpler and substantially humbler one: that works of literature constitute a distinctive class of cultural artefact, and so are as worthy of study as any other class of cultural artefact. In particular – and notwithstanding the poststructuralist chestnut that understands the category of person as writing's echo – a literary artefact is an attestation of human consciousness, one perhaps with more density in this respect than, say, a shard of pottery (the study of which I admittedly know nothing about). To be sure, the privileging of human consciousness by the Western philosophical tradition (and the human exceptionalism that has motivated it) may be, as some versions of the posthumanist critique urge us to recognise, the siren's song that has led us to the present brink of global environmental catastrophe. Nevertheless, consciousness is valuable enough to me – and, I suppose, to those who bankroll universities – to justify the study of an artefact that remains one of its key historical attestations, albeit certainly just one among many others. There may be a great deal more to literature than this, and on most days I tend to think that there is. But, for me, there need not be.

Query 2: Even if the works of Chaucer are 'great', do they and their study do more harm than good?

When I first read the *Canterbury Tales*, which was after I had already earned an MA in English (having taken courses part-time while still immersed in my software engineering career), I was completely awestruck. Never had I encountered a work of literature that possessed such a dazzlingly combination of compelling storytelling, intellectual power, depth of insight, enchanting style and frequent, stupendous moments of sheer, infectious playfulness. A couple years later when I began my PhD programme, it was by no means inevitable that I would become a medievalist (see above for my fondness for nineteenth-century novels), yet the more literary experience I gained, the more Chaucer continued to emerge from the crowd. The eventual acquaintance that I gained with the rest of his works confirmed the qualities that I experienced in the *Tales* and added several others. From that point to this day, when I am asked (as it seems literature professors frequently are),'What is the best book of all time', I always unhesitatingly name the *Tales*, followed by 'of course'.

Nonetheless, I must recognise – prompted by the several scholars cited in the preceding chapters – that Chaucer's still *de facto* position as the Father of English poetry carries with it a set of values that has served, and continues to serve, as a legitimating framework for some deeply entrenched injustices. Many of those injustices, obviously, are encapsulated by the phrase 'white male Eurocentric canon', and the social, cultural, political and institutional forces that have created that canon in their own image, and have installed Chaucer as its English fountainhead, continue to have deeply detrimental impact, albeit one becoming more visible as such every day. Moreover, as many critics have also pointed out, Chaucer's works themselves are scarcely passive vehicles of those forces. Rather, those forces have not had to search very far to find in those works ideologically amenable content, which is to say, those works themselves are part of those forces.

Embarrassingly belatedly, I have become aware of a personal dimension of this aspect of Chaucer's works and their study. My grandparents on one side emigrated to the US in the early twentieth century from a rural village in the Guangdong Province of China; on the other side are Shenandoah Valley Mennonites, ultimately of Swiss-German ancestry. I readily pass as white in most situations, and I am, alas, only slowly coming to realise the extent to which, consciously and unconsciously, I have sought to ensure that passing. I am still coming to grips with how much a desire to be whiter than I am has shaped my behaviour and decisions. Looking back now almost three decades, I cannot say that my attraction to Chaucer – and to a period of English literary history that includes no authors of colour – was not a manifestation of this desire. As Jonathan Hsy has recently explored so incisively, medievalists of colour often experience intrusive inquiries about why *they* would want to be a medievalist;[1] conversely, therefore, my choice to be a medievalist has necessarily added to my cover.

As mentioned above, I continue to believe that Chaucer's works are great, and at this point, having devoted so much time and energy to the study of those works, I doubt that I would survive the cognitive dissonance of fully embracing the possibility that they have done more harm than good. But I cannot in good conscience argue against those who build an informed case for that possibility. To use an analogy, my appreciation of Chaucer's works lies somewhere on the continuum between an appreciation of the Weminuche Wilderness mountains at sunset and of Versailles at the height of tourist season. Both are spectacular, but, on balance, I believe we would be entirely better off without the latter.

Last words and a final query: where does all this leave the value of literature? If you have found your way through this book to this final sentence, you know where.

Note

1 Jonathan Hsy, *Antiracist Medievalisms: From 'Yellow Peril' to Black Lives Matter* (Leeds: Arc Humanities Press, 2021). Hsy both answers the question and exposes (explodes) its assumptions; see especially his initial discussion of disidentification on pp. 4–5.

References

Abrams, M. H. and Stephen Greenblatt (eds), *The Norton Anthology of English Literature*, 7th edn, 2 vols (New York: W. W. Norton, 2000).
Alonso, Carlos J., 'Editor's Column: My Professional Advice (to Graduate Students)', *PMLA*, 117:3 (2002), 401–6.
Alter, Robert, *Canon and Creativity: Modern Writing and the Authority of Scripture* (New Haven: Yale University Press, 2000).
Altieri, Charles, *Reckoning with the Imagination: Wittgenstein and the Aesthetics of Literary Experience* (Ithaca: Cornell University Press, 2015).
Alworth, David J., 'Critique, Modernity, Society, Agency: Matters of Concern in Literary Studies', in Felski and Muecke (eds), *Latour and the Humanities*, pp. 275–99.
Appadurai, Arjun, 'Introduction: Commodities and the Politics of Value', in Arjun Appadurai (ed.), *The Social Life of Things: Commodities in Cultural Perspective* (Cambridge: Cambridge University Press, 1986), pp. 3–63.
Arner, Lynn, *Chaucer, Gower, and the Vernacular Rising: Poetry and the Problem of the Populace after 1381* (University Park: Pennsylvania State University Press, 2013).
———, 'Why Do We Care More About Chaucer Than Gower?', *The Gower Project*, https://thegowerproject.wordpress.com/2015/01/03/why-do-we-care-more-about-chaucer-than-gower/ (2017; accessed 21 July 2017).
Arnold, Matthew, *Culture and Anarchy* (Cambridge: Cambridge University Press, 1993).
Ashe, Laura, 'How to Read Both: The Logic of True Contradictions in Chaucer's World', *SAC*, 42 (2020), 111–46.
Ashton, Gail and Louise Sylvester, *Teaching Chaucer* (Basingstoke: Palgrave Macmillan, 2007).
Attridge, Derek, *The Singularity of Literature* (London: Routledge, 2004).

———, *The Work of Literature* (Oxford: Oxford University Press, 2015).
Baechle, Sarah and Carissa M. Harris, 'The Ethical Challenge of Chaucerian Scholarship in the Twenty-First Century', *ChR*, 56:4 (2021), 311–21.
Bahr, Arthur, *Fragments and Assemblages: Forming Compilations of Medieval London* (Chicago: University of Chicago Press, 2013).
Bahr, Arthur and Alexandra Gillespie, 'Medieval English Manuscripts: Form, Aesthetics, and Literary Text', *ChR*, 47:4 (2013), 346–60.
Bell, David F., 'A Moratorium on Suspicion?', *PMLA*, 117:3 (2002), 487–90.
Bellah, Robert N., Richard Madsen, William M. Sullivan, Ann Swidler and Steven M. Tipton, *Habits of the Heart: Individualism and Commitment in American Life*, 3rd edn (Berkeley: University of California Press, 2007).
Benjamin, Walter, *The Work of Art in the Age of Its Technological Reproducibility, and Other Writings on Media*, ed. Michael W. Jennings, Brigid Doherty and Thomas Y. Levin, trans. Edmund Jephcott, Rodney Livingstone and Howard Eiland and others (Cambridge, MA: Belknap Press of Harvard University Press, 2008).
Bennett, Tony, *Formalism and Marxism* (London: Methuen, 1979).
Benson, C. David, *Chaucer's Drama of Style: Poetic Variety and Contrast in the* Canterbury Tales (Chapel Hill: University of North Carolina Press, 1986).
Berger, Peter L. and Thomas Luckmann, *The Social Construction of Reality: A Treatise in the Sociology of Knowledge* (New York: Anchor Books, 1966).
Bérubé, Michael, 'Introduction: Engaging the Aesthetic', in Michael Bérubé (ed.), *The Aesthetics of Cultural Studies* (Malden: Blackwell, 2005), pp. 1–27.
———, *Rhetorical Occasions* (Chapel Hill: University of North Carolina Press, 2006).
Best, Stephen and Sharon Marcus, 'Surface Reading: An Introduction', *Representations*, 108:1 (2009).
Bjork, Robert E. (ed.), *Old English Shorter Poems: Wisdom and Lyric* (Cambridge, MA: Harvard University Press, 2014).
Bloom, Harold, *Shakespeare: The Invention of the Human* (New York: Riverhead Books, 1998).
———, *The Western Canon: The Books and School of the Ages* (New York: Harcourt Brace, 1994).
Boccaccio, Giovanni, *The Life of Dante (Trattatello in Laude Di Dante)*, trans. Vincenzo Zin Bollettino (New York: Garland, 1990).
———, *Opere in Versi, Corbaccio, Trattatello in Laude Di Dante, Prose Latine, Epistole* (Milano: R. Ricciardi, 1965).

Boltanski, Luc and Laurent Thévenot, *On Justification: Economies of Worth*, trans. Catherine Porter (Princeton: Princeton University Press, 2006).

Bourdieu, Pierre, *Distinction: A Social Critique of the Judgement of Taste*, trans. Richard Nice (Cambridge, MA: Harvard University Press, 1984).

———, *The Field of Cultural Production*, ed. Randal Johnson (New York: Columbia University Press, 1993).

———, *The Logic of Practice*, trans. Richard Nice (Stanford: Stanford University Press, 1990).

Burke, Michael (ed.), *The Routledge Handbook of Stylistics*, 1st edn (London; New York: Routledge, 2014).

Burrow, J. A., 'Should We Leave Medieval Literature to the Medievalists?', *Essays in Criticism*, 53:3 (2003), 278–83.

Butler, Judith, 'The Future of the Humanities Can Be Found in Its Public Forums', *MLA Newsletter*, 52:4 (2020), 2–3.

Cady, Diane, *The Gender of Money in Middle English Literature: Value and Economy in Late Medieval England* (Cham: Palgrave Macmillan, 2019).

Callard, Agnes, *Aspiration: The Agency of Becoming* (New York: Oxford University Press, 2018).

Cannon, Christopher, *The Making of Chaucer's English: A Study of Words* (Cambridge: Cambridge University Press, 1998).

Cantó Milà, Natàlia, *A Sociological Theory of Value: Georg Simmel's Sociological Relationism* (Bielefeld: Transcript Publishing, 2005).

Carey, John, *What Good Are the Arts?* (Oxford: Oxford University Press, 2006).

Carruthers, Mary, '"Micrological Aggregates": Is the New Chaucer Society Speaking in Tongues?', *SAC*, 21 (1999), 1–26.

Casanova, Pascale, *The World Republic of Letters*, trans. Malcolm DeBevoise (Cambridge, MA: Harvard University Press, 2004).

Cawsey, Kathy, *Twentieth-Century Chaucer Criticism: Reading Audiences* (Farnham: Routledge, 2011).

Cerquiglini, Bernard, *In Praise of the Variant: A Critical History of Philology*, trans. Betsy Wing (Baltimore: Johns Hopkins University Press, 1999).

Chaganti, Seeta, 'Boethian Abolition', *PMLA*, 137:1 (2021), 144–54.

———, 'Boethian Privilege and the Abolitionist Position' (lecture given at the Sewanee Medieval Colloquium, University of the South, 9 April 2021).

———, 'B-Sides: Chaucer's "The House of Fame"', *Public Books*, www.publicbooks.org/b-sides-chaucers-the-house-of-fame/ (2019; accessed 14 September 2021).

———, 'B-Sides: "Sir Gawain and the Green Knight"', *Public Books*, www.publicbooks.org/b-sides-sir-gawain-green-knight/ (2017; accessed 14 September 2021).

———, *Strange Footing: Poetic Form and Dance in the Late Middle Ages* (Chicago: University of Chicago Press, 2018).
Chaucer, Geoffrey, *Chaucer's Poetry: An Anthology for the Modern Reader*, ed. E. T. Donaldson, 2nd edn (New York: Ronald Press, 1975).
———, *The Norton Chaucer*, ed. David Lawton (New York: W. W. Norton, 2019).
———, *The Riverside Chaucer*, gen. ed. Larry D. Benson, 3rd edn (Boston: Houghton Mifflin, 1987).
Citton, Yves, 'Fictional Attachments and Literary Weavings in the Anthropocene', in Felski and Muecke (eds), *Latour and the Humanities*, pp. 200–24.
Cohen, Philip G. (ed.), *Devils and Angels: Textual Editing and Literary Theory* (Charlottesville: University Press of Virginia, 1991).
Cohen, Stephen, 'Between Form and Culture: New Historicism and the Promise of a Historical Formalism', in Mark David Rasmussen (ed.), *Renaissance Literature and Its Formal Engagements* (New York: Palgrave, 2002), pp. 17–41.
Connor, Steven, 'Doing without Art', *NLH*, 42:1 (2011), 53–69.
———, *Theory and Cultural Value* (Oxford: Blackwell, 1992).
Cooper, Helen, 'Averting Chaucer's Prophecies: Miswriting, Mismetering, and Misunderstanding', in McCarren and Moffat (eds), *A Guide to Editing Middle English*, pp. 79–93.
Crocker, Holly A., Kathy Lavezzo, Jessica Rosenfeld, Mark Miller and Kellie Robertson, letter from MLA Chaucer Division to Marianne Hirsch and Margaret Ferguson, email attachment (19 April 2013).
Da Rold, Orietta and Elaine Treharne (eds), *Textual Cultures: Cultural Texts* (Cambridge: D. S. Brewer, 2010).
Dagenais, John, 'That Bothersome Residue: Toward a Theory of the Physical Text', in A. N. Doane and Carol Braun Pasternack, *Vox Intexta: Orality and Textuality in the Middle Ages* (Madison: University of Wisconsin Press, 1991), pp. 246–59.
de Man, Paul, *Blindness and Insight: Essays in the Rhetoric of Contemporary Criticism*, 2nd edn (Minneapolis: University of Minnesota Press, 1983).
———, *The Resistance to Theory* (Minneapolis: University of Minnesota Press, 1986).
Derrida, Jacques, *The Truth in Painting*, trans. Geoffrey Bennington and Ian McLeod (Chicago: University of Chicago Press, 1987).
Dewey, John, *Theory of Valuation* (Chicago: University of Chicago Press, 1939).
Dillon, George L., 'Whorfian Stylistics', *Journal of Literary Semantics*, 11:2 (1982), 73–7.
Dinshaw, Carolyn, *Getting Medieval: Sexualities and Communities, Pre- and Postmodern* (Durham: Duke University Press, 1999).

———, *How Soon Is Now?: Medieval Texts, Amateur Readers, and the Queerness of Time* (Durham: Duke University Press, 2012).
Donaldson, E. Talbot, *Speaking of Chaucer* (London: Athlone Press, 1970).
Dromi, Shai M. and Eva Illouz, 'Recovering Morality: Pragmatic Sociology and Literary Studies', *NLH*, 41:2 (2010), 351–69.
Eagleton, Terry, 'Bodies, Artworks, and Use Values', *NLH*, 44:4 (2013), 561–73.
———, *The Event of Literature* (New Haven: Yale University Press, 2012).
———, *How to Read a Poem* (Malden: Wiley-Blackwell, 2007).
———, *The Ideology of the Aesthetic* (Malden: Blackwell, 1990).
———, *Literary Theory: An Introduction* (Minneapolis: University of Minnesota Press, 1983).
Easthope, Antony, *Literary into Cultural Studies* (London: Routledge, 1991).
———, 'Literary Value Again: A Reply to Steven Connor', *Textual Practice*, 5:3 (1991), 334–6.
Echard, Siân and Stephen Partridge, 'Introduction: Varieties of Editing: History, Theory, and Technology', in Siân Echard and Stephen Partridge (eds), *The Book Unbound: Editing and Reading Medieval Manuscripts and Texts* (Toronto: University of Toronto Press, 2004), pp. xi–xxi.
Edmondson, George, 'Naked Chaucer', in Scala and Federico (eds), *The Post-Historical Middle Ages*, pp. 139–60.
Edwards, A. S. G., 'Gladly Wolde He Lerne? Why Chaucer Is Disappearing from the University Curriculum', *Times Literary Supplement* (1 July 2021), pp. 7–8.
Edwards, Suzanne M., ' "Burn All He Has, but Keep His Books": Gloria Naylor and the Proper Objects of Feminist Chaucer Studies', *ChR*, 54:3 (2019), 230–52.
English, James F., *The Global Future of English Studies* (New York: John Wiley, 2012).
———, 'Literary Studies', in Tony Bennett and John Frow (eds), *The SAGE Handbook of Cultural Analysis* (London: SAGE, 2008), pp. 126–44.
Evans, Ruth, 'The Chaucer Society, Victorian Medievalism, and the Nation-State: Englishness and Empire', *The Chaucer Blog*, https://chaucerblog.net/2018/03/the-chaucer-society-victorian-medievalism-and-the-nation-state-englishness-and-empire/ (2018; accessed 4 January 2020).
———, 'An Interim Report on the Standard Edition(s) of The Works of Geoffrey Chaucer', *The Chaucer Blog*, https://chaucerblog.net/2017/10/an-interim-report-on-the-standard-editions-of-the-works-of-geoffrey-chaucer/ (2017; accessed 9 January 2022).
———, 'On Not Being Chaucer', *SAC*, 44 (2022), 3–26.

———, 'What Is a Chaucer?' (paper presented at the MLA Convention, 9 January 2015).
———, 'Update on MLA Proposals and Chaucerians' Responses', email to New Chaucer Society membership (20 April 2013).
Farrell, Thomas J., 'The Value of the Canterbury Tales Project, and Textual Evidence in the Emendation of *Canterbury Tales* III.117', *JEGP*, 120:1 (2021), 93–129.
Fekete, John, 'Introductory Notes for a Postmodern Value Agenda', in John Fekete (ed.), *Life after Postmodernism: Essays on Value and Culture* (New York: St. Martin's Press, 1987), pp. i–xix.
Fellows, Jennifer, 'Author, Author, Author …: An Apology for Parallel Texts', in McCarren and Moffat (eds), *A Guide to Editing Middle English*, pp. 15–24.
Felski, Rita, ' "Context Stinks!" ', *NLH*, 42:4 (2011), 573–91.
———, 'Introduction', *NLH*, 45:2 (2014), v–xi.
———, 'Latour and Literary Studies', *PMLA*, 130:3 (2015), 737–42.
———, *The Limits of Critique* (Chicago: University of Chicago Press, 2015).
———, 'The Role of Aesthetics in Cultural Studies', in Michael Bérubé (ed.), *The Aesthetics of Cultural Studies* (Malden: Blackwell, 2005), pp. 28–43.
———, *Uses of Literature* (Malden: Blackwell, 2008).
Felski, Rita, and Stephen Muecke (eds), *Latour and the Humanities* (Baltimore: Johns Hopkins University Press, 2020).
Fish, Stanley, 'Interpreting the Variorum', *Critical Inquiry*, 2:3 (1976), 465–85.
———, *Is There a Text in This Class?: The Authority of Interpretive Communities* (Cambridge, MA: Harvard University Press, 1980).
———, 'What Is Stylistics and Why Are They Saying Such Terrible Things About It?', in Seymour Benjamin Chatman (ed.), *Approaches to Poetics: Selected Papers from the English Institute* (New York: Columbia University Press, 1973), pp. 109–52.
———, 'What Is Stylistics and Why Are They Saying Such Terrible Things about It?-Part II', *Boundary 2*, 8:1 (1979), 129–46.
———, 'Why No One's Afraid of Wolfgang Iser', *Diacritics*, 11:1 (1981), 2–13.
Fishelov, David, *Dialogues with/and Great Books: The Dynamics of Canon Formation* (Brighton: Sussex Academic Press, 2010).
Flannery, Mary C., 'Good Fun: Cecily Chaumpaigne and the Ethics of Chaucerian Obscenity', *ChR*, 56:4 (2021), 360–77.
Fradenburg, L. O. Aranye, *Sacrifice Your Love: Psychoanalysis, Historicism, Chaucer* (Minneapolis: University of Minnesota Press, 2002).

Frank, Robert W. and Edmund Reiss, 'Bringing Confort and Mirthe', *ChR*, 1:1 (1966), 1–3.
Franke, William, *The Revelation of Imagination: From Homer and the Bible through Virgil and Augustine to Dante* (Evanston: Northwestern University Press, 2015).
Frow, John, *Cultural Studies and Cultural Value* (Oxford: Clarendon Press, 1995).
——, 'On Literature in Cultural Studies', in Michael Bérubé (ed.), *The Aesthetics of Cultural Studies* (Malden: Blackwell, 2005), pp. 44–57.
——, 'On Midlevel Concepts', *NLH*, 41:2 (2010), 237–52.
——, *The Practice of Value: Essays on Literature in Cultural Studies* (Crawley: University of Western Australia, 2013).
Gagnier, Regenia, *The Insatiability of Human Wants: Economics and Aesthetics in Market Society* (Chicago: University of Chicago Press, 2000).
Gallagher, Catherine and Stephen Greenblatt, *Practicing New Historicism* (Chicago: University of Chicago Press, 2000).
Gates, Henry Louis, Jr., *Loose Canons: Notes on the Culture Wars* (Oxford: Oxford University Press, 1992).
Gillespie, Alexandra, 'The History of the Book', *New Medieval Literatures*, 9 (2007), 245–77.
Goodstein, Elizabeth S., *Georg Simmel and the Disciplinary Imaginary* (Stanford: Stanford University Press, 2017).
Graff, Gerald, *Professing Literature: An Institutional History* (Chicago: University of Chicago Press, 1987).
Green, Bryan S., *Literary Methods and Sociological Theory: Case Studies of Simmel and Weber* (Chicago: University of Chicago Press, 1988).
Green, Richard Firth, Rev. of *Poets and Power from Chaucer to Wyatt*, by Robert J. Meyer-Lee, *SAC*, 30 (2009), 387–9.
Greenblatt, Stephen, *Shakespearean Negotiations: The Circulation of Social Energy in Renaissance England* (Berkeley: University of California Press, 1988).
—— (ed.), *The Norton Anthology of English Literature*, 10th edn, 6 vols (New York: W. W. Norton, 2018).
Grigely, Joseph, *Textualterity: Art, Theory, and Textual Criticism* (Ann Arbor: University of Michigan Press, 1995).
Guillory, John, *Cultural Capital: The Problem of Literary Canon Formation* (Chicago: University of Chicago Press, 1993).
——, 'It Must Be Abstract', in Robert Alter (ed.), *Pleasure and Change: The Aesthetics of Canon* (Oxford: Oxford University Press, 2004), pp. 65–75.
Hanna, Ralph, 'Analytical Survey 4: Middle English Manuscripts and the Study of Literature', *New Medieval Literatures*, 4 (2001), 243–64.

——, *London Literature, 1300–1380* (Cambridge: Cambridge University Press, 2005).

——, 'Piers Plowman and the Radically Chic', *The Yearbook of Langland Studies*, 13 (1999), 179–92.

——, *Pursuing History: Middle English Manuscripts and Their Texts* (Stanford: Stanford University Press, 1996).

Hansen, Elaine Tuttle, *Chaucer and the Fictions of Gender* (Berkeley: University of California Press, 1992).

Harman, Graham, 'Entanglement and Relation: A Response to Bruno Latour and Ian Hodder', *NLH*, 45:1 (2014), 37–49.

Harris, Carissa M., *Obscene Pedagogies: Transgressive Talk and Sexual Education in Late Medieval Britain* (Ithaca: Cornell University Press, 2018).

Hartman, Geoffrey, 'The Passing of the Canon', in Robert Alter (ed.), *Pleasure and Change: The Aesthetics of Canon* (Oxford: Oxford University Press, 2004), pp. 53–64.

Harvard Humanities Working Group, 'The Teaching of the Arts and Humanities at Harvard College: Mapping the Future', https://scholar.harvard.edu/files/sdkelly/files/mapping_the_future_12_april_2013.pdf (2013; accessed 4 January 2020).

Hennion, Antoine, 'From ANT to Pragmatism: A Journey with Bruno Latour at the CSI', in Felski and Muecke (eds), *Latour and the Humanities*, trans. Muecke, pp. 52–75.

Hilmo, Maidie, *Medieval Images, Icons, and Illustrated English Literary Texts: From Ruthwell Cross to the Ellesmere Chaucer* (Aldershot: Ashgate, 2004).

Hirsch, E. D., *Validity in Interpretation* (New Haven: Yale University Press, 1967).

Hirsch, Marianne, 'D023--Possible MLA Division Changes: Your Advice Needed', email to Kellie Robertson, Holly A. Crocker, Kathy Lavezzo, Jessica Rosenfeld and Mark Miller (28 March 2013).

Horobin, Simon, 'Thomas Hoccleve: Chaucer's First Editor?', *ChR*, 50:3–4 (2015), 228–50.

Horowitz, Damon, 'From Technologist to Philosopher: Why You Should Quit Your Technology Job and Get a Ph.D. in the Humanities', *The Chronicle of Higher Education*, www.chronicle.com/article/from-techn ologist-to-philosopher (2011; accessed 4 January 2020).

Hoy, David Couzens, *The Critical Circle: Literature, History, and Philosophical Hermeneutics* (Berkeley: University of California Press, 1982).

Hsy, Jonathan, *Antiracist Medievalisms: From 'Yellow Peril' to Black Lives Matter* (Leeds: Arc Humanities Press, 2021).

Hunter, Ian, *Culture and Government: The Emergence of Literary Education* (Basingstoke: Macmillan Press, 1988).
Ingham, Patricia Clare, 'Why Chaucer Now?', *The Chaucer Blog*, https://chaucerblog.net/2015/05/why-chaucer-now/ (2015; accessed 4 January 2020).
Iser, Wolfgang, *The Act of Reading: A Theory of Aesthetic Response* (Baltimore: Johns Hopkins University Press, 1978).
Jaeger, C. Stephen, 'Aura and Charisma: Two Useful Concepts in Critical Theory', *New German Critique*, 38:3 (2011), 17–34.
Jagot, Shazia, 'Students from All Backgrounds Need Access to the Literature of Every Age', *Times Higher Education*, www.timeshighereducation.com/blog/students-all-backgrounds-need-access-literature-every-age (2021; accessed 14 September 2021).
Jahner, Jennifer, *Literature and Law in the Era of Magna Carta* (Oxford: Oxford University Press, 2019).
Jakobson, Roman, 'Closing Statement: Linguistics and Poetics', in Thomas Albert Sebeok (ed.), *Style In Language* (Cambridge, MA: Technology Press of Massachusetts Institute of Technology, 1960), pp. 350–77.
Jay, Paul and Gerald Graff, 'Fear of Being Useful', *Inside Higher Ed*, www.insidehighered.com/views/2012/01/05/essay-new-approach-defend-value-humanities (2012; accessed 4 January 2020).
Johnson, Eleanor, 'Against Order: Medieval, Modern, and Contemporary Critiques of Causality', in *Chaucer and the Subversion of Form*, ed. by Thomas A. Prendergast and Jessica Rosenfeld (Cambridge: Cambridge University Press, 2018), pp. 61–82.
———, *Practicing Literary Theory in the Middle Ages: Ethics and the Mixed Form in Chaucer, Gower, Usk, and Hoccleve* (Chicago: University of Chicago Press, 2013).
Johnston, Michael and Michael Van Dussen (eds), *The Medieval Manuscript Book: Cultural Approaches* (Cambridge: Cambridge University Press, 2015).
Jusdanis, Gregory, *Fiction Agonistes: In Defense of Literature* (Stanford: Stanford University Press, 2010).
Kamolnick, Paul, 'Simmel's Legacy for Contemporary Value Theory: A Critical Assessment', *Sociological Theory*, 19:1 (2001), 65–85.
Karpik, Lucien, *Valuing the Unique*, trans. Nora Scott (Princeton: Princeton University Press, 2010).
Kelemen, Erick, 'Critical Editing and Close Reading in the Undergraduate Classroom', *Pedagogy: Critical Approaches to Teaching Literature, Language, Composition, and Culture*, 12:1 (2012), 121–38.
Kerby-Fulton, Kathryn, Maidie Hilmo, and Linda Olson, *Opening Up Middle English Manuscripts: Literary and Visual Approaches* (Ithaca: Cornell University Press, 2012).

Kerby-Fulton, Kathryn, and with Denise Despres, 'Fabricating Failure: The Professional Reader as Textual Terrorist', *The Yearbook of Langland Studies*, 13 (1999), 193–206.
Kermode, Frank, *Pleasure and Change: The Aesthetics of Canon*, ed. Robert Alter (Oxford: Oxford University Press, 2004).
Khwaja, Waqas, 'Reimagining the Humanities in a Transcultural, Post-Truth World', in Waseem Anwar and Nosheen Yousaf (eds), *Transcultural Humanities in South Asia: Critical Essays on Literature and Culture* (New York: Routledge, 2022), pp. 28–40.
Kittredge, George Lyman, *Chaucer and His Poetry* (Cambridge, MA: Harvard University Press, 1915).
Klinkenborg, Verlyn, 'The Decline and Fall of the English Major', *New York Times* (23 June 2013), New York edition, p. SR10.
Knapp, Ethan, 'Chaucer Criticism and Its Legacies', in Seth Lerer (ed.), *The Yale Companion to Chaucer* (New Haven: Yale University Press, 2006), pp. 324–56.
Knapp, Peggy A., 'Aesthetic Attention and the Chaucerian Text', *ChR*, 39:3 (2005), 241–58.
———, *Chaucerian Aesthetics* (New York: Palgrave Macmillan, 2008).
Knapp, Steven, *Literary Interest: The Limits of Anti-Formalism* (Cambridge, MA: Harvard University Press, 1993).
Knight, Stephen, 'Textual Variants: Textual Variance', *Southern Review*, 16:1 (1983), 44–54.
Kolbas, E. Dean, *Critical Theory and the Literary Canon* (Boulder: Westview Press, 2001).
Konchar Farr, Cecelia, *The Ulysses Delusion: Rethinking Standards of Literary Merit* (Basingstoke: Palgrave Macmillan, 2016).
Krebs, Paula M., 'Our Majors Can Fix Things', *MLA Newsletter*, 53:1 (2021), 1, 5.
Lahire, Bernard, *La Condition littéraire: la double vie des écrivains* (Paris: Découverte, 2006).
———, 'The Double Life of Writers', trans. Gwendolyn Wells, *NLH*, 41:2 (2010), 443–65.
———, *The Plural Actor*, trans. David Fernbach (Cambridge: Polity, 2011).
Langland, William, *Piers Plowman: The B Version*, ed. George Kane and E. Talbot Donaldson (London: Athlone Press, 1975).
Latour, Bruno, 'An Attempt at a Compositionist Manifesto', *NLH*, 41:3 (2010), 471–90.
———, *An Inquiry into Modes of Existence: An Anthropology of the Moderns*, trans. Catherine Porter (Cambridge, MA: Harvard University Press, 2018).
———, *Pandora's Hope: Essays on the Reality of Science Studies* (Cambridge, MA: Harvard University Press, 1999).

———, *Reassembling the Social: An Introduction to Actor-Network-Theory* (Oxford: Oxford University Press, 2005).

———, 'Why Has Critique Run out of Steam? From Matters of Fact to Matters of Concern', *Critical Inquiry*, 30:2 (2004), 225–48.

Lawton, David, *Chaucer's Narrators* (Cambridge: D. S. Brewer, 1985).

———, *Voice in Later Medieval English Literature: Public Interiorities* (Oxford: Oxford University Press, 2017).

Leck, Ralph M., *Georg Simmel and Avant-Garde Sociology* (Amherst, NY: Humanity Books, 2000).

Leitch, Vincent B., William E. Cain, Laurie A. Finke, John McGowan, T. Denean Sharpley-Whiting and Jeffrey J. Williams (eds), *The Norton Anthology of Theory and Criticism*, 3rd edn (New York: W. W. Norton, 2018).

Lerer, Seth, *Chaucer and His Readers: Imagining the Author in Late-Medieval England* (Princeton: Princeton University Press, 1993).

———, 'The Endurance of Formalism in Middle English Studies', *Literature Compass*, 1 (2003), 1–15.

——— (ed.), *Reading from the Margins: Textual Studies, Chaucer, and Medieval Literature* (San Marino: Huntington Library Press, 1996).

Levine, Caroline, *Forms: Whole, Rhythm, Hierarchy, Network* (Princeton: Princeton University Press, 2015).

Levine, George, 'Introduction: Reclaiming the Aesthetic', in George Levine (ed.), *Aesthetics and Ideology* (New Brunswick: Rutgers University Press, 1994), pp. 1–28.

———, 'The Real Trouble', *Profession* (1993), 43–5.

———, 'Saving Disinterest: Aesthetics, Contingency, and Mixed Conditions', *NLH*, 32:4 (2001), 907–31.

Levinson, Marjorie, 'What Is New Formalism', *PMLA*, 122:2 (2007), 558–69.

Leypoldt, Günter, 'Degrees of Public Relevance: Walter Scott and Toni Morrison', *MLQ*, 77:3 (2016), 369–93.

———, 'Singularity and the Literary Market', *NLH*, 45:1 (2014), 71–88.

Liu, Alan, 'The Power of Formalism: The New Historicism', *ELH*, 56:4 (1989), 721–71.

Lomuto, Sierra, 'Becoming Postmedieval: The Stakes of the Global Middle Ages', *postmedieval*, 11:4 (2020), 503–12.

———, 'A White Canon in a World of Color', *Medievalists of Color*, http://medievalistsofcolor.com/race-in-the-profession/a-white-canon-in-a-world-of-color/ (2019; accessed 4 January 2020).

Love, Heather, 'Care, Concern, and the Ethics of Description', in Felski and Muecke (eds), *Latour and the Humanities*, pp. 107–31.

———, 'Close but Not Deep: Literary Ethics and the Descriptive Turn', *NLH*, 41:2 (2010), 371–91.
Lumiansky, R. M., *Of Sondry Folk: The Dramatic Principle in the Canterbury Tales* (Austin: University of Texas Press, 1955).
Lynch, Deidre Shauna, *Loving Literature: A Cultural History* (University of Chicago Press, 2015).
Machan, Tim William, 'Chaucer's Poetry, Versioning, and Hypertext', *Philological Quarterly*, 73:3 (1994), 299–316.
———, '"I Endowed Thy Purposes": Shakespeare, Editing, and Middle English Literature', *Text*, 13 (2000), 9–25.
———, 'Middle English Text Production and Modern Textual Criticism', in A. J. Minnis and Charlotte Brewer (eds), *Crux and Controversy in Middle English Textual Criticism* (Cambridge: D. S. Brewer, 1992), pp. 1–18.
———, *Textual Criticism and Middle English Texts* (Charlottesville: University Press of Virginia, 1994).
Manly, John M. and Edith Rickert, *The Text of the Canterbury Tales: Studied on the Basis of All Known Manuscripts*, 8 vols (Chicago: University of Chicago Press, 1940).
Marcus, Sharon, Heather Love and Stephen Best, 'Building a Better Description', *Representations*, 135:1 (2016), 1–21.
Marshall, Helen and Peter Buchanan, 'New Formalism and the Forms of Middle English Literary Texts', *Literature Compass*, 8:4 (2011), 164–72.
Massumi, Brian, *99 Theses on the Revaluation of Value* (Minneapolis: University of Minnesota Press, 2018).
Matthews, David, *The Making of Middle English, 1765–1910* (Minneapolis: University of Minnesota Press, 1999).
McCarren, Vincent P. and Douglas Moffat (eds), *A Guide to Editing Middle English* (Ann Arbor: University of Michigan Press, 1998).
McDonald, Peter D., 'Ideas of the Book and Histories of Literature: After Theory?', *PMLA*, 121:1 (2006), 214–28.
McGann, Jerome J., *A Critique of Modern Textual Criticism* (Chicago: University of Chicago Press, 1983).
McGillivray, Murray, 'Towards a Post-Critical Edition: Theory, Hypertext, and the Presentation of Middle English Works', *Text*, 7 (1994), 175–99.
McKenzie, D. F., *Bibliography and the Sociology of Texts* (Cambridge: Cambridge University Press, 1999).
Meyer-Lee, Robert J., 'Abandon the Fragments', *SAC*, 35 (2013), 47–83.
———, *Literary Value and Social Identity in the Canterbury Tales* (Cambridge: Cambridge University Press, 2019).

———, *Poets and Power from Chaucer to Wyatt* (Cambridge: Cambridge University Press, 2007).
Meyer-Lee, Robert J. and Catherine Sanok (eds), *The Medieval Literary: Beyond Form* (Cambridge: D. S. Brewer, 2018).
Milac, Louis T., 'Unconscious Ordering in the Prose of Swift', in Jacob Leed (ed.), *The Computer and Literary Style: Introductory Essays and Studies* (Kent, Ohio: Kent State University Press, 1966), pp. 79–106.
Miles, Laura Saetveit and Diane Watt, 'Introduction: Women's Literary Culture and the Medieval English Canon: Gender and Genre', *SAC*, 42 (2020), 285–93.
Miller, J. Hillis, 'Stevens' Rock and Criticism as Cure, II', *The Georgia Review*, 30:2 (1976), 330–48.
Miller, Mark, *Philosophical Chaucer: Love, Sex, and Agency in the Canterbury Tales* (Cambridge: Cambridge University Press, 2004).
———, 'Why Do We Care About Chaucer?', *The Chaucer Blog*, https://chaucerblog.net/2014/05/what-do-we-care-about-chaucer/ (2014; accessed 4 January 2020).
Miller, Timothy S., 'Hyper Chaucer', www.thefishinprison.com/hyper-chaucer.html (accessed 17 October 2021).
Millett, Bella, 'What Happened to Electronic Editing?', in Vincent Gillespie and Anne Hudson (eds), *Probable Truth: Editing Medieval Texts from Britain in the Twenty-First Century* (Turnhout: Brepols, 2013), pp. 39–54.
Minnis, A. J. and A. B. Scott, with David Wallace (eds), *Medieval Literary Theory and Criticism c. 1100–c. 1375: The Commentary Tradition* (Oxford: Clarendon Press, 1988).
Minnis, Alastair and Ruth Evans, letter from NCS President and Executive Director to Marianne Hirsch and Margaret Ferguson, email attachment (17 April 2013).
MLA Teagle Foundation Working Group, 'Report to the Teagle Foundation on the Undergraduate Major in Language and Literature', *Profession*, 2009, 285–312.
Mohanty, Satya P., 'Can Our Values Be Objective? On Ethics, Aesthetics, and Progressive Politics', *NLH*, 32:4 (2001), 803–33.
Mooney, Linne R., 'Chaucer's Scribe', *Speculum*, 81:1 (2006), 97–138.
Moretti, Franco, *Graphs, Maps, Trees: Abstract Models for Literary History* (London: Verso, 2007).
Morse, Charlotte C., 'From "Ricardian Poetry" to Ricardian Studies', in A. J. Minnis, Charlotte C. Morse and Thorlac Turville-Petre (eds), *Essays on Ricardian Literature: In Honour of J. A. Burrow* (Oxford: Clarendon Press, 1997), pp. 316–44.
———, 'What the Clerk's Tale Suggests about Manly and Rickert's Edition and the Canterbury Tales Project', in A. J. Minnis (ed.), *Middle English*

Poetry: Texts and Traditions: Essays in Honour of Derek Pearsall (Woodbridge: York Medieval Press, 2001), pp. 41–56.

Mosser, Daniel W., 'Reading and Editing the *Canterbury Tales*: Past, Present, and Future (?)', *Text*, 7 (1994), 201–32.

Muecke, Stephen, 'An Ecology of Institutions: Recomposing the Humanities', in Felski and Muecke (eds), *Latour and the Humanities*, pp. 31–51.

Mukařovský, Jan, *Aesthetic Function, Norm and Value as Social Facts*, trans. Mark E. Suino (Ann Arbor: University of Michigan, 1970).

Mukherjee, Ankhi, *What Is a Classic? Postcolonial Rewriting and Invention of the Canon* (Stanford: Stanford University Press, 2014).

Nichols, Stephen G., 'Introduction: Philology in a Manuscript Culture', *Speculum*, 65:1 (1990), 1–10.

Nolan, Maura, 'Making the Aesthetic Turn: Adorno, the Medieval, and the Future of the Past', *Journal of Medieval and Early Modern Studies*, 34:3 (2004), 549–75.

Olson, Clair C., 'The Interludes of the Marriage Group in the *Canterbury Tales*', in Beryl Rowland (ed.), *Chaucer and Middle English Studies in Honour of Rossell Hope Robbins* (Kent: Kent State University Press, 1974), pp. 164–72.

Olson, Glending, 'Making and Poetry in the Age of Chaucer', *Comparative Literature*, 31 (1979), 272–90.

Otaño Gracia, Nahir I., 'Borders and the Global North Atlantic: Chaucer, Pilgrimage, and Crusade', *English Language Notes*, 58:2 (2020), 35–49.

Owen, Charles A., 'The *Canterbury Tales*: Beginnings (3) and Endings (2 + 1)', *Chaucer Yearbook*, 1 (1992), 189–211.

Patterson, Lee, *Acts of Recognition: Essays on Medieval Culture* (Notre Dame: University of Notre Dame Press, 2010).

———, *Chaucer and the Subject of History* (Madison: University of Wisconsin Press, 1991).

———, 'Chaucer's Pardoner on the Couch: Psyche and Clio in Medieval Literary Studies', *Speculum*, 76:3 (2001), 638–80.

———, 'The Disenchanted Classroom', *Exemplaria*, 8:2 (1996), 513–45.

———, 'Introduction: Critical Historicism and Medieval Studies', in Lee Patterson (ed.), *Literary Practice and Social Change in Britain, 1380–1530* (Berkeley: University of California Press, 1990), pp. 1–14.

———, *Negotiating the Past: The Historical Understanding of Medieval Literature* (Madison: University of Wisconsin Press, 1987).

———, 'On the Margin: Postmodernism, Ironic History, and Medieval Studies', *Speculum*, 65:1 (1990), 87–108.

———, 'The Parson's Tale and the Quitting of the *Canterbury Tales*', *Traditio*, 34 (1978), 331–80.

———, *Temporal Circumstances: Form and History in the 'Canterbury Tales'* (Basingstoke: Palgrave Macmillan, 2006).

———, 'The Return to Philology', in John H. Van Engen (ed.), *The Past and Future of Medieval Studies* (Notre Dame: University of Notre Dame Press, 1994), pp. 231–44.

Pearsall, Derek, 'Authorial Revision in Some Late-Medieval English Texts', in A. J. Minnis and Charlotte Brewer (eds), *Crux and Controversy in Middle English Textual Criticism* (Cambridge: D. S. Brewer, 1992), pp. 39–48.

———, 'Editing Medieval Texts: Some Developments and Some Problems', in Jerome J. McGann (ed.), *Textual Criticism and Literary Interpretation* (Chicago: University of Chicago Press, 1985), pp. 92–106.

———, 'Medieval Literature and Historical Enquiry', *The Modern Language Review*, 99:4 (2004), xxxi–xlii.

———, 'The Value/s of Manuscript Study: A Personal Retrospect', *Journal of the Early Book Society*, 3 (2000), 167–81.

Perkins, Nicholas, *The Gift of Narrative in Medieval England* (Manchester: Manchester University Press, 2021).

Poovey, Mary, *Genres of the Credit Economy: Mediating Value in Eighteenth- and Nineteenth-Century Britain* (Chicago: University of Chicago Press, 2008).

Prendergast, Thomas A., 'Canon Formation', in Marion Turner (ed.), *A Handbook of Middle English Studies* (Hoboken: John Wiley, 2013), pp. 239–51.

———, *Chaucer's Dead Body: From Corpse to Corpus* (London: Routledge, 2004).

———, 'Introduction: Writing, Authenticity, and the Fabrication of the Chaucerian Text', in Prendergast and Kline (eds), Rewriting Chaucer, pp. 1–9.

Prendergast, Thomas A. and Barbara Kline (eds), *Rewriting Chaucer: Culture, Authority, and the Idea of the Authentic Text, 1400–1602* (Columbus: Ohio State University Press, 1999).

Prendergast, Thomas A., and Jessica Rosenfeld (eds), *Chaucer and the Subversion of Form* (Cambridge: Cambridge University Press, 2018).

Price, Leah, 'From The History of a Book to a "History of the Book"', *Representations*, 108:1 (2009).

Readings, Bill, *The University in Ruins* (Cambridge, MA: Harvard University Press, 1996).

Robinson, Peter, 'The History, Discoveries, and Aims of the *Canterbury Tales* Project', *ChR*, 38:2 (2003), 126–39.

———, 'Response to Roger Bagnall Paper: Integrating Digital Papyrology', in Jerome J. McGann (ed.), *Online Humanities Scholarship: The Shape of Things to Come* (Houston: Rice University Press, 2010), pp. 99–108.

Roger, Euan and Sebastian Sobecki, 'Geoffrey Chaucer, Cecily Chaumpaigne, and the Statute of Laborers: New Records and Old Evidence Reconsidered', *ChR*, 57:4 (2022), 407–37.

Rooney, Ellen, 'Form and Contentment', *MLQ*, 61:1 (2000), 17–40.
Rose, Christine M., ' "Diverse Folk Diversely They Seyde": Teaching Chaucer in the Nineties', *Exemplaria*, 8:2 (1996), 443–8.
Ross, Trevor, *The Making of the English Literary Canon: From the Middle Ages to the Late Eighteenth Century* (Montreal: McGill-Queen's University Press, 1998).
Rubery, Matthew and Leah Price, 'Introduction', in Matthew Rubery and Leah Price (eds), *Further Reading* (Oxford: Oxford University Press, 2020), pp. 1–11.
Salisbury, Eve, 'Rethinking the Place of the Author', *MLA Commons*, https://mla.hcommons.org/groups/middle-english/forum/topic/rethinking-the-place-of-the-author/ (2015; accessed 13 October 2021).
Scala, Elizabeth, *Absent Narratives, Manuscript Textuality, and Literary Structure in Late Medieval England* (New York: Palgrave Macmillan, 2002).
——, 'Historicists and Their Discontents: Reading Psychoanalytically in Medieval Studies', *Texas Studies in Literature and Language*, 44:1 (2002), 108–31.
——, 'The Gender of Historicism', in Scala and Federico (eds), *The Post-Historical Middle Ages* (New York: Palgrave Macmillan, 2009), pp. 191–214.
Scala, Elizabeth, and Sylvia Federico (eds), *The Post-Historical Middle Ages* (New York: Palgrave Macmillan, 2009).
Scholes, Robert, *English after the Fall: From Literature to Textuality* (Iowa City: University of Iowa Press, 2011).
——, 'The English Curriculum after the Fall', *Pedagogy*, 10:1 (2010), 229–40.
Sebastian, John T., 'Chaucer and the Theory Wars: Attack of the Historicists? The Psychoanalysts Strike Back? Or a New Hope?', *Literature Compass*, 3:4 (2006), 767–77.
Seyhan, Azade, 'Why Major in Literature – What Do We Tell Our Students?', *PMLA*, 117:3 (2002), 510–12.
Short, Mick, *Exploring the Language of Poems, Plays and Prose* (London: Longman, 1996).
Simmel, Georg, *The Philosophy of Money*, trans. Tom Bottomore and David Frisby (London: Routledge & Kegan Paul, 1978).
Simpson, James, *Reform and Cultural Revolution* (Oxford: Oxford University Press, 2002).
Skiveren, Tobias, 'Postcritique and the Problem of the Lay Reader', *NLH*, 53:1 (2022), 161–80.
Smith, Barbara Herrnstein, *Contingencies of Value: Alternative Perspectives for Critical Theory* (Cambridge, MA: Harvard University Press, 1988).

Soderholm, James (ed.), *Beauty and the Critic: Aesthetics in an Age of Cultural Studies* (Tuscaloosa: University of Alabama Press, 1997).
Solberg, Emma Margaret, 'Response to "#MeToo, Medieval Literature, and Trauma-Informed Pedagogy"', *New Chaucer Studies: Pedagogy and Profession*, 2:2 (2021), 134–53.
Sotirova, Violeta (ed.), *The Bloomsbury Companion to Stylistics* (London: Bloomsbury Academic, 2016).
Spearing, A. C., *Medieval Autographies: The 'I' of the Text* (Notre Dame: University of Notre Dame Press, 2012).
———, *Textual Subjectivity: The Encoding of Subjectivity in Medieval Narratives and Lyrics* (Oxford: Oxford University Press, 2005).
Stimpson, Catharine R., 'Introduction', *Profession* (1991), 5.
Stockwell, Peter, *Cognitive Poetics: An Introduction*, 2nd edn (London: Routledge, 2019).
Symes, Carol, 'Manuscript Matrix, Modern Canon', in Paul Strohm (ed.), *Middle English* (Oxford: Oxford University Press, 2007), pp. 7–22.
Tanselle, G. Thomas, *Textual Criticism and Scholarly Editing* (Charlottesville: University Press of Virginia, 1990).
Taylor, Andrew, 'Session 3 (Papers): "In Praise of the Middle English Variant"', *The New Chaucer Society Newsletter*, 29:1 (2007), 2.
Theile, Verena, and Linda Tredennick (eds), *New Formalisms and Literary Theory* (Basingstoke: Palgrave Macmillan, 2013).
Tinkle, Theresa, *Gender and Power in Medieval Exegesis* (New York: Palgrave Macmillan, 2010).
———, 'The Wife of Bath's Textual/Sexual Lives', in George Bornstein and Theresa Tinkle (eds), *The Iconic Page in Manuscript, Print, and Digital Culture* (Ann Arbor: University of Michigan Press, 1998), pp. 55–88.
Toolan, Michael, *The Stylistics of Fiction: A Literary-Linguistics Approach* (London: Routledge, 1990).
Trigg, Stephanie, *Congenial Souls: Reading Chaucer from Medieval to Postmodern* (Minneapolis: University of Minnesota Press, 2002).
Turner, James, *Philology: The Forgotten Origins of the Modern Humanities* (Princeton: Princeton University Press, 2014).
Turner, Marion, *Chaucer: A European Life* (Princeton: Princeton University Press, 2019).
Turville-Petre, Thorlac, 'Editing Electronic Texts', in Vincent Gillespie and Anne Hudson (eds), *Probable Truth: Editing Medieval Texts from Britain in the Twenty-First Century* (Turnhout: Brepols, 2013), pp. 55–70.
Underwood, Ted and Jordan Sellers, 'The Longue Durée of Literary Prestige', *MLQ*, 77:3 (2016), 321–44.

Vaughan, Míċeál F., 'Creating Comfortable Boundaries: Scribes, Editors, and the Invention of the Parson's Tale', in Prendergast and Kline (eds), *Rewriting Chaucer*, pp. 45–90.
Viswanathan, Gauri, *Masks of Conquest: Literary Study and British Rule in India* (New York: Columbia University Press, 1989).
Wallace, David, *Chaucerian Polity: Absolutist Lineages and Associational Forms in England and Italy* (Stanford: Stanford University Press, 1997).
——, (ed.), *The Cambridge History of Medieval English Literature* (Cambridge: Cambridge University Press, 1999).
Warren, Michelle R., 'Post-Philology', in Patricia Clare Ingham and Michelle R. Warren (eds), *Postcolonial Moves: Medieval Through Modern* (New York: Palgrave Macmillan, 2003), pp. 19–45.
Watson, Nicholas, 'Response to the New Chaucer Society Conference, New York, July 27–31, 2006', *The New Chaucer Society Newsletter*, 28:2 (2006), 1–5.
Weber, Max, *The Vocation Lectures*, ed. David Owen and Tracy B. Strong, trans. Rodney Livingstone (Indianapolis: Hackett Publishing, 2004).
Weinstein, Deena and Michael A. Weinstein, *Postmodern(ized) Simmel* (London: Routledge, 1993).
Wellek, René and Austin Warren, *Theory of Literature* (New York: Harcourt Brace, 1949).
Williams, Raymond, *Marxism and Literature* (New York: Oxford University Press, 1977).
Willinsky, John, 'Matthew Arnold's Legacy: The Powers of Literature', *Research in the Teaching of English*, 24:4 (1990), 343–61.
Wimsatt, W. K., with Monroe C. Beardsley, *The Verbal Icon: Studies in the Meaning of Poetry* (Lexington: University of Kentucky Press, 1954).

Index

Actor-Network Theory 13, 83–5, 90, 102, 126, 222
Adorno, Theodor W. 73
Agnes Scott College 176–80
Alonso, Carlos J. 6, 123
Althusser, Louis 133
Altieri, Charles 72
Alworth, David J., 126
Arendt, Hannah 170
Arner, Lynn 161–2
Arnold, Matthew 160
Ashe, Laura 105, 107, 109
Attridge, Derek 73, 80, 86
axiological approach to value, definition of 100
axiological environment, definition of 83

Baechle, Sarah 177
Bahr, Arthur 24, 32
Balthaser, Benjamin 93
Barthes, Roland 164
Beardsley, Monroe C. 39, 41, 43
Bell, David F. 5
Benjamin, Walter 117, 118, 236
Berger, Thomas 197
Best, Stephen 191, 202
Bloom, Harold 6, 105, 155
Boccaccio, Giovanni
    Trattatello in laude di Dante 13, 112–19, 121, 137, 181
Boethius, Anicius Manlius Severinus 226–9

book history 6, 20
Bordalejo, Barbara 26
Bourdieu, Pierre 10, 56, 77, 93, 171, 197
Burrow, John 45
Buss, Sarah 96
Butler, Judith 2

Cady, Diane 131
Cannon, Christopher 32, 146
Canterbury Tales 19–20, 27, 33, 43, 48, 52, 54, 156, 161, 176, 202, 225, 228, 239
    dramatic approach to 212–14
    General Prologue, first sentence of 204–6
    Merchant's Tale 212–13, 225
    Parson's Tale 68, 193–4, 199, 200, 203, 205
    Squire's Tale 190, 192–3, 199
    Wife of Bath's Prologue 23, 32
Canterbury Tales Project 26, 33
Cantó Milà, Natàlia 102
Carruthers, Mary 24
Cerquiglini, Bernard 20
Chaganti, Seeta 226–9, 235
cognitive poetics 231
Connor, Steven 7, 74, 75, 78, 86
constellation, axiological network, definition of 111, 197
crisis in literary studies 2, 4, 6, 15, 16, 122

Index 261

Crocker, Holly, Kathy Lavezzo, Jessica Rosenfeld, Mark Miller, and Kellie Robertson
 Letter to the MLA Executive Council 145–7
cultural studies 6, 9, 30, 45–50, 106, 125

Dagenais, John 23
Dangarembga, Tsitsi 137, 141
de Man, Paul 218, 219, 233, 235
defamiliarisation 13, 120–2, 181, 223
Depres, Denise 40
Derrida, Jacques 73, 133
descriptive reading 125, 190, 194, 202, 230
Dewey, John 81
Dinshaw, Carolyn 236
distant reading 20, 92, 125, 190, 202
Donaldson, E. T. 30, 52
Dromi, Shai M. 128

Eagleton, Terry 9, 81, 83
Easthope, Antony 86
Edwards, Suzanne 177, 178
Empson, William 170
English, James F. 123
Evans, Ruth 141–9
Evans, Ruth and Alastair Minnis
 Letter to the MLA Executive Council 142–7

Fekete, John 74
Felski, Rita 8, 74, 80–1, 90, 122, 126, 190, 191
Fish, Stanley 9, 81, 86, 87, 189, 194–8, 218
Floyd, George 226
formalism 86, 107, 118, 120–2, 194, 208
 see also New Criticism
Foucault, Michel 74
Fradenburg, Aranye 24, 56
Frow, John 74, 77, 79, 80
Furnivall, Frederick J. 147

Gadamer, Hans-Georg 165
Gallagher, Catherine 44, 46, 47
Gates, Jr, Henry Louis 135–8, 140, 141, 157, 160, 164, 167, 179
Geertz, Clifford 44
genealogical approach to literary value, definition of 74
Gillespie, Alexandra 24, 32
Goodstein, Elizabeth S. 101
Gower, John 156, 158, 162
Graff, Gerald 5, 151–5
Green, Richard Firth 65
Greenblatt, Stephen 44, 46, 47, 209
Guillory, John 10, 56, 75, 78, 105, 165, 167–9, 172–3

Hanna, Ralph 25, 33–8, 40, 44, 47, 49, 146
Harris, Carissa 177, 224–6, 228
Hartman, Geoffrey 165–7, 168, 169
hermeneutic circle 14, 195, 196, 200
Hilmo, Maidie 24, 53
Hirsch, E. D. 204, 218
historicism 6, 9, 12, 20, 28, 30, 31, 32, 38, 44–52, 56, 201, 208–21
Hoccleve, Thomas 53
Horowitz, Damon 154–5
Hsy, Jonathan 240
Hunter, Ian 10

Illouz, Eva 128
Indiana University South Bend
 English major mission statement 150, 151, 152
Ingham, Patricia Clare 148
interlinked networks of value, definition of 83, 109
interpretation, axiological definition of 198
interpretive communities 196–8
Iser, Wolfgang 231

Jagot, Shazia 183
Jakobson, Roman 204
Jay, Paul and Gerald Graff
  'Fear of Being Useful' 151–5
Johnson, Eleanor 31, 41
Jusdanis, Gregory 8

Kane, George 30
Karpik, Lucien 96, 130, 170
Kelemen, Erik 61
Kempe, Margery 165
Kerby-Fulton, Kathryn 40
Kermode, Frank 163, 164–72, 173, 174
Khwaja, Waqas 183
Kittredge, George Lyman 21
Knapp, Ethan 21, 27
Knapp, Peggy 8, 19, 40
Knapp, Steven 76, 86
Kolbas, E. Dean 73

Lacan, Jacques 133
Langland, William
  Piers Plowman 20, 40, 49, 146, 156, 158, 159
Latour, Bruno 83, 86
Lawton, David 53, 192–3, 196, 199, 200, 201, 206
Lee, David Dodd 93
Lerer, Seth 31, 46
Levinas, Emmanuel 73
Levine, George 6–7, 75
literary valuing, abstract formulation of 81
Liu, Alan 31
Lomuto, Sierra 182
loose binding, definition of 102–7
Love, Heather 202
Lowes, John Livingston 21
Luckmann, Peter 197
Lynch, Deidre Shauna 128

Machan, Tim William 19, 21, 29–30, 38, 46, 47, 51, 124, 147
Manly, J. M. 33

manner, textual, definition of 86
manuscript studies, 6, 12, 19–58, 202
  definition of 20–1
Marcus, Sharon 191, 202
Marx, Karl 3, 30, 89, 101
Massumi, Brian 131
Matthews, David 21, 147
Mattox, Jake 17
McDonald, Peter 74
McGann, Jerome J. 20
McGillivray, Murray 26
McKenzie, D. F. 20
method wars 190
Meyer-Lee, Gabriel 129
Meyer-Lee, Robert J.
  Poets and Power from Chaucer to Wyatt 71, 125, 127
Milic, Louis 195
Miller, Mark 156–62, 163, 164, 166, 167, 169, 174
Millet, Bella 27
MLA
  'Report to the Teagle Foundation on the Undergraduate Major in Language and Literature' 8–9, 76
  proposal to eliminate the Chaucer Division 141–9
Mohanty, Satya 75
Mooney, Linne R. 66
Morse, Charlotte 26, 44
Mukařovský, Jan 77, 80, 81, 120–2, 164
Mukherjee, Ankhi 136–7
Muscatine, Charles 30

network of literary valuing, definition of 83–5
New Chaucer Society 24, 25, 32, 48, 141–9
New Criticism 5, 21, 29–31, 32, 34, 36, 37–9, 41–3, 52, 157
New Economic Criticism 92
New Formalism 31–3, 40–1

New Historicism *see* historicism
New Philology 23, 60
Nichols, Stephen 23, 56
Nolan, Maura 3
Norton Anthology of English Literature 7, 39
Nussbaum, Martha 105

ontological approaches to literary value, definition of 73–4
Otaño Gracia, Nahir 183

Patterson, Lee 14, 31, 190, 193–4, 199, 200, 203, 206, 208–21, 222, 223, 224, 225, 229
Pearsall, Derek 22, 25, 45, 56
Pinkhurst, Adam 54, 66
pizza 54, 103, 104, 108, 111, 144, 159
Poovey, Mary 10
poststructuralism 30, 38, 191, 193, 198, 239
Prendergast, Thomas 46, 147, 163–4, 169, 174
Propp, Vladimir 202

racial passing 178, 240
Rickert, Edith 33
Riverside Chaucer 21–2, 24, 88, 201
Robinson, Peter 26

Saussure, Ferdinand de 102, 196
Scase, Wendy 64
Scholes, Robert 153–4, 169, 174
Sellers, Jordan 202
Seyhan, Azade 107–9, 151, 152
Shakespeare, William 5, 37, 47, 55, 106, 124, 143, 147, 155
    Othello 106, 124, 138

Shelley, Percy Bysshe 105
Sidney, Sir Philip 3, 76, 105, 215
Simmel, Georg
    Philosophy of Money 13, 89, 100–2
Sir Gawain and the Green Knight 163–4, 165
skills-based justification for literary studies 150–6
Smith, Barbara Hernstein 9, 81, 84, 90, 100, 104
Solberg, Emma Margaret 206
Spearing, A. C. 234
stylistics 107, 189, 194–6, 204, 218
surface reading 92, 190, 191, 202, 235

Tanselle, G. Thomas 56
Taylor, Andrew 25
Tinkle, Theresa 22–4, 32, 33, 34, 46, 53
Toolan, Michael 195, 196
Trigg, Stephanie 21, 23, 25, 46, 147
Trilling, Lionel 166
Turner, James 232
Turner, Marion 24, 193–4, 196, 199, 200 201, 203, 206
Turville-Petre, Thorlac 27

Underwood, Ted 202

value, differential theory of 100–2

Wallace, David 44, 65
Watson, Nicholas 48
Weber, Max 217–20
Widsith 117, 118
Wimsatt, W. K. 39, 41, 43, 202
Wordsworth, William 164, 166

Milton Keynes UK
Ingram Content Group UK Ltd.
UKHW032000111224
452466UK00004B/9